W9-ABN-861

A CONCISE HISTORY OF SPAIN

The rich cultural and political life of Spain has emerged from its complex history, from the diversity of its peoples, and from continual contact with outside influences. This updated edition traces that history from prehistoric times to the present, focusing particularly on culture, society, politics, and personalities. Written in an engaging style, it introduces readers to key themes that have shaped Spain's history and culture. These include its varied landscapes and climates; the impact of waves of diverse human migrations; the importance of its location as a bridge between the Atlantic and the Mediterranean and Europe and Africa; and religion, particularly militant Catholic Christianity and its centuries of conflict with Islam and Protestantism, as well as debates over the place of the church in modern Spain. Illustrations, maps, and a guide to further reading, major cultural figures, and places to see make the history of this fascinating country come alive.

WILLIAM D. PHILLIPS, JR., is Professor Emeritus of History at the University of Minnesota and directed the Center for Early Modern History there from 2001 to 2008. His previous publications include *Slavery in Medieval and Early Modern Iberia* (2013), *Testimonies from the Columbus Lawsuits* (edited, 2000), *The Worlds of Christopher Columbus* (with Carla Rahn Phillips, 1992, recipient of the "Spain in America" [Second] Prize, awarded by the Spanish government), *Historia de la esclavitud en España* (1990), and *Slavery from Roman Times to the Early Transatlantic Trade* (1985).

CARLA RAHN PHILLIPS is Union Pacific Professor Emerita in Comparative Early Modern History at the University of Minnesota. Her previous publications include *The Treasure of the San José: Death at Sea in the War of the Spanish Succession* (2007, winner of the Award for Excellence in World History and Biography/Autobiography of the Professional and Scholarly Publishing division of the American Association of Publishers), and *Spain's Golden Fleece: Wool Production and the Wool Trade from the Middle Ages to the Nineteenth Century* (1997, with William D. Phillips, Jr., winner of the 1998 "Leo Gershoy Award" of the American Historical Association).

CAMBRIDGE CONCISE HISTORIES

This is a series of illustrated 'concise histories' of selected individual countries, intended both as university and college textbooks and as general historical introductions for general readers, travellers, and members of the business community.

A full list of titles in the series can be found at:
www.cambridge.org/concisehistories

A CONCISE HISTORY OF SPAIN

WILLIAM D. PHILLIPS, JR.

AND

CARLA RAHN PHILLIPS

CAMBRIDGE
UNIVERSITY PRESS

CAMBRIDGE
UNIVERSITY PRESS

University Printing House, Cambridge CB2 8BS, United Kingdom

Cambridge University Press is part of the University of Cambridge.

It furthers the University's mission by disseminating knowledge in the pursuit of education, learning and research at the highest international levels of excellence.

www.cambridge.org
Information on this title: www.cambridge.org/9781107109711

© William D. Phillips, Jr. and Carla Rahn Phillips 2010, 2016

First published 2010
Second edition 2016

Printed in the United Kingdom by TJ International Ltd. Padstow Cornwall

A catalogue record for this publication is available from the British Library

Library of Congress Cataloguing in Publication data
Phillips, William D.
A concise history of Spain / William D. Phillips, Jr. and Carla Rahn
Phillips. – Second edition.
pages   cm. – (Cambridge concise histories)
Includes bibliographical references and index.
ISBN 978-1-107-10971-1 (hardback : alkaline paper)
1. Spain – History.   I. Phillips, Carla Rahn, 1943–   II. Title.
DP17.P55   2015
946 – dc23   2015023289

ISBN 978-1-107-10971-1 Hardback
ISBN 978-1-107-52505-4 Paperback

CONTENTS

ILLUSTRATIONS

Unless otherwise indicated, photos were taken by the authors.

MAPS

PREFACE

In modern times, Spain has often been perceived as different from other countries in Europe, with a pejorative connotation to that difference. In part, at least, that perception stems from a lack of knowledge about the history of Spain. Yet, in a certain sense Spain is different from the rest of Europe, in the diversity of its population and in its close contacts with civilizations outside Europe, in historical times and into the present as well. In writing this book, we have aimed to survey the long and complex history of Spain and its regions in a form accessible to an interested readership from various backgrounds. Whether those readers are serious students of Spain or casual travelers, we hope this book will provide a useful introduction to the complex history of a fascinating country. To best accomplish this, we pay due attention to all of the periods of the Spanish past, rather than concentrating on the more recent centuries. We also try to pay due attention to the many voices contending over the Spanish past.

As we planned and produced the book, we identified a series of themes that we could follow through the millennia. Among the themes we chose were the diverse populations mentioned above and the difficult and varied ecology of the Iberian Peninsula. The location of Spain between the Atlantic and the Mediterranean – and, by extension, between Europe and Africa – placed it in continual contact and potential conflict with other countries and other civilizations, from prehistoric times through the medieval centuries. In the early chapters, we discuss how waves of in- and out-migration by a diversity of peoples shaped not only the demographic character of Spain but also its political and social character. For example, medieval Spain had a unique history in the coexistence of Christian, Muslim, and Jewish communities. At the same time, however, centuries of conflict between Christian and Islamic political power eventually forged religious militancy on both sides. In the Christian kingdom that emerged victorious at the end of the medieval period, religious identity permeated every aspect of Spanish life. The implications of that religious identity – and opposition to it – persist even into the present day, and one cannot understand Spanish history without taking it into account.

Another theme we follow is the challenge of power. During the early modern period, roughly from 1500 to 1800, the Habsburg dynasty and its Bourbon successors presided over the world's first global empire. In the process of administering that empire, the Spanish bureaucracy had to deal with issues emanating from all corners of the earth – a precursor to the modern challenges of globalization. By 1650, Spain had lost dominance in Europe to its rivals, but the Spanish Empire persisted until the early nineteenth century, and a few remnants lasted even longer. The legacy of Spain's history as a global power continues to color Spanish political life into the present, not least in its role as an intermediary between Europe and the Islamic world, and Europe and Latin America.

The rich cultural life of Spain emerged from the diversity of peoples who inhabited the land and from continual contact with outside influences as well. In a concise history, we cannot do justice to such diversity. As an attempt to remedy that lack, in the Guide to Further Information we mention major cultural figures and sites where interested readers can supplement the brief mentions in the text.

This book reflects our decades-long interest in Spain and its people over time. We have been studying, visiting, and teaching about Spain throughout our academic careers and have published both separately and together on a wide range of topics. In addition to learning from our own research and teaching, we have benefited from scholarship in related fields. In particular, we have learned from participation in the Society for Spanish and Portuguese Historical Studies (SSPHS) (now the Association for Spanish and Portuguese Historical Studies [ASPHS]), an international organization based in the United States that celebrated its fortieth anniversary in 2009. Throughout its existence, the SSPHS/ASPHS has provided an important venue for lively debate and intellectual exchange among established scholars and those starting out in their careers. In that organization, as well as in professional meetings and while doing research and writing, we have learned from so many scholars, archivists, librarians, and editors, that it is impossible to thank them individually. We are also grateful to the editorial team at Cambridge University Press, particularly Helen Waterhouse and Marigold Acland for inviting us to undertake this project, and to Leigh Mueller and the anonymous readers who helped us immeasurably in strengthening the text. This is a small book on a vast topic. We take full responsibility for choosing what to emphasize, what to leave out, and how to interpret the overall trajectory of Spanish history. We also take full responsibility for any errors that remain, despite our best efforts.

The Program for Cultural Cooperation between Spain's Ministry of Culture and United States universities provided partial support for the first edition of this publication.

In memory of David A. Vassberg (1936–2014), Carolyn P. Boyd (1944–2015), and Christopher Schmidt-Nowara (1966–2015): valued friends, colleagues, and traveling companions on the journey toward understanding the Spanish past.

NOTE ON THE SECOND EDITION

We have taken the opportunity of this second edition to change the final chapter to reflect changes through the early autumn of 2014, particularly the abdication of King Juan Carlos I and the accession of Felipe VI. We have also corrected some minor errors that we and others noted in the first edition. We wish to express our appreciation to Liz Friend-Smith for her continuing support for the project.

I

The land and its early inhabitants

~

The Iberian Peninsula occupies several crucial crossroads, providing connections between Europe and Africa, the Mediterranean and the Atlantic, and Europe and the Atlantic world. Spain's connections with Africa date from prehistoric times. When Muslim rulers controlled most of Spain during the Middle Ages, the close relationship with the North African world intensified. Today, Spain is the destination of choice for African would-be immigrants to Europe. Spain's connections with the rest of Europe are powerful as well, defined by history and geography and enhanced by the ties of the European Union. Spain's connections with Latin America date from the period of exploration and empire-building in the late fifteenth century. In our times, Spain provides an important link between Europe and Latin America, with the greatest number of flights between the two continents, the largest investment in Latin America of any European country, and the most Latin American immigrants in Europe. For the world as a whole, Spain is a major center of tourism. In 2007 Spain ranked second in the world in the number of tourists, according to the World Tourism Organization. In that year, some 59.2 million tourists entered the country, compared to a Spanish population of about 45 million, a clear indication of Spain's continuing importance as a nexus of travel, transportation, and exchange.

This is a concise history of Spain, which we understand to mean a modern country that shares the Iberian Peninsula with Portugal. All of those geographical terms have a complex history, however. The Greeks called the whole peninsula "Iberia," and the Romans called it "Hispania." Between the end of the Roman Empire and the eighteenth century, "Spain" was more a term of convenience than a political reality, and other terms have come and gone to describe the land and its peoples. When the Muslims held Spain, they called the part they controlled "al-Andalus," an area that varied in geographical extent as the area under Islamic control waxed and ultimately waned. Medieval Jews called the country "Sefarad." Christian Spain in the Middle Ages contained a number of kingdoms and smaller entities. Castile and Aragon were the most prominent of those kingdoms and, by the end of the Middle Ages, controlled a large portion of the peninsula. The marriage of their rulers Isabel of Castile and Fernando of Aragon marked the origin of the modern definition of Spain. Since the eighteenth century, the political geography of Spain has remained more or less constant: the Iberian Peninsula with the exception of Portugal, Andorra, and Gibraltar. In modern times, most writers employ the Greek word "Iberia" to refer to the peninsula and a descendant of the Roman word "Hispania" to refer to Spain. In other words, Spain and Iberia are not equivalent, although they were both equivalent and coterminous in Greek and Roman times, referring to the peninsula as a whole.

That Portugal developed as an independent kingdom was also a product of history and happenstance. In the later Middle Ages, the western part of the peninsula was developed mainly by conquerors and settlers from Galicia in the northwest, whose overlord was the king of León. In the twelfth century, Afonso Henriques, count of Portugal, worked to secure papal recognition of Portugal's independence and of his status as its king. Nonetheless, Portugal could have been joined with Spain on several occasions. A Castilian invasion failed in the fourteenth century. Isabel and Fernando in the late fifteenth and early sixteenth centuries secured marriage alliances with the Portuguese ruling house that could have led to a unified peninsula, but the deaths among the marriage partners ended that effort. Felipe II of Spain secured the Portuguese throne in 1580, and Spain and Portugal had the same Habsburg rulers until 1640. In that year, a revolt began that eventually restored Portuguese independence and enshrined resistance to Spain as a part of Portugal's national identity. In short, Spain has rarely been identical to Iberia and, for most of its long history, Spain itself was a theoretical concept or a term of convenience overlaid on a patchwork of kingdoms and regions with shifting boundaries. In the present day, leaders of regional political movements contest the notion of Spain as an indivisible entity, instead looking back to ancient and medieval antecedents for their modern self-definition.

As part of this regional complexity, Iberia has always been multiethnic, multireligious, and multicultural. One way to trace modern regionalism is to examine the peninsula's different languages, both historic and current. Most of the languages of the peninsula are so-called "Romance" languages derived from Latin, a legacy of the centuries-long Roman occupation and control of Hispania. The language spoken by the greatest number of present-day

Iberians and Spanish-speakers throughout the world is Castilian, the descendant of the language of medieval Castile. Most non-Spaniards call this language "Spanish." It was exported to the Spanish Empire in the Americas and the Philippines, and is the language with the third-highest number of speakers in the world today, following Chinese and English. The regime of Francisco Franco in the mid twentieth century tried to make Spanish or Castilian the only language of Spain, but linguistic identity persevered and provided a strong component of regional struggles for increased recognition and autonomy during the regime.

Among the other Romance languages in the peninsula, Portuguese is the official language of Portugal, and its close cousin Gallego, the language of Galicia, is seeing a revival in northwestern Spain, spoken and written on local radio and television stations and in the publishing industry. The Catalan language is prominent in education and the media as the mother tongue of many residents of Catalonia. Catalan is intimately related to the medieval language of the south of France, the *langue d'oc* or Occitan. In medieval times, Catalans took their language to Valencia and the Balearic Islands in the course of conquering those areas. Today the languages in those regions are somewhat different from but closely related to Catalan.

Aside from the Romance languages, other languages have also figured prominently in Spanish history. The most unusual is the Basque language, Euskerra, one of Europe's oldest spoken languages, going back to prehistoric times. With the language in decline by the nineteenth century, Basque intellectuals revived its use and developed a written form, which it had formerly lacked. Since then, the use of Euskerra has been associated with

Basque nationalism and the quest for various degrees of autonomy from the Spanish government. The most extreme element of the nationalist movement, known as ETA, from the Basque phrase "Homeland and Freedom," aims at total independence from Spain and has waged a campaign of terrorism and extortion since 1968.

The Arabic language came to Iberia with the Islamic conquerors in the eighth century and remained the language of the political elite of al-Andalus. In parts of Spain, Arabic remained current into the seventeenth century. It strongly influenced Castilian and the other Romance languages in the peninsula and eventually contributed variants of nouns from "algebra" to "zenith" to languages throughout Europe. Arabic is coming back into Spain with the immigration of Muslims from North Africa and elsewhere in the Islamic world, and with the contemporary conversion of some native Spaniards to Islam and their exposure to the language of the Qur'ān.

For centuries, Hebrew was the common language of the flourishing Jewish communities of medieval Spain. It influenced and was influenced by both Arabic and the Romance languages. Largely extirpated or driven underground by the expulsion of the Jews at the end of the fifteenth century, Hebrew has returned to Spain from the mid twentieth century onward with the establishment of communities of Jews from Morocco and other parts of North Africa and the Middle East.

The various historical languages of Iberia serve as a potent reminder of other facets of regional difference. Underlying everything is the geology of the peninsula, comprising a diverse series of zones from glaciers in the high northern mountains to a small area of true desert in the southeast near Elche. Iberia's mountain ranges, which were formed millions of years ago, separate and define Spain's distinctive regions. In the northeast, the Pyrenees divide Spain from France with peaks that reach to over 11,000 feet. The valleys and low mountains of the Basque country connect the Pyrenees with the Cantabrian Mountains (Cordillera Cantábrica), with a maximum height of some 8,500 feet, which stretch across most of the rest of northern Spain, separating a narrow coastal strip of land from the interior of the peninsula. At the western end of the Cantabrian range is Asturias, with its daunting coastal cliffs and mountainous interior. The coastal mountains and valleys of Galicia in the extreme northwest of Spain are similar to those of Asturias. Galicia's coastline is dominated by *rías*, fingers of the Atlantic Ocean probing into the interior between hills, similar to the fiords of Scandinavia, though less dramatic.

South of the western edge of the Cantabrian ranges, the mountains of León slope southward onto a huge plateau called the Northern Meseta, with an average altitude of 2,300 to 2,600 feet. To the east it is bounded by the Iberian Mountains (Cordillera Ibérica), with peaks as high as 7,500 feet. Farther eastward lie the Ebro River valley in Aragon and Catalonia and the rich plains of Valencia near the Mediterranean coast. The southern edge of the Northern Meseta meets the Central Mountains (Cordillera Central), a mountain chain north and west of Madrid whose ranges include the Somosierra, Guadarrama, and Gredos.

Farther south, the Southern Meseta has an average altitude of 2,000 to 2,300 feet. The high plains of the two Mesetas, comprising about 36 percent of the Iberian Peninsula, are isolated from one another. They are high enough and large enough to give Spain a mean altitude of nearly 2,200 feet, second only to Switzerland in Europe and double the European average. Over 56 percent of the surface area of Spain lies between 1,300 and 3,300 feet. In many places, a traveler can descend from the high plains into impressive mountain ranges before reaching plains at lower altitudes. Madrid, in the center of the country, has the highest elevation of any European capital, with its airport almost exactly 2,000 feet above sea level.

The Southern Meseta's eastern edge lies between the mountains of the Cordillera Ibérica (which also borders the Northern Meseta) and the even more daunting Baetic Mountains (Cordillera Bética), which separate the southeastern desert and coastal plain from the Southern Meseta. The Sierra Morena mountain range marks the southern border of the Southern Meseta. South and west of the Sierra Morena, the Guadalquivir River valley, a broad and rich agricultural plain, slopes southwestward toward the Atlantic Ocean. Farther east, the Sierra Nevada Mountains, south of Granada and the other southern ranges, rise to peaks ranging from 3,300 to 11,500 feet. As their name implies, the mountain-tops of the Sierra Nevada are snow-capped all year, providing a stunning contrast with the hot plains and coastal areas in the rest of Andalusia.

Over the centuries, the difficult topography of Spain has limited agriculture and hampered long-distance transport, separating seaports from inland plains and cities and hindering commercial development. Before the advent of

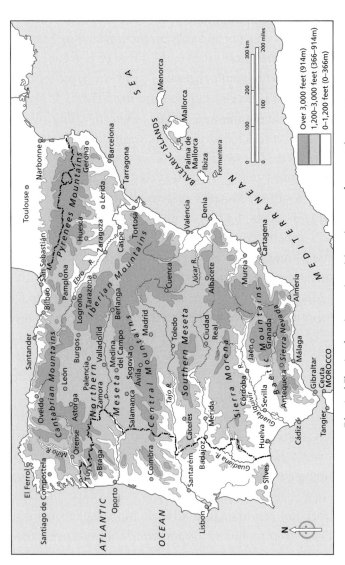

MAP 1.1 Physical Iberia, showing major cities, rivers, and mountain ranges.

the railroads, topography put a premium on goods that could be easily moved, or better yet that could move themselves, such as livestock.

The rivers of the peninsula provide little opportunity for transport by boat or barge. They tend to make short, rapid descents from their origins in the mountains, and most suffer from variations in flow according to erratic and unpredictable rainfall. Many Spanish rivers, even those with considerable volume, flow through steep banks that make them very difficult to use as sources for irrigation.

Despite these limitations, before the nineteenth century Spanish rivers carried considerable boat traffic along their navigable stretches. In modern times, roads and railroads supplanted the rivers as thoroughfares, with the exception of the lower reaches of the largest rivers. Nonetheless, the major rivers of Spain help to define the regions through which they flow and have been the scenes of important historical developments. One historian has even suggested that we might best understand the medieval history of Spain by tracing the changes in political control of the major river valleys.

Only one of the largest Spanish rivers flows into the Mediterranean: the Ebro, rising in the Cantabrian Mountains, flowing through the valleys of Aragon, and reaching the sea 565 miles from its source, after traversing the delta it created. In Roman times the river had a significant seaport at Amposta, then located on the Mediterranean coast and now located, due to silting and the formation of the delta, about 16 miles from the sea. Historically, the Ebro formed the spine of a series of routes into the center of the peninsula. The city of Zaragoza has been, since its

Roman foundation, the principal inland crossing point of the Ebro, a fact that assured the city's prominence.

The northernmost of the major rivers that flow into the Atlantic is the Duero, rising in the Sierra de Urbión and flowing through the grain- and wine-producing regions of Old Castile and northern Portugal. The Duero and its valley formed a frontier zone between al-Andalus and the Christian kingdoms in medieval times, as Christian forces began to wrest control of the peninsula from the Muslims. In the eighteenth century, the Duero and some of its tributaries in Old Castile served as the nexus of a major effort at canal-building. The canals still remain but fell into disuse when the railroads came in the nineteenth century. The Duero is navigable for only a short distance before it reaches the Atlantic at the Portuguese city of Porto. The lower Duero (Portuguese Douro) today supports a system of barge carriers for wine and other goods.

Farther south is the Tajo River ("Tagus" in English), rising in the Sierra de Albarracín and flowing around the tall hill that defines Toledo, a military strongpoint since its founding by the Romans. Its conquest from the Muslims in 1085 by Alfonso VI of Castile marked an important step in the Castilian move into central Iberia. A favored residence of medieval kings, Toledo housed an important Jewish community whose synagogues still stand as a tourist destination. During the Spanish Civil War, Toledo was the scene of a famous siege, an event more important for propagandistic than strategic reasons. From central Spain, the Tajo flows into Portugal, where it is called the Tejo, and farther on forms the great estuary upon which Lisbon is located.

Still farther south, the Guadiana (Arabic "Wadi Ana") rises in the province of Cuenca and flows through La Mancha and southern Extremadura. These historically underpopulated areas were the location of winter pastures for Spain's famous Merino sheep, the vast migratory flocks that produced the finest of wools from the thirteenth century onward. In ancient and medieval times, there was considerable boat transport on the navigable stretches of the Guadiana, centering on Mérida and then on the lower reaches south of the waterfall at Pulo do Lobo in Portugal. As the Guadiana passes through Extremadura, four large dams form the main links of a project of the 1950s and 1960s to provide electric power and water for irrigation in a broad area around the city of Badajoz. After defining part of the border between Spain and southeastern Portugal, and providing a navigable stretch of some 43 miles, the Guadiana reaches the Atlantic between Ayamonte in Spain and Vila Real de Santo António in Portugal.

The southernmost major river in Spain is the Guadalquivir, flowing through a rich agricultural region that forms the heartland of Andalusia. The region and the river enriched the city of Córdoba, the Corduba of Roman times, which later served as a principal Islamic city and the capital of the Islamic caliphate in Spain from the tenth to the eleventh centuries. Its mosque and other cultural monuments make modern Córdoba a major destination for cultural tourism.

In historic times, ships could travel on the Guadalquivir as far upstream as Córdoba. Today, ocean-going vessels can only travel as far upriver as Seville, where important episodes have played out in every period of Spain's history.

Legendarily founded by Hercules and likely established by Julius Caesar, the city the Romans called "Hispalis" later became the capital of a major Muslim kingdom. Its reconquest in the thirteenth century assured Christian control of the Guadalquivir valley. Seville was the official port for all traffic to Spain's American empire in the sixteenth and seventeenth centuries and retains a rich architectural legacy from that period. The Guadalquivir reaches the Atlantic at the Bay of Cádiz, which takes its name from its major city, the oldest in Western Europe.

Iberia has two distinct areas of climate, one rainy and the other semi-arid. The wetter region, which geographers call the pluvial zone, encompasses most of the north coast and the northern half of the western coast, from Lisbon northward through Galicia. The region has cool summers, mild winters, and frequent rain throughout the year. The verdant hillsides seem to promise good growing conditions for crops, but in fact the hills, valleys, and overabundant rain in Galicia have hindered grain production through the centuries, forcing its inhabitants to rely on the sea and to import food and export people. The semi-arid remainder of the peninsula shares a climate with its Mediterranean neighbors, with mild winters along the coast and colder and more severe winters in the interior. Summers are hot and dry, and the other seasons bring unpredictable rainfall.

Variations in wind and rainfall year by year and decade by decade depend largely on changes in the path of the westerly winds over the North Atlantic Ocean. These winds pick up warm, moist air as they pass over the Gulf Stream and deliver rain to Europe, more in the north and less in the south. Changes in the path of the westerlies result from alterations in the systems of sea-level atmospheric pressure. There are permanent areas of low pressure in the north and high pressure in the south, usually known as the Icelandic low and the Azores high (or, sometimes, as the Bermuda high in the western hemisphere). The variations in pressure and the relations between the two systems make up a system called the North Atlantic Oscillation. When the pressure in the north is relatively low compared with much higher pressure in the south, that is known as a high North Atlantic Oscillation index. It allows the westerlies to blow strongly into Northern Europe, bringing cool summers and mild winters and increased rain to that region, whereas the Mediterranean region tends to be drier. When pressure is higher in the north and the Icelandic and Azores pressures are close to one another, this defines a low North Atlantic Oscillation index. The westerlies then reach Europe farther to the south than usual, allowing north and northeast winds to bring cold weather into northwest Europe and stormy, wet weather into the Mediterranean lands.

The story of human habitation in the peninsula has unfolded against a background of the constraints represented by the environment and its notable extremes of topography and climate. At the same time, Iberia's position between two continents and bordering two seas has meant that human populations have had relatively easy access to the peninsula. These population movements into Iberia over thousands of years played a major role in shaping both its prehistory and its history.

The fossil remains of the earliest Europeans found to date rest in northern Spain, east of the city of Burgos in the Sierra de Atapuerca. These remains suggest that a population of hominids (of the genus *Homo*) has been living in the peninsula for over a million years. Though such a population seems very ancient, it is fairly recent among hominid remains, some of which date as far back as seven million years in Africa. Early humans began to leave Africa by the northeast, with the earliest waves making their way into Asia. Somewhat later, some groups began to migrate west into Europe. They were certainly in the Caucasus Mountains by around 1.7 million years ago.

That Atapuerca became a center for the study of early humans in Europe happened almost by chance. Gold mining in the area during the nineteenth century impelled the Sierra Company, a British enterprise, to build a railway from Burgos to the mines. One deep cut went through the Sierra de Atapuerca, exposing ancient layers of sedimentation. After the mines gave out and the railroad fell into disuse in the 1920s, animal and human remains eventually appeared. The first and most important find, at a site called the Sima del Elefante ("Pit of the Elephant"), occurred in 1976 with the discovery of human teeth and part of a jawbone, dated by experts to be as old as 1.2 million years.

The abundance of slightly more recent bones at Atapuerca, particularly at the Gran Dolina site, have allowed archeologists to build a full picture of life in the area over three-quarters of a million years ago. The inhabitants lived by scavenging and hunting some twenty-five species of animals, including large ones such as rhinoceros, mammoth, and bison. They butchered the animals and disposed of their bones in the cave. They did the same for humans, making the hominids at Atapuerca some of the earliest documented cannibals.

Near the Gran Dolina, archeologists also investigated the Sima de los Huesos ("Pit of Bones"), where they found, in addition to the bones of animals, the largest assemblage of ancient hominid bones found anywhere in the world: some thirty individuals, along with one well-preserved ax head. These individuals lived much later and were probably unrelated to those in the Gran Dolina. The remains have been identified as examples of *Homo heidelbergensis* ("Heidelberg man"), a species active in that part of Spain some 400,000 years ago, during the Old Paleolithic period (500,000 to 100,000 years ago). The thirty individuals found in the Sima de los Huesos were all in their late teens or twenties and showed signs of injuries. They seem to have been placed intact in an uninhabited cave. Whether this signifies a deliberate burial of the dead or a simple disposal of individuals killed in some form of combat remains open to speculation.

Later groups of hominids also entered Spain. Neanderthals arrived around 200,000 years ago and established settlements scattered throughout the peninsula. In fact, Neanderthal remains were first discovered at Gibraltar in 1848, but their identification as a separate species came later, when other fossil material turned up at Neanderthal in Germany in 1856. Scientists once thought that the Neanderthals died out around 35,000 years ago, but they may have survived in the Iberian Peninsula for much longer: Neanderthal remains have been found in Gibraltar that date to as recently as 24,000 years ago.

These various finds show that Neanderthals in Iberia coexisted with other Stone Age cultures, including representatives of modern humans (*Homo sapiens sapiens*) who settled throughout the peninsula during the Upper

Paleolithic period (45,000 to 10,000 years ago). The earliest dated from some 35,000 years ago, representing members of the Aurignacian culture, widespread in Europe. They brought improved implements on their migrations, notably tools of bone, antler, and flint. They likely sewed skins and furs together for clothing, because archeologists have found needles for that purpose among their remains. The Solutreans, coming from North Africa and bringing the hunting bow with them, replaced the Aurignacians in Iberia about 20,000 years ago. In turn, the Magdalenian culture, which came from Northern Europe and whose hunters pursued reindeer, displaced the Solutreans about 17,000 years ago. Finally, the last Paleolithic culture replaced the Magdalenians in Iberia about 10,000 years ago.

Archeological sites from these Paleolithic cultures abound throughout the Iberian Peninsula, including many with cave paintings. Perhaps the most famous is at Altamira in northern Spain, on the low coastal plain at the center of the Cantabrian coast. The Upper Paleolithic cave paintings of Altamira are some of the best examples found thus far and date from 18,500 to 14,000 years ago. Produced by using locally obtained pigments mixed with animal fat, they depict food animals – horses, bison, red deer, and reindeer, among others – in various poses, some of them wounded. Scholars debate the significance of the paintings. They likely were not for decorative purposes, as they appear far back in the cave, isolated from the inhabited portions near the entrance. Perhaps the paintings figured in initiation rites for young hunters. Perhaps they represent attempts to establish spiritual and material links between the group and their food supply. Certainly they are some of the best early realistic paintings in all of human history.

The animals depicted in the cave paintings were well adapted to the conditions of the last ice age and they tended to become scarcer when the climate warmed significantly some 12,000 years ago. Warming temperatures across the world melted Arctic ice and glaciers in the northern hemisphere, thereby flooding coastal lowlands. In the Iberian Peninsula, as the animal populations decreased, the Stone Age cultures turned toward gathering shellfish along the coasts for their sustenance.

Around 8,000 years ago, Neolithic (New Stone Age) peoples entered the peninsula; they with them better stone tools – hence their name – but, more importantly, early techniques of agriculture and animal husbandry. With their arrival, the pace of change in the human population quickened, and the newcomers displaced older human groups. Supported by agriculture, as well as hunting and gathering, they were able to form larger communities and to live a more settled existence.

About 3,400 years ago, copper tools appeared in the peninsula, and along with them evidence of copper mining and smelting. The most important archeological site for this period is Los Millares, near Almería in southeastern Spain. Most Copper Age sites include fortifications and carefully constructed stone tombs. By around 2,200 years ago, Bronze Age groups made their appearance in Iberia. Metal deposits exist in many parts of the peninsula, including gold deposits in river sands, copper in the south, and silver in the west. Sources of tin exist in both the south and the northwest. Lead and iron deposits are located in the same general areas as tin, though human groups did not mine them as early. Scientists have identified two Bronze Age cultures in Spain, one along the Mediterranean coast, and the other along the Atlantic coast, presumably related to the incursions – respectively – of the Iberians and the Celts.

The Iberians entered Spain from North Africa, possibly with eastern origins, and spread along the Mediterranean coast. They brought with them knowledge of agriculture, mining, and working metals, including bronze. They also worked stone, using large blocks for construction, and carving blocks for statues, most notably the so-called "Dama de Elche." From the merchants of the Mediterranean, they learned writing and the coining of money and developed a written language whose alphabet derived from Greek and Phoenician. The Iberian language is now mostly lost, except for inscriptions on stone and lettering on coins. Celtic culture came in a series of waves with peaks in the ninth and seventh centuries BCE. Coming from the north, the Celts entered Iberia via the western Pyrenees and spread along the Atlantic coast, supporting themselves primarily by herding. Toward the end of the Bronze Age, knowledge of working iron spread through the Celtic region. For generations, scholars assumed that the spread of Celtic culture was due to movement of peoples. Recent specialists have suggested that a diffusion of ideas and techniques, rather than migration, was probably more responsible.

However they spread, Celtic and Iberian cultural forms influenced local peoples and, in the center of the peninsula, blended with one another to produce a composite culture that Greek and Roman writers described: the latter called them "Hispani." They had a warrior aristocracy at the top of their society and a free class of workers beneath them. Further down the social scale were slaves, usually prisoners of war but also individuals who had voluntarily given up their freedom in exchange for the protection of a local strongman. They had no large kingdoms but instead grouped themselves in independent cities ruled by elites. Their settlements tended to be on fortified hillsides or in fortified villages on the flat lands of the Southern Meseta. Various cities formed temporary alliances in times of danger but resisted long-term associations. Economically, they practiced herding and agriculture. They also produced ceramics, cloth from wool and linen, iron weaponry, and baskets. Mining the metal resources in their areas gave them a product to trade with the merchants from the Mediterranean and elsewhere.

Southwestern Spain became a major nexus for the Atlantic Bronze Age, with its people exchanging Iberian metals with northwest Europe for tin, which they combined with native copper to make bronze. The Atlantic coast of southwest Iberia was the site of the legendary place called Tartessos that figured in mythology from the Greeks forward. It was the scene of some of the labors of Hercules, later considered to be one of the founders of Spain. According to legend, Hercules split apart Europe and Africa and created the Strait of Gibraltar, known to the ancients as the Pillars of Hercules. In Greek legends, Herakles (Hercules) is supposed to have tended the cattle of Geryon, the king of Tartessos. The Greek historian Herodotus (fifth century BCE) related stories about Arganthonios, another ruler of Tartessos, and noted the region's richness in metals. Traditionally described as a city, Tartessos is more properly the name of the region along the lower reaches of the Guadiana and Guadalquivir rivers and of the indigenous people who settled and developed the area. Tartessos became a famous ancient center of trade and eventually attracted Phoenician invaders, who ultimately conquered it.

The interest of Mediterranean merchants in Spain began with the Phoenicians around 800 BCE. They, and later the Greeks and the Carthaginians, established a series of trading posts that the Greeks called *clerukia*. With relatively large populations – 1,000 or so in each settlement – their main purpose was to trade with local suppliers and send goods back to their home areas. The merchants were interested primarily in the ordinary and precious metals that abounded in Iberia, including silver, copper, and lead. They were also interested in the produce of the sea. Lacking refrigeration, the peoples of the ancient Mediterranean world used other means to preserve food. After bringing fish ashore, they would clean and dry some of the catch for sale. From some species, they would remove the fillets, dry and salt them, and thus be able to trade them widely without losing much to spoilage. They also made use of the skin, bones, and entrails of the catch, which they processed in large stone vats in the sun. With salt and spices added, the mixture would steep, ferment, and eventually form a thick sauce called *garon*, that kept well and could therefore be transported long distances.

Ancient Mediterranean merchants traveling to Spain were also interested in timber, because many parts of the Mediterranean world are semi-arid and faced constant problems in finding adequate supplies of wood. Peoples living around the Mediterranean had to manage their forests very carefully, and some areas in the

Mediterranean basin do not produce forests at all, forcing inhabitants to import what timber they needed. The
Phoenicians were in that latter category and sought timber in Spain. Tradition holds that Phoenicians founded
the city of Cádiz in 1100 BCE, giving it a history of over
3,000 years. Almost assuredly, the foundation occurred
later, after 800 BCE. Even so, Cádiz is Western Europe's
oldest city, known to its founders as Gadir, a name the
Romans changed to Gades.

In addition to Cádiz, the Phoenicians founded other
trading bases in southern Iberia, including Malaca
(Málaga) and Onuba (Huelva) on the southern coast, and
an outpost on the island of Ibiza. Resident agents of businesses based in the Phoenician home cities – mainly Tyre
and Byblos – lived in these outposts and traded wares such
as gold jewelry and Greek pottery. Phoenician colonies
in Iberia even weathered the subjugation of their home
cities by the Babylonians in the sixth century BCE. They
remained active in Iberia and connected with the new
trading system organized by the Carthaginians, themselves of Phoenician origin.

After the Phoenicians, other outsiders began to form
communities in Iberia. Even before the Greeks themselves arrived, their goods – pottery and bronze – were
common in Iberia, brought in by the Phoenicians. The
Greeks reached Iberia as an outcome of their pattern
of expansion in the ancient period. Their ancient home
in the Balkan Peninsula is even more mountainous than
Iberia and has a limited amount of good grain land. As
their population grew, the Greeks planted colonies far
from Greece proper, in a process sometimes called "bud-
ding." A group of people from an overpopulated Greek

city-state would move elsewhere and establish a daughter-city, whose people would share and maintain the customs of the mother-city. Following this custom, the Greeks colonized all of the shoreline of Anatolia; the area around the Black Sea, especially its southern shore; southern Italy and Sicily; southern France; and finally eastern Iberia, where they established a major presence. Most of the Greek colonies in the western Mediterranean were founded from the major settlement at Massalia (modern Marseille).

After setting up several trading stations along Spain's Mediterranean shore, Greek colonizers founded the first true Greek city in Iberia around the sixth century BCE, and called it Emporion. The name relates to the English word "emporium," a place where trade is conducted, and that seems to have been its major function; it became the most important of the Greek city-states in eastern Iberia. The Romans called it Emporiae. In modern times, Spaniards call the area's major city Ampurias, and Catalans call it Empuries.

The Greeks and the Phoenicians introduced a number of important plants to Iberia, among them the grapevine and the olive tree. From the time of their introduction until the present day, these well-adapted plants made Spain a major producer of wine and olive oil. The olive tree will grow in about two-thirds of Spain – the warmer and more arid regions. It requires some rain, of course, but it requires above all sunlight and warm winter temperatures. Olive trees will not grow in the pluvial, or rainy, regions of the north and northwest, because the temperatures are not warm enough in the summer and rain is too abundant year-round. In modern times, olive trees grow nearly everywhere in Spain that the climate can support them, but their main region is the southern quarter of the peninsula, where one can see vast areas stretching in every direction with almost nothing but olive trees. The Greeks and the Phoenicians also brought writing into the Iberian Peninsula, and the Iberians probably learned their alphabet from the Phoenicians. The Greeks also brought metal coinage, primarily in silver, and the Iberians learned from them how to produce their own coinage.

The people of Carthage also established themselves in Iberia. Carthaginians were descendants of the Phoenicians and continued the Phoenician tradition of trading in the western Mediterranean, into North Africa, and into the Iberian Peninsula. They also established a colony on the island of Ibiza (Ebusus). Carthage sat across the Mediterranean from Rome, and its remains are close to the modern city of Tunis. The Carthaginians and the Romans became rivals for a number of reasons, but particularly over possession of Sicily, a very prosperous and productive island in the ancient period. It was a breadbasket for the central Mediterranean and exported wheat in various directions.

The Carthaginians also came to think that they could establish a large presence in the Iberian Peninsula, a decision that intensified their long-term struggle with the Romans. A family of Carthaginian generals and highly placed politicians called the Barcas coordinated much of the Carthaginian activity in Iberia. Hamilcar Barca suggested to his superiors that Spain would be a good counterweight to Rome. He entered Spain in 236 BCE with a Carthaginian army and virtually independent military authority, perhaps with the objective of conquering all of Spain. Some local leaders and city-states joined with

Barca; others did not, but he achieved some success and a series of notable conquests during his career. Hamilcar Barca built a number of fortresses in Spain, some of which grew into cities. One town at the southeastern tip of the Iberian Peninsula was among the most successful. The Romans would call it Nova Carthago (New Carthage), and modern Spaniards call it Cartagena.

At the time when Barca entered Spain, there was no unified political authority. Instead, various city-states and tribal groups lived in more or less disconnected areas throughout the peninsula, in addition to various Greek cities and trading posts on the Mediterranean coast. The Greek enclaves in Spain each had close ties to their home cities and to Rome, but they functioned as independent entities. The Romans made separate treaties with the Greek enclaves in Spain, whose leaders essentially paid for Roman military protection in case they were attacked. The Romans also made an agreement in 226 BCE with the Carthaginians, establishing the Ebro River as the division between their spheres of influence in Spain, with the Romans to the north and the Carthaginians to the south.

The Romans became increasingly interested in Spain because of Carthaginian activities there. Matters reached a critical point in 209 BCE, after Hamilcar Barca's son Hannibal attacked Saguntum, a town south of the Ebro – technically in the Carthaginian sphere. Saguntum's leaders had nonetheless appealed to Rome for help, but, as Hannibal besieged the town, Roman help failed to arrive. The townspeople defended themselves to the last man, and their efforts became famous in Spanish history as a tale of endurance and patriotic sacrifice. Only after the siege ended did Rome prepare for full-scale war against Carthage.

By the time the Romans were ready, Hannibal had launched an invasion of Italy from Spain, entering Gaul and crossing the Alps in the winter with his troops and war elephants. He won some engagements against Roman forces, but Rome ultimately prevailed. Under Publius Cornelius Scipio, the Roman army drove the Carthaginians from Spain in 206 BCE. Four years later, Scipio's forces put an end to the Second Punic War at the battle of Zama in North Africa, near Carthage, and for that victory he acquired the name Scipio Africanus. The Romans then had to decide what they would do with the places they had won from Carthage in Spain.

FIGURE 1.1 The Picos de Europa (Peaks of Europe, Cantabria) represented a formidable obstacle to communication between interior regions and the northern coast for much of Spanish history.

FIGURE 1.2 Many scholars think that the so-called "Toros de Guisando" (Bulls of Guisando) near Ávila date from the second century BCE, and that the Romans moved them to their present site.

2

Ancient legacies

∽

A formative period for Spanish history began with the Roman conquest at the end of the third century BCE. Roman political control thereafter expanded over most of the peninsula and lasted through the fourth century CE, as Iberia became one of the most Romanized portions of the empire. Fundamental components of Iberian life were set in place and continued to influence later developments long after the Roman Empire ended. Roman innovations and foundations underlay many medieval and modern developments in Spain and remain strong and apparent in Spain today in such areas as language, law, and religion.

Initially, the process of Romanization in Iberia proceeded slowly, as the Romans followed the pattern that their ancestors had set in taking over the Italian Peninsula, making treaties with groups who agreed to join them voluntarily and conquering those who chose to resist. Nonetheless, it took about 200 years for the Romans to establish full control in Iberia, whereas they conquered Gaul in a decade. The difficult terrain and the traditions of local rule in Iberia made the Roman conquest extraordinarily difficult, and there was scarcely a year in two centuries that did not see fighting in one or more regions.

Soon after the conquest, the Romans divided the area into two parts: Hispania Citerior and Hispania Ulterior

(Closer and Farther Spain, respectively). All they really controlled by the end of the Punic Wars was a band along the Mediterranean coast and beyond Gibraltar as far as Cádiz. That was the part of the peninsula with the greatest number of towns and cities, and the part longest influenced by the other Mediterranean civilizations. Because larger political entities did not exist previously in Iberia, the Romans had to deal separately with one small group after another. They focused on cities and towns in this segmented expansion, making treaties with existing towns and tribes that agreed to join the Roman world, and giving their inhabitants affiliate Roman status. Towns or regions that resisted they forced into submission, often through long wars. This was the case with Numantia, which fell only after a lengthy siege.

Though the Romans had become involved in what they called Hispania only to thwart the ambitions of Carthage, they were quick to recognize the advantages the peninsula offered. These ranged from the psychological – as one historian said, they could claim to have reached the end of the world where Hispania touched the boundless ocean – to the practical and mundane. Control of the peninsula would help secure the sea routes to western Gaul, Britain, and the mouth of the Rhine. The Roman republic and later Roman emperors benefited from taxes on land and profits from mineral exploitation in the peninsula. Several would-be emperors owned profitable estates there, and in fact launched from Hispania their campaigns to secure the imperial throne. Merchants and bureaucrats also established themselves successfully in the peninsula as the Romans settled in.

Rome's authority in the inland areas of the peninsula spread slowly, reaching its fullest extent only after two centuries. Even then, the peninsula remained incompletely Romanized, but in the cities, regardless of their origin, a process of acculturation began almost immediately after the Romans moved in, and proceeded as local and imported customs interacted and blended. The Romans imposed their law, and members of the local elite who wished to deal with the Roman authorities and to function in the new system had to learn Roman law and the Latin language. Elements of Roman law and Romance variants of Latin remain in Spain today. Intermarriage fostered biological integration and cultural assimilation as well. Prominent among those who intermarried were Roman soldiers who remained in Spain and received land when their enlistments ended. Later, Roman immigrants who sought opportunities in Spain secured local marriages and the connections they brought. Roman religion, including the cult of the emperor and the many mystery religions of Roman or eastern Mediterranean origin, spread to Spain with the immigrants and became established there.

An important key to understanding the Roman period in Spain is the story of the towns and cities that linked the various parts of the peninsula together for the first time and connected it to the wider Mediterranean world. In some cases, the Romans created new municipalities, often by offering land to retiring and disabled soldiers. Newly created municipalities under direct Roman control were called "colonies," whose inhabitants were Roman citizens enjoying tax privileges. The implantation of colonies began very early on. In 206 BCE, the Roman general Publius Cornelius Scipio established a colony of veteran soldiers at the new town of Itálica, near Seville, now an important archeological site. Other colonies joined existing municipalities, such as the small town of Mérida, or Tarragona (Roman Tarraco), already a sizeable city and the chief town of the Cessetani tribe. Tarraco became the capital of Hispania Citerior. In time, indigenous communities became associated with the Romans and received the title of *municipia* (sing., *municipium*). Officials of such towns received full Roman citizenship and the ordinary inhabitants became Latin citizens, a lesser status that did not confer tax exemptions.

Where the terrain permitted, Romans laid out their towns on a common, rectilinear pattern with the principal north–south street, called the *cardus*, intersecting with the main east–west street, the *decumanus*, usually to form a main square. The construction of public works also aided in the Romanization of a town. On being incorporated into the Roman world, both new towns and restructured existing towns received civic improvements of various types. Most Roman municipalities had walls, bridges over local rivers, and aqueducts to assure the water supply. The aqueduct of Segovia is the most prominent one remaining today, but portions of others exist in Mérida and Tarragona. Roman houses followed a typical Mediterranean pattern, with rooms opening into a central atrium and presenting an easily fortified face to the street. Tile roofs and stone, brick, or plaster exteriors provided a durable structure, relying on local materials. This model persisted through medieval times in both Christian and Islamic Spain and was the style exported by Spaniards to the Americas. In addition to practical structures such as aqueducts and bridges, most Roman towns had temples (later churches), public baths, schools, and, in the case of larger towns and cities, stadiums, race courses, and elaborate theatres and amphitheatres.

The most important cities of Roman Spain gained that status because they offered strategic advantages. Tarraco, the capital of Hispania Citerior, sat on a strategic hilltop, which its previous rulers, the Cessetani, had already walled. With their huge pre-Roman lower courses, Roman additions, and medieval repairs, Tarraco's walls remain impressive in the twenty-first century. Only five days from Rome by sea, Tarraco also had a road link to the Ebro valley and thus quick access to the interior of Spain. One of the most prominent cities inland from Tarraco was Caesar Augusta (now Zaragoza/Saragossa), whose name indicates its foundation as a colony by Emperor Augustus between 19 and 15 BCE. Roman Caesar Augusta had a bridge over the Ebro River that offered access to a wide area of the Iberian interior. Modern Zaragoza overlays and obscures the Roman constructions, but visitors can still sense the importance of its strategic location. The natural harbor at today's Cartagena on the Mediterranean served as an ideal site for a town in Carthaginian times, and the Romans made it a prominent port for the entire southeastern region of Hispania Citerior. They also minted coins there.

In the southwest of Hispania Ulterior, Roman ships and boats came up the Guadalquivir River as far as Corduba (modern Córdoba), where a major bridge spanned the river. The city was a Roman regional capital, founded as a *municipium* in the second century BCE and made a

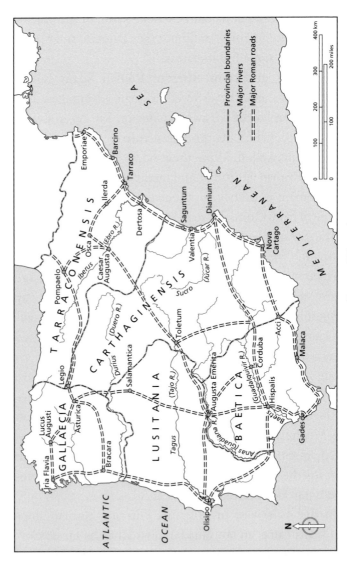

MAP 2.1 Roman Hispania.

colony of army veterans under Julius Caesar and Augustus. Though Córdoba's Islamic monuments and city plan are its most prominent features today, in Roman times the city impressed visitors with its aqueducts, temples, and public baths, plus a theatre and an amphitheatre. Down the Guadalquivir River from Córdoba, near Itálica, lay the town of Hispalis (Seville), which was in existence from the time of Julius Caesar. In fact, he may have founded it himself during his short tenure as governor of Hispania Ulterior in 61 and 60 BCE. Hispalis became a prominent river port with access to the Atlantic Ocean, which undoubtedly explains its ascendancy over Itálica. In Roman times, Hispalis was fully walled and had an aqueduct – part of which is still standing – to provide water to the citizenry. At the mouth of the Guadalquivir, Gades (Cádiz) was already an ancient city when the Romans arrived. With its huge bay and ideal defensible site, Gades served as a strategic port on Rome's Atlantic shipping routes and gained additional wealth from fishing. Julius Caesar gave the city's residents full Roman citizenship, and the urban infrastructure included temples, an aqueduct, a theatre, and an amphitheatre.

Mérida, on the Guadiana River in western Spain near the Portuguese border, retains many architectural and engineering reminders of its Roman past. The city began life as Augusta Emerita, a colony for the veterans of Augustus's campaigns in the northwest of the peninsula. It retains its Roman bridge, the remains of several aqueducts, a theatre, an amphitheatre, and a number of other monuments. In addition, the city's stunning National Museum of Roman Art, built in 1986, houses an impressive collection of Roman statuary, mosaics, and diverse objects of art, commerce, warfare, and common household use. Many other towns and cities all over the Iberian Peninsula also conserve architectural remains and artifacts of their Roman past. For example, Barcelona (the Roman Barcino) has an unusual Roman museum one storey down from modern street level, where visitors walk through several blocks of Roman streets, alongside the foundations of Roman buildings. The huge Roman aqueduct of Segovia, the best preserved in the peninsula, has long served as the emblem of the city.

Even today, Latin adjectival forms often appear in formal usage for Spanish cities and other institutions: matritense for Madrid; onubense for Huelva, the Roman Onuba; abulense for Ávila; hispalense for Seville, among many others. Madrid's oldest university is the Universidad Complutense, originally founded in Alcalá de Henares, the Roman Complutum.

Despite these pervasive remnants of the Roman presence in Spain, the process of Romanization was never complete throughout the peninsula. Eastern and southern Hispania assimilated most completely into the Roman world, following their long tradition of contact with successive Mediterranean civilizations. Farther to the west and north, Roman influence faded, with some notable exceptions. The northern mountainous areas were the least affected by contact with Rome; indeed, some areas take pride in the fact that Rome never conquered them. Throughout the peninsula, urban areas were more romanized than rural areas, and urban elites assimilated more completely than poorer segments of the population. Within many cities of Roman Hispania, Jewish communities began to form in the second century CE, populated by refugees who fled westward following the Romans' destruction of the temple of Jerusalem in the first century CE. From then on, the Jewish communities in Iberia maintained a continuous existence and developed a rich culture, creating the Sephardic branch of European Jewry.

During the Roman period, the rural economy of Iberia changed considerably. Smallholdings, characteristic of pre-Roman days, declined as peasant farmers competed unsuccessfully with larger holdings amassed by Roman immigrants and members of the local elite. The large landowners could afford to acquire slaves and operate on a much larger scale, producing for a network of markets both within and outside Iberia. The Roman style of villa – a large complex with the owner's residence, housing for the workers, barns, and workshops – spread in the more Romanized portions of the peninsula.

Large landowners sold their products in urban markets all over Roman Spain, and exported products by sea to other markets around the Mediterranean and elsewhere. Olive oil traveled in large pottery amphorae to Italy and the Rhine valley. Wine also traveled to Italy; the ruins of Pompeii contain amphorae for Spanish wine. Exports from Hispania also included wheat, flax, wool, and esparto grass, both in their raw states and processed into biscuit, cloth, rope, and baskets. Spanish-produced pottery and glass also made their way into the export markets of the Mediterranean and up the Rhone and other rivers into continental Europe. The ancient mineral trade in gold, silver, copper, cinnabar, and lead also continued in the early centuries of Roman rule. As the easily extracted deposits ran low and production in other Roman provinces increased, however, Spain's role as a leading supplier declined.

Some of the earliest Mediterranean traders to reach Iberia came because of the abundant fish available along the coasts. Fishing and fish processing continued to be highly developed in Roman times. Entrepreneurs salted and exported fish and fish products at numerous coastal locations where bays or sheltered beaches lay close to supplies of salt. The town of Baelo Claudia was an important center of the fish-salting industry. Founded in the time of the emperor Claudius (41–54 CE) as a *municipium*, Baelo Claudia lay on the Atlantic coast between Gibraltar (the Mons Calpe of the Romans) and Cape Trafalgar and had important ties with Tangier in North Africa. The archeological remains of Baelo Claudia today show the installations where freshly caught fish were salted, either whole or filleted, and packed in pottery vessels for transport. Baelo Claudia also produced the widely popular fish sauce the Romans called *garum*, known to earlier inhabitants as *garon*. Omnipresent in the western Roman world, *garum* had an honored place in Rome's imperial kitchens, as well as in the homes of more modest citizens. To produce *garum*, workers dumped layers of fish, fish parts, salt, and various flavorings into stone vats under the hot sun, and then let the mixture ferment for several weeks. The process resulted in a pungent sauce that would keep for months, or even years, in clay pots. That meant that merchants could export *garum* for long distances and reach a wide range of consumers. *Garum* sold throughout the ancient Mediterranean for centuries, but Baelo Claudia suffered an earthquake in the second century CE that cut its easy access to the hinterland. The settlement declined thereafter and finally was abandoned in the seventh century.

Due to Spain's importance in the Roman world, there were frequent contacts and migrations between Italy and Hispania. The emperors Trajan and Hadrian were born in Spain, and the Emperor Theodosius I as well. Marcus Aurelius, the emperor and Stoic philosopher, was of Spanish ancestry, though born in Rome. In philosophy and literature, Seneca, Quintilian, Martial, and Lucan were all born in Hispania, of either Hispanic or Roman parentage. Wherever they traveled, the Romans brought their religions with them, including the civic cult of allegiance to Rome and later emperor-worship. Roman soldiers who had served in distant parts of the empire adopted religions from the eastern Mediterranean and beyond, adding them to the panoply of cults that flourished under Rome.

Of fundamental importance for the later history of Spain, Christianity came early to Iberia, certainly as early as the second century. There are even traditions that Saint James and Saint Paul preached in Spain. The early history of Iberian Christianity is obscure, though it was probably linked initially with the establishment of Jewish communities in eastern and southern Spain during the early Jewish diaspora in the second century. By the third century, the details of Christian history in Iberia become clearer. By then, Christian communities were large enough to have their own bishops and to maintain ties with the papacy in Rome. The persecution of Christians by Roman authorities in Hispania occurred sporadically. The bishop of Tarraco, Fructuosus, and two of his lieutenants suffered martyrs' deaths by burning in 259 CE, and the patron saints of Hispalis, Justa and Rufina, also fell victim to martyrdom under the Romans in the late third century.

Early in the fourth century, Christianity received recognition as a legal religion throughout the Roman Empire, and thereafter expanded rapidly. By the 390s it became the legal and official religion of the empire, under Emperor Theodosius I. By then, Christianity had become fully established in Spain. The most important early act of the Spanish church occurred at the Council of Toledo in 400, when the clergy announced their allegiance to the Nicene Creed as the basis of their faith. The church in Spain remained largely independent of secular authority, having secured immunity from taxation and the right to judicial autonomy from Roman authorities.

Over the course of the third and fourth centuries, the western portions of the Roman Empire experienced economic and demographic alterations. Popular histories often refer to this as the decline of the Roman Empire, but the decline did not affect all parts of the empire equally. The eastern provinces continued to be stronger and more politically coherent; most changes took place in the west. There, the population declined due to a variety of causes, and the remaining population drifted away from the large cities toward increasingly self-sufficient estates in the countryside. Imperial defense suffered from these changes in the west, and the Romans found it more and more difficult to maintain their northern frontiers against the tide of outside groups that wanted to penetrate the empire. By the late fourth century, there were separate emperors in the eastern and western portions of the empire, as well as separate military commands.

Early in the second decade of the fifth century, one of the Germanic groups, the Visigoths, entered Spain, initiating a new period in Spanish history. Their story began in northeastern Europe, but it is important to trace their origins and early history for the insights that history brings to their later career in Spain. Like other Germanic groups, the Visigoths formed from the amalgamation of several related and unrelated groups in a process that scholars have dubbed "ethnogenesis." After a period of wandering through Eastern Europe, they established themselves in the late third century in the area of Dacia to the north of the Danube River. During this period, they adopted certain Roman customs, serving as federates of the empire and furnishing troops and local leaders in return for an annual subsidy. While in Dacia they gained considerable respect for Roman institutions and accepted conversion to the Arian variety of Christianity.

Their conversion was due in large measure to the work of Ulfila (or Wulfila, 310–81), the son of Cappadocian parents living among the Visigoths as prisoners captured in Visigothic raids and then enslaved. Many of the Cappadocians and some of the Visigoths were already Christian. With the addition of new converts, the Christians among the Visigoths made up a sufficiently large number for them to feel justified in petitioning the authorities to name a bishop to lead them. They nominated Ulfila for the office, and he traveled into the Roman Empire and received ordination from a group of bishops, among them Eusebius, at this time bishop of Nicomedia. Ulfila's ordination was to prove a mixed blessing. He became an Arian Christian and converted his flock accordingly. Shortly after he left the Roman Empire, however, the Council of

Nicea declared Arianism – the belief that God the Son was a lesser figure than God the Father – a heresy, leaving Ulfila and his flock outside the definition of Catholic Christian orthodoxy.

Despite this doctrinal discrepancy, the fact that Ulfila converted the Visigoths meant that they absorbed much of the classical Christian tradition. Ulfila's main tool for conversion was his Gothic Bible, a product of many years' work. In the process, Ulfila transformed Gothic into a written language, devising an alphabet for the purpose based on the Greek alphabet. Ulfila had great success in converting the Visigoths. Within twenty years after his death, the entire nation had embraced Arian Christianity.

During the same period, the Visigoths increasingly wanted to move into the Roman Empire, for a number of reasons. Like other Germans, the Visigoths had traded with the empire and had come to appreciate the advantages of Roman civilization and the ecology of the Mediterranean region. Having adopted agriculture from the Romans, they recognized that the lands around the Mediterranean offered better conditions for agriculture. Those lands were more arid and intrinsically poorer than the lands of Northern Europe, but they were easier to plow and manage, given the tools and techniques available at the time.

Ancient farming techniques relied on the so-called "scratch plow" and on simple harnessing devices for draft animals. Such techniques worked well on the light soils of the Mediterranean and the Middle East. They were only marginally effective for most of the lands north of the Alps and the Pyrenees, however, which had abundant rainfall, dense vegetation, and heavy, compact soil. By the tenth and eleventh centuries, the invention and diffusion of new, heavier plows and better harnesses would make it easier to cultivate the lands in Northern Europe, but those days were still far in the future as the Visigoths looked longingly toward the south. Even so, the Roman agricultural techniques that the Visigoths and other Germanic groups adopted allowed a rise in population, which created demand for more lands with more friable soils.

In addition to the pressure from their own numbers, the Visigoths and other Germanic groups faced pressure from the invasion of nomadic Huns from central Asia in the fourth century and from its intensification in the early fifth. To escape the Huns, the Germans sought to enter Roman territory. At this point, the Visigoths had formed up as an amalgamation of several Gothic groups, some outsiders, and even some Huns and Alans (Iranian nomads). In 376, the eastern emperor, Valens, allowed the Visigoths to enter Moesia, south of the Danube in the southeastern Balkans, as the first full group of northern outsiders to enter the boundaries of the empire.

The Visigoths continued to act as federates of the empire under their Christian chief Fridigern, but disputes with the Romans over promised subsidies soon arose. The Visigoths then violated the terms of their agreement and ravaged Moesia and a large part of Thrace, where only the cities could resist them. Emperor Valens rallied an army and tried to check their expansion, but the Visigoths, aided by some Ostrogothic horsemen, inflicted a defeat on the Roman army at Adrianople and killed the emperor himself on August 9, 378. That was a major military defeat and an even more chilling psychological blow, given that an alien army had defeated Roman troops on Roman soil. The new emperor, Theodosius, took up the imperial defense and was able to reach an agreement with the Visigoths in 382. They would remain in Moesia as self-governing vassals and would supply the empire with troops.

That situation continued throughout the lifetime of Theodosius, but on his death in 395 the Visigoths reconsidered their position. They seem to have distrusted the new emperor and may have feared that a settled life would cause them to stagnate and lose power. In any case, the Visigothic nobles chose Alaric of the Balthas family as their king and agreed to follow his lead. Theodosius may have promised Alaric a command in the Roman army. If so, his death removed an incentive for the new king to abide by the terms of federation. Instead, Alaric led the Visigoths on a rampage through Thrace, Macedonia, and Greece, plundering the countryside but generally sparing the towns. The Roman military chief in the west, Stilicho, though nominally under the authority of the western emperor, Honorius, took an army to the Peloponnesus and intercepted Alaric. After some desultory fighting, the two leaders came to an agreement and disengaged their forces. Thereafter, in 397, the eastern government of Arcadius granted Alaric the title of *magister militum* (chief military commander) in Illyricum, a province along the eastern coast of the Adriatic. Apparently, Stilicho had persuaded Alaric to help bring Illyricum under western Roman authority and out of eastern control.

The story of the Visigoths for the next decade and a half is complicated. It seems to have depended in part on the desires and plans of Alaric, who apparently still wanted a high imperial command for himself and a worthwhile homeland for his followers. Aided by a diversionary tactic conducted by the Ostrogoth Radagaisus, Alaric invaded Italy and occupied Milan in hopes of capturing the Emperor Honorius. Stilicho raised the siege and pursued Alaric to Pollentia, where, early in 402, he inflicted a sharp defeat on the Visigoths. Alaric agreed to move back to Illyricum, but the next year he tried another invasion of Italy and again was repelled.

At that point in their history, the Visigoths in all probability numbered no more than 100,000 people, with 4,000 to 5,000 members of the elite and perhaps 25,000 to 30,000 warriors. The total numbers included significant non-Gothic elements, plus ex-slaves and ex-soldiers who joined with the Visigoths during their Italian campaigns. Still hoping to secure an area for his followers to settle, Alaric again invaded the Italian Peninsula and moved quickly toward Rome, placing it under siege. He demanded a huge ransom from the city, and because imperial aid from Honorius in Ravenna was not forthcoming, the Roman Senate acceded to his demands. Alaric then opened negotiations with the government of Honorius, demanding the provinces of Noricum, Venetia, Istria, and Dalmatia for the Visigoths. Even though Alaric eventually scaled back his demands to the single province of Noricum, Honorius and his advisers refused.

Once again, Alaric marched on Rome. He forced the Senate to elect Priscus Attalus as a rival emperor, but Attalus proved no more accommodating than Honorius. In August 410, the Visigoths entered Rome and sacked the city for four days. As they wanted mainly moveable goods, they did not inflict too much physical damage on the city, but they dealt a harsh psychological blow to the Romans. The Visigoths also secured a number of important captives in Rome, among them Emperor Attalus and Galla Placidia, sister of Honorius. Traditionalists among the Romans blamed their plight on Christianity, which had become the sole legal religion of the empire in the 390s. In their view, Christianity had caused a collapse in the Roman system that allowed the Visigoths to break into the empire. That accusation motivated the Christian theologian Augustine, bishop of Hippo, to write *The City of God*, in which he drew a sharp distinction between the inevitable progress of Christianity and the often-disturbing vicissitudes of the secular sphere.

From Rome, Alaric led his people on a rapid advance through southern Italy, with Africa as his apparent goal. At Rhegium, the ships for the initial passage to Sicily were wrecked, and, before Alaric could reach Naples to find other transportation, he died and was given a river burial in the Basentus. The Visigoths elected Ataulf as Alaric's successor. Originally anti-Roman, Ataulf soon became disillusioned with his Gothic followers, according to the contemporary writer Osorius, and decided to integrate his people into what remained of the Roman system. He reached an accommodation with Honorius and agreed to enter Gaul and return it to imperial authority. Accordingly, he entered southern Gaul, establishing strongpoints at the towns of Narbonne, Toulouse, and Bordeaux. He also persuaded Galla Placidia to marry him, an event that caused her brother Honorius to withdraw his support. Ataulf then raised Priscus Attalus again to the imperial title and began probing expeditions into the Iberian Peninsula, but he failed to accomplish much more before his death in 415.

By then, other Germanic groups had crossed the borders into the Roman Empire, just as the Visigoths had done, and Roman forces in the west could not expel them. After Ataulf died, the Visigoths elected Wallia as their king, and he tried to revive Alaric's dream of an African homeland for his people. Once again, shipwrecks caused him to abandon the project, but he still needed a source of grain. To secure it, Wallia reached an agreement with Honorius' general Constantius. For a suitable supply of food, the Visigoths would return Ataulf's widow Galla Placidia to her brother and would undertake to drive the other Germanic tribes from Iberia in service to Rome.

Spain was not immune from the internal problems that beset the later Roman Empire. The *Pax Romana*, and the subsequent demobilization of troops, had weakened the peninsula's ability to withstand invasion. In fact, Roman taxation had become so severe that some inhabitants actually welcomed invading barbarians as an alternative to Roman rule. In the years from 409 to 415, three other barbarian groups entered Roman Spain: the Suevi, the Vandals, and the Alans. At the end of the first five years of invasion, they had established themselves in the west and south of the peninsula: the Suevi and some Vandals in Gallecia (later Galicia) in the northwest, the main body of the Vandals in Baetica in the southwest, and the Alans in Lusitania south of the Duero. The remaining parts of the peninsula stayed in Roman hands.

Wallia began the reconquest of Iberia – a task not fully completed until 585 – and was rewarded with Roman recognition of the Visigothic sway in southern Gaul. With this, the Visigothic kingdom established a capital at Toulouse, and Wallia renounced sovereignty over the Spanish lands he had conquered. The Visigoths maintained this compact until 456. Under Theodoric I, they pushed the Vandals from Spain into Africa in 429 and later forced the Suevi from Galicia. They virtually annihilated the Alans. In 456 the Visigothic king, Theodoric II (453–66), renounced imperial sovereignty and began the conquest of additional territory in both Gaul and Spain on his own authority. Euric (467–85), the successor of Theodoric II, was able to secure the entire peninsula, with the exception of the northwest and some pockets of Hispano-Roman resistance. At his death, Euric was probably the most powerful ruler in Western Europe.

Soon after Euric's death, the Franks in northern Gaul began to challenge Visigothic control. The Franks' conversion to Catholicism in 496 was an additional spur to their plans to drive out the Arian Visigoths. Aided by native Catholics in Visigothic territory, by 508 King Clovis and the Franks had pushed the Visigoths from all of Gaul, with the exception of Septimania. The Visigoths lost their capital of Toulouse and temporarily made Narbonne their political center. In the middle of the sixth century, a claimant to the Visigothic throne, Athanagild, asked for assistance from the eastern Roman emperor, Justinian, who sent an army to help secure the throne for Athanagild. In the process, the Byzantine army gained a block of territory in the southeastern portion of Hispania, stretching roughly from the mouth of the Guadalquivir in the west to that of the Júcar River in the east. Although they lost most of it after Justinian's death, Byzantine influence remained strong in southeastern Spain from the 550s to the 620s. Athanagild's main contribution to Visigothic rule in Spain was to establish the capital at Toledo. There it was to remain for as long as the kingdom lasted.

Visigothic legal development shows their accommodation to Roman practice and, at the same time, marks their increasing sophistication. Like other Germanic tribes, they had amassed a large corpus of customary usages, which formed the basis for their legal practice. Major differences existed between Roman written law and Germanic customary law, which had no mechanism to create new laws. In the absence of trained lawyers and judges, interpretations of customary law relied on the collective memory of the elder men of the group. While the Visigothic capital was still in Toulouse, Euric commissioned Leon of Narbonne, a Gallo-Roman jurist, to prepare a national law code for the Goths, written in Latin and based on the older Visigothic laws and customs. In addition, elements of Roman law, including canon legislation, entered the code. The code of Euric applied only to the Visigoths; they allowed the Gallo- and Hispano-Romans living among them to keep Roman law. In 506, Alaric II provided a uniform legal code for those populations, the *Lex romana visigothorum*, which later became known as the *Brevium Alarici regis*, or, in English, the Breviary of King Alaric. The Breviary was a compilation of Roman law actually in force in the Visigothic kingdom, with defunct or conflicting legislation deleted.

King Chindaswinth (ruled 642–53) wished to establish one territorial law for all the peninsula and Septimania, instead of the Roman practice, continued by the early Visigoths, of allowing subject peoples to keep their own laws. Expanded by his successors, the Visigothic law code was known as the *Liber iudiciorum*, the *Lex visigothorum*, or, much later the *Fuero Juzgo*. The code included civil and penal legislation, administrative law, and some political regulations. Unlike the Franks or Anglo-Saxons, the Visigothic legislators consciously introduced new laws and did not merely record customs. An examination of the code shows a complete absence of customary usages, and many scholars have assumed that Germanic customary law fell out of use as Roman law took hold. Instead, the legal codes of Spain's various medieval Christian kingdoms reveal that customary law survived alongside the *Liber iudiciorum*, often in direct contradiction to its provisions.

Arian and Catholic versions of Christianity remained in conflict in the Visigothic kingdom. As governance disintegrated in the later Roman Empire, bishops began to provide many of the services that government officials had once administered. In the formative period of the Visigothic monarchy, members of the ruling class were Arians, whereas their subjects were Catholics, and this religious gulf was a source of constant conflict. The Catholic Hispano-Romans and Suevi regarded their Visigothic conquerors as heretics as well as barbarians and often agreed to support Frankish or Byzantine invasions against their Arian rulers.

To ease these problems and to avoid others, King Reccared announced his conversion to Catholicism in 586. The conversion was largely due to the work of Leander, bishop of Seville. He presided over the third Council of Toledo in 589, when the rest of the royal family, the higher Arian clergy, and most of the Visigothic nobility publicly announced their adherence to Catholicism. They had ample reasons to convert, as many Visigoths had already done. The Visigothic monarchs seemed to have believed that the clergy would make more willing and tractable allies than the lay magnates. Moreover, the Catholic religious hierarchy enjoyed great political power over their flocks and would find it easier to relate to a Catholic monarchy.

Despite these advantages, the alteration of Visigothic religious practices created several upheavals. First, the event marked the beginning of the virtual extinction of the Gothic language in Spain. Latin had served for administrative pronouncements as early as King Euric's code a century earlier. Gothic had survived only as the language of the Arian church. After Arianism was condemned and anathematized, Reccared ordered the seizure and destruction of all Arian books that the authorities could find. As a result, not a single Gothic text has survived in Spain. Vulgar Latin completely replaced Gothic as a spoken language. Some 100 words of Gothic origin are present in modern Spanish, but most scholars believe that they entered Latin before the Visigoths got to Spain, through Germanic connections with the Roman army.

Visigothic administration emanated from the monarchy, with kings theoretically elected by the nobility and the bishops – Arian at first and then Catholic. Royal rule was supposed to be pious, merciful, and just; a king who departed from custom was no longer king. As the Visigothic code expressed the concept: "King you will be, if you do right, and if you do not do right, you will not be king." Despite such lofty principles, the political life of Visigothic Spain was far from placid. The centrifugal power of the nobility always posed a potential threat to monarchical authority. The nobility tried hard to maintain the principle of elective kingship, while almost every king tried to secure hereditary succession for his heir. Unrest, and at times civil war, followed the death of kings, as nobles raised an elected claimant, while the deceased king's designated heir rallied support in opposition. Sometimes, one or the other side sought outside support. The invasion of Justinian's Byzantine army was the product of a succession crisis, as was the later Muslim invasion. In their attempt to check noble power, after 589 the kings relied increasingly on the national councils of the Catholic clergy.

These national councils, which met at Toledo eighteen times from 589 to 710, resembled the Frankish Marchfields and Mayfields and the Anglo-Saxons' Witenagemots. Called by the kings, the councils were in part an outgrowth of the national synods of the Spanish church and included a majority of clerics and a smaller number of lay lords. The councils dealt with both ecclesiastical and secular matters, and the kings specified at the beginning of each session what secular matters the council could address. Councils could petition or initiate new legislation, but the kings were free to accept or refuse what they wished. Councils had no power over taxation but did have a limited judicial function.

In the field of education, the Roman municipal schools disappeared soon after the Germanic conquests, as did the individual masters of rhetoric. Although the Jewish communities retained their own academies where professors read and discussed books with their students, the church carried out the bulk of education under the Visigoths. Monasteries were the first to claim educational jurisdiction, and Valencia had the first Spanish monastery school in the late fifth century. The monasteries trained boys destined for the clergy as well as those who simply desired an education. They also provided public lectures in connection with the divine office and independent lectures each day, for six or seven hours in winter and three or four hours in summer. The monasteries also maintained libraries, and although they frowned upon pagan authors, their libraries retained some classical knowledge. The education of females took place almost wholly within the home; any female education outside the home occurred separately from male education.

Cathedrals later began to operate schools as well, with establishments in Zaragoza and Seville, and the most influential one in Toledo. With the establishment of Toledo as the Visigothic capital, that city also became the most important educational center in the peninsula, with one cathedral school and one school operated in connection with the nearby monastery of Agali. These schools aimed above all to educate the sons of the nobility, and the study of liberal arts alternated with physical education. The study of law and medicine continued, but the curriculum emphasized other topics, while jousting, horseback riding, and other martial sports replaced the Roman gymnasia.

Most writers in the Visigothic period had some connection with the church. Paulus Orosius was a well-known writer in the period of transition between late Roman and early Visigothic rule. Of Hispano-Roman ancestry, Orosius was born in Bracara (modern Braga) in the late fourth century, and in the years 415 to 420 visited St. Augustine at Hippo and St. Jerome near Jerusalem. Orosius wrote a universal history (possibly the first by a Christian), in which he revealed himself as a patriotic Spaniard and an ardent devotee of the Roman Empire. Far from condemning the Visigoths for their sack of Rome in 410, he saw them as the only hope for a united Spain and a revitalized Roman Empire. Most of the clerical writers focused on theology and Christian apologetics. The poets among them included Draconcius and Bishop Eugene II of Toledo. Braulio, bishop of Zaragoza in the late seventh century, wrote lives of saints and letters in excellent Latin, and was familiar with the Latin classics. Julian (late seventh century) wrote a biography of Wamba, a Visigothic king, as well as theological and apologetical works in good Latin. Idacius wrote a history of the Visigothic invasion.

There were also some specifically lay writers. Several Visigothic kings left evidence of their literary skill, in particular Reccared, Chindaswinth, Recceswinth, and Sisebute. Among the nobles, a certain Duke Claudius was also a writer, and a Count Lorenzo had a massive library. Indeed, the possession of large libraries with many and beautiful manuscripts became a favored status symbol among the kings and the aristocracy of Visigothic Spain.

The highest point of Visigothic culture arrived with Isidore of Seville (560–636), brother of Leander, archbishop of Seville. Educated at the cathedral school that his brother established in the city, Isidore learned Latin, Greek, and Hebrew, and in 599 he succeeded his brother as archbishop there. His subsequent career shows that he managed to combine the life of a scholar with that of a man of affairs. Active in the political life of the kingdom, he attended the Council of Toledo in 589 when his brother secured Reccared's conversion. He also presided over a general church council at Seville in 619 and at the national council of Toledo in 633. Isidore also produced his own monastic rule, which stressed an active life defined by hard work as well as piety.

In his cultural initiatives as archbishop, Isidore founded schools for children, seminaries for the education of clerics, and monasteries. He enlarged the already sizeable cathedral library at Seville and reorganized its *scriptorium*, insisting on accuracy, beauty, and excellence in the work of his copyists. Isidore also became a prolific writer, and history remembers him best for his literary efforts. As a historian, he wrote a *History of the Goths, Vandals, and Suevi* and a literary history, *De viris illustribus* (*On Illustrious Men*). His theological works included an Old Testament gloss and commentaries on various aspects of Christian dogma. His best work, without doubt, is his *Etymologiae*, written late in his life.

The *Etymologies*, its title in English, is an encyclopedic work in which Isidore first explained the philological basis of each term he included, and then proceeded to include all knowledge he could find relating to it. Wherever possible, he substituted Christian authorities for pagan ones. After Isidore's death in 636, his disciple Braulio organized the encyclopedia and divided it into twenty books. Books I and II deal with the Roman *trivium* (grammar, rhetoric, and logic) and Book III treats the *quadrivium* (arithmetic, geometry, astronomy, and music). The other books cover an astonishing range of topics, from medicine, law, and kingship, to food, dress, and furniture, and everything in between.

In short, Isidore intended to compile an encyclopedia of all existing knowledge based on the sources available to him. For philosophy, he relied on Plato, Aristotle, and Seneca. For theology, he relied on Origen, Tertullian, Augustine, and Gregory the Great, and for grammar and rhetoric he used Cicero and Quintilian. For history, he summarized Sallust, Livy, Jerome, Orosius, and Hidacius, and for law he used Ulpian and the Theodosian code. Isidore also recorded works of the poets Virgil, Horace, Ovid, Lucan, and Lucretius. He based his architectural knowledge on Vitruvius, and he was familiar with the scientific works of Hesiod, Democritus, Pliny, Varro, and Columela. He also relied on the encyclopedic works of Boethius and Cassiodorus. Historians have often derided Isidore for his naive acceptance of his sources, and for his uncritical amassing of information. Despite that criticism, many of the classical writings that he collected would have been lost, had he not compiled them.

Isidore's *Etymologiae* became a crucial text for medieval education, and most well-equipped medieval libraries had a copy. The Venerable Bede knew Isidore's work in early eighth-century England. References to Isidore also abound in the writers of the Carolingian Renaissance in France. Until Vincent of Beauvais wrote his *Speculum* in the thirteenth century, the *Etymologiae* was the most easily available work covering so wide a range of topics. With the advent of printing in the fifteenth century, Isidore's work experienced a new period of popularity. Ten editions of the *Etymologiae* appeared in print between 1477 and 1577, and many other editions have appeared since then. In fact, the first complete English translation was published in 2006 – testimony to the enduring appeal and significance of this early encyclopedia.

The Visigothic kingdom of Spain exemplified an uneven blending of Germanic and Roman institutions and customs, but the continuities from Roman times are more significant than any changes made by the Visigoths. Partly that is due to the latter's small numbers – perhaps 100,000 Visigoths in a population of several million Hispano-Romans. Roman traditions were already entrenched in language, law, and religion before the Visigoths arrived, and that, too, helps to explain their dominance. The continuity is readily apparent in archeological investigations showing that material life hardly changed with the transition. Few Visigothic buildings survive, because medieval structures superseded them. Nonetheless, by 711 the Visigoths had created, from their own and their adopted customs, a monarchical state quite similar to other early kingdoms in Western Europe. What they might eventually have accomplished is unknowable, for the kingdom abruptly fell before the sweep of Islamic conquest.

The last Visigothic king of Spain was Roderick, elected in 710 by a group of nobles in defiance of the late King Witiza, who had hoped that his son Akhila would succeed him. After Roderick's election, Akhila withdrew to the northeast of the peninsula, raised the banner of civil war, and declared himself the ruler. There is some rather circumstantial evidence that some of Akhila's Visigothic supporters, along with a certain Julian (possibly the Byzantine exarch of Ceuta), encouraged the Muslims to attack Roderick and aided the invaders for a time. The records are incomplete, and later chroniclers preserved unverifiable legends and stories that developed over the years. Without doubt, however, Roderick faced divisions within the ruling class, in addition to the lingering disaffection of the Hispano-Roman subjects of the Visigothic monarchy.

In July 710, a reconnaissance force of 400 Muslims from North Africa crossed the strait and landed on the Iberian Peninsula at a place just west of Gibraltar. This initial foray, and the lack of resistance to their incursion, encouraged the Muslims to organize a large invasion force the following spring. Berber forces numbering 7,000 to 12,000 men, under the leadership of Ṭāriq ibn Ziyād, the governor of Tangier, crossed the strait and established a base camp at the foot of the Roman Mons Calpe, now renamed the hill of Ṭāriq, Gibraltar. Roderick hurried from the north with his army to meet the invaders, but it was too late. Roderick lost the battle and his life, and effective resistance to the Islamic invasion collapsed. The Visigothic kingdom, and with it Iberia's ancient history, had come to an abrupt end.

FIGURE 2.1 In the remains of fortification walls in Tarragona (Catalonia), the huge stones at the base are thought to date from the sixth century BCE. The middle courses date from the time of the Roman general Scipio (*c.* 200 BCE), and the top courses from the time of Caesar Augustus (late first century BCE).

FIGURE 2.2 The great aqueduct of Segovia is one of the most dramatic remnants of the Roman period in Spain.

FIGURE 2.3 The elaborate proscenium of the Roman theatre in Mérida (Extremadura), along the "silver road," evokes the wealth and cultural sophistication of the province of Lusitania.

FIGURE 2.4 Besides bridges and aqueducts, roads were important Roman contributions to the economic infrastructure of Iberia. This road, in the Gredos range of the Central Mountains, is still used by transhumant livestock.

FIGURE 2.5 This crown, bearing the name of King Recceswinth (mid seventh century CE), represents the Christian identity of Visigothic Spain. Crafted of gold and adorned with precious stones, it was made to hang in church as a votive offering – in other words, in fulfillment of a sacred vow.

FIGURE 2.6 San Pedro de la Nave, *c.* 680–711 (Zamora), is one of the few churches that still retain their Visigothic character. When a dam-building project threatened its existence in 1930–2, it was moved, stone by stone, to its present site at El Campillo, at the insistence of a local architect.

3

Diversity in medieval Spain

~

The fall of the Visigothic monarchy marked the beginning of the Islamic phase of Spain's history. From 711 to 1492, Muslims controlled varying portions of Iberia, and their long presence had a profound influence on Spanish culture long after they lost political control. From their origins in the Arabian Peninsula during the time of the prophet Muhammad (*c.* 570–632), the Muslims spread quickly and widely throughout the Middle East and across North Africa. They conquered cities as they went, fighting when they had to and making deals with local authorities when they could. People who came under Muslim authority had the option of converting to Islam, but they did not have to do so to live peaceably under their new overlords. Christians and Jews, considered "People of the Book" or fellow monotheists, could retain their religion and customs if they refrained from proselytizing, if they paid special taxes, and if they agreed to political restrictions preventing them from having authority over Muslims.

The historical sources, both Christian and Muslim, for the end of the Visigothic monarchy and the conquest and establishment of Islamic Spain are not abundant and come from later periods. Contemporary accounts are not available, and later ones are contradictory and contain legendary accretions. Nonetheless, scholars generally agree on the main outlines of the early years of Muslim consolidation in Spain.

After the defeat of King Roderick in southern Spain, the Muslim commander Ṭāriq ibn Ziyād, commanding a mainly Berber army, sent troops toward Córdoba. They defeated a remnant of the Visigoths on the way and took the city after a long siege. Ṭāriq accepted the allegiance of disaffected groups in the area, including significant elements of the Jewish communities, a segment of the population oppressed by the Visigoths and especially discontented. Ṭāriq himself moved on Toledo, the Visigothic capital, which his forces easily captured, while a detachment of his army secured Córdoba. His immediate overlord Mūsā ibn Nasayr, governor of northwest Africa, arrived in Spain with a force of 18,000, many of them Arabs, and conquered Carmona, Seville, and Mérida. Ṭāriq and Mūsā joined forces in Toledo and wintered there. During the following year Ṭāriq went to the northwest while Mūsā secured the Ebro valley, thanks in part to the conversion to Islam of two prominent Christian families, who remained in control of the local area as the Banū Qasī and the Banū Amrūs. Mūsā advanced on Narbonne beyond the Pyrenees. In Orihuela in the southeast, the local Duke Thodemir made a favorable treaty with the Muslims allowing local autonomy in exchange for tribute in kind. In 714, the caliph in Damascus summoned Mūsā and Ṭāriq to report on their conquests. In their absence, Spain remained in the charge of Mūsā's son ʿAbd al-ʿAzīz, who extended Muslim power in the eastern regions of Iberia.

By early 716 the Muslims had conquered most of the peninsula with the exception of the far northwest and the mountainous regions elsewhere in the north. Within the remainder of the territory, there were undoubtedly pockets of resistance and areas of only nominal allegiance, but Muslim control was probably more effective than that of the late Visigoths. The new Islamic province received the name al-Andalus and came under the ultimate authority of the Umayyad caliph in Damascus. In 716 the caliph placed the newly conquered al-Andalus under the authority of the governor of Tunisia, with a subordinate provincial governor for Spain. Some twenty governors served in al-Andalus from 716 to 756, but their short periods of tenure made it almost impossible to quell rising infighting among the various factions of the leadership.

Muslim Arabs and Berbers formed the core of the invading armies and received a stipend from captured booty. In some cases, as when local landowners had fled their property, certain Muslim warriors gained control of landed estates. This practice occurred in Spain until about 750, creating in the process a large group of Muslim landowners. Friction developed as Arabs received the best lands and Berbers the worst.

After conquering most of Spain, the Muslim governors in al-Andalus made repeated advances into France, taking Narbonne in 719–21 but failing to capture Toulouse. In 725 they tried unsuccessfully to advance up the Rhone valley. In 732 they crossed the western Pyrenees at Roncevalles and took Bordeaux, advancing from there into central France. The Frankish leader Charles Martel met and defeated the invaders between Tours and Poitiers in October 732. Although the Muslim army did not suffer a severe defeat in the battle, the event marked the high point of the Islamic advance in Western Europe.

Economics and psychology help to explain why the Muslims drew back. First, their strategy aimed mainly to gain booty through short, intense campaigns; they disliked long and bitter fighting. Western Europe was relatively poor and backward in the early eighth century, with little easily removable plunder available. The power of the Franks was growing, while internal dissensions in the Islamic world multiplied, making Muslim soldiers harder to recruit, particularly for campaigns that yielded little plunder. In addition, the Muslims likely considered the climate north of the Pyrenees to be hostile and unfamiliar. They made one more raid into the Rhone area in 734, but from then on Charles Martel and his sons gradually but inexorably pushed the Muslims from France and had effectively contained them in Spain by 759.

Conquest, conversion, and assimilation

The conquerors of al-Andalus faced sometimes severe internal problems, and fissures along lines of ethnic and geographical affiliations. Even the elite Arabs split into rival factions: the Qaysites and the Kalbites, groups which had their origins in rivalries in the Arabian Peninsula. Closely resembling political parties, the same factions were also present in Damascus. To retain power, the caliph relied on one group at the expense of the other, changing sides periodically. As he drew his appointees in Spain from the party he favored at any particular time, the factional strife in Damascus gave rise to bitter feuds in Spain as well.

Friction between the Arabs and all other ethnic groups who later converted to Islam was already apparent in the Islamic world. The Arabs were proud of their status as the original Muslims and as the recipients of the best lands in conquered territories; the later converts and their descendants resented the Arabs' assumed superiority. This resentment extended even to the Syrians and was especially acute among the Berbers, the majority of the invaders of Spain, who had contributed mightily to the conquest and then found themselves rewarded with allocations of considerably less desirable lands. Many of them were so disaffected that they joined a Berber revolt that started in Morocco in 740. The caliph sent a contingent of Syrians to Morocco to calm the unrest, but they failed. The survivors among them – some 7,000 out of an original 30,000 – transferred to Spain, where they defeated the Berber rebels in three areas of the south. The Berbers in Spain dispersed and some returned to Morocco. The Syrians remained in Spain.

Overall, relatively few Muslims went to the peninsula. Ṭāriq's mainly Berber forces numbered around 12,000, Mūsā's commanded about 18,000 Arabs, and 7,000 Syrians arrived in 741. The Iberian population at the time of the Muslim incursion has been estimated at anywhere from 4,000,000 to 8,000,000, mainly Christian but with important Jewish communities in the larger cities. Statistically, therefore, the Muslim presence was quite small, but conversions to Islam added to those numbers from the beginning and increased over time.

The converts from Christianity to Islam came from two quite different categories. At the top were members of the Visigothic royal house, high nobles, and influential families such as the Banū Qasī, dominant in the upper Ebro valley, who saw political advantages in joining with the new rulers. But members of the local elite were few in number. Far more numerous were the lowly Visigothic or Hispano-Roman Christians who converted to Islam. They typically occupied low positions in the social hierarchy. Despite these conversions, in the early centuries of Islamic Spain, most Christians retained their ancestral faith, though many adopted Muslim customs and learned Arabic – hence the term for them: Mozarabs (*mozárabes*), or Muslim-like. The sizeable Jewish communities in a number of cities also remained largely true to their faith. Both Christians and Jews lived as "People of the Book" in Islamic Spain, as did their coreligionists in other parts of the Islamic world.

From emirate to caliphate in Muslim Spain

Even though Spain lay far from the center of the caliphate in Damascus, events at the core of the Islamic world had a major unintended impact on al-Andalus, as Muslim Spain began to follow its own political path. In 750 the Abbasid family wrested the Damascus caliphate from the Umayyad dynasty. The scion of the defeated family, 'Abd al-Raḥmān ibn Mu'āwiya, fled to Morocco, where his mother's family had influence. Once there, he sent agents to the opposing groups in al-Andalus. The Qaysite faction refused to treat with him, but the Yemenis welcomed his proposals. He crossed the strait at the head of an army composed of Syrians, Yemenis, and some Berbers with Iberian connections. By May 756, he had destroyed the Qaysite army and had taken the title of emir of al-Andalus in the capital of Córdoba. 'Abd al-Rahmān's action was revolutionary in that he assumed the office on his own and admitted no subordination to a higher authority. After 756, al-Andalus enjoyed de facto political independence, one of the first breaks in the political unity of the Islamic world.

'Abd al-Raḥmān I, as he is traditionally styled, ruled his independent emirate effectively, and strengthened Córdoba as his capital, beautifying the city and building the principal mosque, a structure still impressive after twelve centuries. Córdoba became the focal point of al-Andalus, a position it enjoyed for over 200 years. Nonetheless, 'Abd al-Raḥmān failed to solve his emirate's social problems. Religious and ethnic disunity continued to plague his successors in the eighth and ninth centuries. One emir after another managed to suppress revolts during the years 756 to 822, although at times with difficulty and considerable bloodshed. To rule effectively, without the constant threat of rebellion, the emirs had to consolidate their authority in al-Andalus. Aside from some apparently futile appeals to religious unity, force was the only solution to the chronic instability. Consequently, the emirs created a professional army, dependent on the emir and run by foreign mercenaries, including enslaved soldiers from elsewhere in Europe. Because many of these soldiers were Slavs, their name became synonymous with slave.

Slavery was present in the Islamic world, as it had been throughout the Mediterranean world and the Middle East in ancient and classical times. Muslims were not to enslave Muslims, only non-believers, but if slaves then converted to Islam they did not automatically become free, only eligible for manumission. Enslaved women had duties that included household labor, nursing, and acting as concubines. Enslaved men were artisans and laborers, and some became soldiers. In addition, enslaved soldiers were imported from beyond the bounds of the Islamic world, many from Central and Eastern Europe, as youths. They were converted to Islam and received military training, designed to instill in them complete loyalty to their commanders and their ruler. Islamic rulers from Spain to Egypt made use of these loyal troops, who often were freed in early middle age as they ascended in the ranks; they then formed families of their own.

The army created by the emirs solved the problem of dissent within al-Andalus and fostered conditions for the emirate to flourish culturally. Córdoba remained a vital center of al-Andalus after 'Abd al-Raḥmān I. As his successors expanded and beautified the city, it grew to become one of Europe's largest. Ideas and intellectuals traveled to Spain from the Islamic heartland, and al-Andalus changed from a far-western outpost of the Islamic world to become a vital part of it.

In the intensified Islamic culture of Córdoba, many Christians adopted the manners and dress of the Muslims, and increasing numbers spoke Arabic. Acculturation brought these Christian Mozarabs closer to their Muslim neighbors. By the time of 'Abd al-Raḥmān II (822–52), many Arabized Christians took the final step and converted to Islam. Some church leaders in Córdoba viewed the loss of their fellow believers to the Islamic ranks as a major threat to the continued existence of the Christian community and tried to check the tide of conversions. Their tactics, in extreme form, included courting martyrdom and encouraging their fellow Christians to do the same. Often they staged provocative displays of Christian faith that included denunciations of Islam and its prophet, deliberately seeking martyrdom; the Muslim authorities obliged by arresting and executing the leaders of the movement. The martyrs of Córdoba seem to have had little effect on the overall character of Islamic Spain, but they may in fact have bolstered Christian identity and morale. The Mozarabic community survived, but individuals and groups of Mozarabs unwilling to remain in Muslim lands moved into the Christian-controlled areas far to the north of al-Andalus.

Meanwhile, Islamic leaders in al-Andalus worked to build local power and make themselves less and less subservient to the emirs in Córdoba. When 'Abd al-Raḥmān III became emir in 912, he faced a difficult situation, with central authority weakened beyond a relatively short radius from the capital. Through clever plans and strong tactics, he rebuilt central authority and reasserted control through an increased use of enslaved troops. He also increased the naval presence of the emirate in the Mediterranean and used it against his chief maritime rivals, including the Normans and the newly powerful Fatimid dynasty in North Africa.

The Fatimid dynasty, which later took control of Egypt, had assumed the title of caliph in challenge to the Abbasid caliph in Baghdad, to whom all Muslims owed obedience – at least nominally. The Fatimids based their challenge on their leader's descent from Muhammad's daughter Fatima, wife of Ali, Muhammad's cousin and a figure venerated by the Shi'ites. Although al-Andalus was already an independent emirate, and in practice had little to do with distant Baghdad or the maintenance of its authority, the emirs had every reason to view the rise of the Fatimids with alarm, once they established a power base in Morocco. 'Abd al-Raḥmān III, in an effort to attain greater authority at home and a counterbalance to the Fatimids across the strait, took the title of caliph for himself, making al-Andalus completely independent from higher authority.

This assumption of the title of caliph conformed to 'Abd al-Raḥmān III's program of building his political authority. He reorganized the structure of government in the caliphate of Córdoba, building an effective bureaucracy and a network of loyal provincial governors. That reorganization worked well for him and for his son and successor al-Ḥakam (d. 976), but in the late tenth century and into the eleventh, power slipped away from successive caliphs in two directions. In Córdoba itself, the chamberlains, or chief ministers of the caliphate, increased their own power and marginalized the caliphs. Outside the capital, local towns and cities became increasingly self-directing and independent from Córdoba. With the center unable to hold and with religious enthusiasm insufficient to sustain support for the caliph, political fragmentation became the rule. This fragmentation reached a climax in the early eleventh century, when the last Umayyad caliph, Hishām II, was overthrown and not replaced. In 1031, the various leaders of al-Andalus met in Córdoba and agreed to abolish the caliphate.

Why would they do so? The reasons for the end of the caliphate are still not completely clear, and numerous possibilities suggest themselves. Muslims had been in control in Spain for three centuries by then, and their leaders may have assumed this to have been a permanent and uncontestable situation. Though Christian forces had made advances in the north, Muslims still controlled over two-thirds of the peninsula and particularly the prosperous south and southeast, despite ethnic differences among the various Muslim communities. Moreover, the caliphs after 'Abd al-Raḥmān III were not as capable as their precursors and relinquished authority to their chamberlains. Muhammad ibn Abī 'Amir, with the *nom de guerre* al-Manṣūr (the Victorious), was the first of the chamberlains to attain authority over the caliphate. Yet he and his successors, known as the Amirid dictators, could not hold al-Andalus together. Localism grew as various urban leaders pursued independent courses.

The last caliph, Hishām II, was actually deposed twice, once in 1009 and definitively in 1013, giving way to a situation of seemingly endless squabbles and battles. When the most prominent urban leaders assembled in Córdoba in 1031 and abolished the caliphate, about thirty freestanding city-states emerged. Called the petty or party kingdoms or *taifas* (from the Arabic ṭā'ifa), each kingdom had a capital city and a greater or lesser hinterland; some were controlled by Slavs, some by Arabs, some by Berbers, and others by descendants of the former Hispano-Romans. In 1031, their leaders seem to have believed they could maintain themselves forever in this mosaic of tiny kingdoms. Over the course of the eleventh century, however, conflicts among the city-states multiplied, and the Christians in the north were quick to take advantage of Muslim disunity.

Origins of Christian states in the north

The initial Muslim invasion failed to conquer the mountainous regions in the north, which were isolated, poor, and sparsely populated. Thereafter, Muslim leaders paid little attention to the north and never made a concerted effort to stamp out the independent Christian groups on the borders of al-Andalus. This inattention allowed a space for remnants of the Visigothic ruling class to establish themselves in the Cantabrian Mountains and to join forces with the local elite. The first leader of Christian resistance to the Muslim conquest was Pelayo, who may have been a Visigothic noble – perhaps even associated with Roderick's court. In 718 or thereabouts, he succeeded in rallying enough support to inflict a sharp defeat on a Muslim army in the Cantabrian area known as the Picos de Europa. The battle took its name from a nearby cave with religious connotations: Covadonga (la Cueva de Santa María or Cova dominica).

Although the small battle is important only as the precursor of later engagements, Pelayo was quick to follow up his advantage. He examined his territorial base and encouraged other bands of Christians to join him, referring to his kingdom as Asturias and establishing its capital at Cangas de Onís. Many of the nobles and clergy who joined Pelayo's cause had been associated with the defunct Visigothic kingdom, and the same tensions between nobility and crown continued in Pelayo's movement. Although the clergy proved to be staunch royal allies, the war against al-Andalus did not have strong religious or racial motivations at this early date. The king wanted to expand his area of authority; the nobles wanted land. To secure their goals, they were willing to join forces to fight the Muslims or to deal independently with them, depending on the circumstances.

From Pelayo, the crown passed to Alfonso I (739–57), Visigothic duke of Cantabria and husband of Pelayo's daughter. He shaped a viable Asturian monarchy and began the territorial expansion of the kingdom. Alfonso's reign coincided with major difficulties among the Muslims of al-Andalus. As rebellious Berbers fought Arabs and Arabs fought each other, Muslim forces abandoned the north. Alfonso was able to pursue a vigorous extension of his authority that pushed the area of Christian control south to the valley of the Duero River, east to the Basque country, and west to Galicia. To secure these gains, Alfonso established garrisons at strategic points and attempted, wherever possible, to repopulate conquered areas with Christians. Nonetheless, the frontier between Christianity and Islam remained fluid and discontinuous. A vast, nearly deserted area lay between the areas under Christian and Muslim control, which one side or the other periodically invaded with large armies.

Within his Asturian kingdom, Alfonso I (known as "the Catholic") relied heavily on the clergy, who proved much better allies than the sometimes unruly nobility. The clergy began to frame the war against the Muslims as a religious duty and to censure those reluctant to participate. In return for their political support, Alfonso and his successors granted land to the clergy and built churches, cathedrals, and monasteries that enhanced the power and visibility of the religious establishment. Nonetheless, the intermittent wars against the Muslims responded to material as well as religious motivations.

The death of Alfonso I in 757 coincided with the establishment and consolidation of the independent emirate of 'Abd al-Raḥmān I in al-Andalus. With the end of their internal struggles, the increased Muslim power in the south made it almost impossible for Asturias to expand farther. Alfonso's successors therefore concerned themselves with consolidating monarchical authority by countering noble challenges and moves toward independence. Because of that consolidation, the next great Asturian king, Alfonso II (791–842), inherited a realm that possessed great internal strength and cohesion.

Alfonso II, "the Chaste," successfully repelled three attacks by Muslim forces. He also took advantage of Muslim unrest under al-Hakam I and 'Abd al-Raḥmān II to make several raids into Muslim areas now in Portugal, where he took prisoners and booty and secured fortified towns. He encouraged many Christians living under the emir to move north to resettle the border areas. In his dealings with Christians north of the Pyrenees, Alfonso II entered into alliances with Charlemagne and Louis the Pious, but he took pains to maintain the political independence of his kingdom. He also continued the process of strengthening royal authority and administration, reinstituting the Visigothic legal code known as the *Lex Visigothorum*, *Liber iudiciorum*, or *Fuero Juzgo* (in Castilian translation), which had fallen into disuse. He moved the capital to Oviedo and encouraged the Basques to resist Muslim overlordship.

During Alfonso II's reign, an event occurred that was to have a tremendous impact on Europe and that would focus attention on Christian Iberia. In a field near the town of Iria Flavia in the far northwest of Galicia, local citizens discovered what were believed to be the sepulcher and remains of St. James the Apostle (St. James the Greater). The story of St. James – called "Santiago" in Spain – became one of the dominant myths of Catholic Spain. Even today, Spaniards widely celebrate July 25, the day of St. James the Greater in the Catholic calendar. Santiago was one of the original twelve apostles of Jesus Christ. As the traditional story goes, after the crucifixion and resurrection of Christ, Santiago undertook a mission to convert Spain to Christianity. He met with little success and was in despair when the Virgin Mary appeared to him, standing on a pillar. Her intervention heartened Santiago and inspired the foundation of a church on the spot where later churchmen would build the cathedral of Zaragoza. María del Pilar remains a popular baptismal name for girls, particularly in northern Spain.

Santiago's legend continued with his return to Palestine and his death there. When he died, his followers supposedly placed his body on board a ship that miraculously guided itself to northwestern Iberia. There, among the fiord-like *rías* of Galicia, the boat approached the shore, where a mounted pagan wedding party was riding along the *ría*. The bridegroom's horse stumbled and pitched him into the sea near the ship. Followers of Santiago in the ship saved the man by lifting him aboard, and one of them performed a spontaneous baptism, using as a dipper one of the scallop shells that clung to the bridegroom's clothing. Thereafter, the scallop shell became the lasting symbol of Santiago.

The pagans were gratified and impressed by the quick actions of the Christians, but when the latter asked the local ruler, Queen Lupa, for permission to bury the apostle, his body now resting in a stone coffin, she refused and imprisoned the Christians. They miraculously escaped from their confinement and fled. As bridges fell behind them, they were able to evade Lupa's pursuing troops. These seeming miracles began to attract local attention and led to many conversions to Christianity. Queen Lupa then feigned a change of heart and offered a plot for Santiago's burial. She told his followers to go up a nearby mountain and fetch the oxen there to pull the stone coffin to the burial place. She did not tell them that the mountain was the territory of a dragon and that the oxen were actually wild bulls. When the dragon challenged them, the Christians showed him the sign of the Cross, the mere sight of which caused his demise. Then they found the wild bulls, which became docile as they approached and allowed themselves to be yoked like oxen to move the coffin. By now, Lupa herself had become a believer and allowed the body to be buried in one of her fields. A small shrine marked the spot, but both were lost until the time of King Alfonso II, when a hermit discovered the shrine in a field marked by burning stars. In a burst of piety, local Christians soon built a church on the spot. They called the place Compostela, from the Latin *Campus Stellae*, or Field of Stars, and a town grew around it named for Santiago.

Santiago de Compostela became one of the most popular and important centers of Christian pilgrimage in all of medieval Europe, outranked only by Rome. Its pilgrim traffic declined in the sixteenth century due to wars and the rise of Protestantism, reducing the number of Northern European pilgrims. In the late twentieth century, however, interest in walking the road to Santiago enjoyed a resurgence, and the pilgrimage remains popular in the early twenty-first century among believers and non-believers alike. True pilgrims begin the trek in Paris at the Tour Saint-Jacques, and proceed south through the French countryside to the Pyrenees and the border with Spain. From there, they travel westward along one of two principal routes, sometimes through large cities that grew to cater to pilgrims, but more often through the countryside. As in the Middle Ages, chapels and churches mark the route, and hostels along the way provide lodging and food for the pilgrims.

The ninth-century growth of the town of Santiago in Galicia indicated the strengthening of Christian control in the area and the growing fame of the pilgrimage route. From its early nuclei in the Cantabrian Mountains and Galicia, Christian territory gradually expanded southward into Muslim-controlled areas, with the raiders sacking towns, destroying crops and seizing animals, collecting loot and captives for ransom or enslavement, and encouraging Mozarabs to return with the raiders and take up residence in Christian areas.

In the eighth and early ninth centuries, the lands of the valley of the Duero River were largely deserted. The Muslims had never settled the region extensively, and many Muslims left after the Berber revolt in the 740s. Late in the ninth century and into the tenth, the Christians began to establish settlements in the lands along the northern bank of the Duero, with strong points at Zamora and Toro, enabling the Asturian king Ordoño II to move his capital south from Oviedo to León. The Christian lands thereafter became the kingdom of León.

In the northeast of the peninsula, the growth of Christian control had close connections with the Frankish kingdom to the north. During the eighth century the Carolingians had pushed the Muslims south to the Pyrenees, and Charlemagne (742–814) wanted to push them even farther south and to establish a series of marches (or defensive frontier provinces) on the Iberian side of the mountains. He thought he saw his chance when the Muslim governor of Zaragoza asked for Frankish aid in his rebellion against the Umayyad emir, Hishām I.

The rebellion was not just a local Spanish Muslim squabble but reflected high politics in the wider Mediterranean world. At that point, the Umayyads were newcomers as rulers in Spain, while the Abbasids still ruled as caliphs in Baghdad and claimed authority over the entire Islamic world. In 778, Charlemagne led his army across the mountains into Spain by the western pass of Roncevalles, to help the Muslim governor regain Zaragoza. In Pamplona, he secured the friendship of local Christians, who provisioned his army on credit. Then he moved toward Zaragoza. Even with the aid of Muslim rebels, his siege of the city failed, and the Franks retreated along the route by which they had entered the peninsula, but they failed to pay their debts to the local Christian community. At Roncevalles, the locals ambushed Charlemagne's rear guard, resulting in the deaths of the heroes Roland and Anselm, among many others. This affair deterred Charlemagne from Spanish excursions for some years.

In later centuries, beginning in the late eleventh, the story became legend and eventually served as the basis for the great French medieval epic, *La Chanson de Roland* (*The Song of Roland*). The epic reflects eleventh- and twelfth-century concerns during the early Christian crusades into the eastern Mediterranean and significantly departs from the historic events. Rather than telling the story of a Frankish–Christian alliance with dissident Spanish Muslims, and a final battle that pitted Christians against Christians over an unpaid debt, the epic fictionalizes the events as a great Christian–Islamic confrontation.

Charlemagne himself never returned to Spain, but his forces established the Spanish March, beginning with the conquest of Gerona in 785. In 797, nearly twenty years after the debacle in Zaragoza and Roncevalles, Charlemagne sent an envoy to the Abbasid caliph Hārūn al-Rashīd to seek an alliance against the Umayyads of Spain. The alliance came to nothing, but Hārūn sent as a gift to Charlemagne an elephant that for years impressed the king's supporters and terrified his enemies. In 801 many small towns near Barcelona, and – most important of all – Barcelona itself, came under Christian control. Tarragona and Tortosa were conquered a decade later, and added to the Spanish March, the whole of which was placed under the duchy of Aquitaine.

Soon, members of the local elite grew restive under the duchy's control. Much of the area, including lands in French territory, joined with Barcelona to form the county of Barcelona (later emerging as Catalonia). Although the counts at first recognized the overlordship of the Carolingians, before the end of the century Catalonia had become an independent state. The independence of the whole Spanish March was assured by the progressive weakness of Charlemagne's descendants. The attitude of the clergy in this area clearly indicated the diminishing authority of the Franks south of the Pyrenees. Whereas the clergy had formerly sought resolution of church questions at the Frankish court, they began to take their problems directly to the pope, or at least to the count of Barcelona.

By the middle of the ninth century, the entire northern section of the peninsula, from Galicia eastward along the Bay of Biscay and the southern slopes of the

Pyrenees to Barcelona, was in Christian hands. Beginning from Asturias and its successor state León, as well as from Navarre, Aragon, and the county of Barcelona, the various Christian states in the north of the peninsula would eventually expand southward into Muslim territory. In the ninth and tenth centuries, however, no one could predict that Christian forces would prevail. Islamic Spain was still in the ascendancy, and al-Andalus had become one of the gems of the Islamic world.

The apogee of Muslim Spain

Islamic Spain at its height was a part of the wider Islamic world stretching from the Indus River to the Atlantic Ocean. It was a rich world, based initially on plunder and later enjoying a Golden Age based on agriculture, animal husbandry, mining, artisan production, and trade. Throughout this Islamic world, the common adherence to one religion and the unifying effects of the Arabic language, a single legal code, and common commercial practices all fostered commercial activity. Muhammad himself had been a merchant, and the high regard for merchants expressed in the Qur'ān reinforced the value of trade and its practitioners.

Nonetheless, despite the importance of cities and trade, the Islamic world remained predominantly rural, and the Muslims in Spain were responsible for introducing a wide range of agrarian improvements. They continued to make use of existing crops such as wheat, olives, and wine grapes (the latter despite religious prohibitions). Especially in the southern and southeastern regions, the Muslims also brought in new crops and new ways to produce them. Various citrus fruits, the fig, and the almond all came to Spain with the Muslims, as did sugar cane, rice, and saffron. Where feasible in the lower river valleys, they extended irrigated agriculture by building new projects or by expanding earlier ones dating back to the Romans. The Muslims had wide experience with irrigation works, learning about them in conquered areas from Syria to Spain and adopting and adapting the most efficient techniques. In animal husbandry, they developed the selective breeding of cattle, sheep, and horses, and introduced the ass from Egypt. They also raised domesticated chickens, peacocks, and doves.

Islamic cities were crucial nexus points for trade in rural produce, mined minerals, and, above all, in artisan production. While urban life in the rest of Western Europe languished between the fading of the Roman Empire and the twelfth century, the cities of Islamic Spain flourished. Córdoba, capital of first the emirate and then the independent caliphate, was the largest city in Islamic Spain, probably containing more than 100,000 inhabitants. Zaragoza, Toledo, Seville, Granada, Almería, and Málaga each had between 15,000 and 40,000. As in ancient times, the south and southeast of the peninsula continued to be the most vibrant and developed part.

The cities of Islamic Spain produced a wide range of goods from the metals mined in the peninsula, including weaponry, fine gold work, and minted gold coins. Leather goods produced from local hides also occupied an important place in artisan production; even today, words associated with leather, such as "cordovan" and "morocco," date from the leather industries of Islamic Spain. Other skilled artisans wove cloth from wool, cotton, linen, and silk, all produced in the peninsula. The Muslims introduced the production of paper – a Chinese invention – to Spain in the ninth century, and developed an export industry from the tenth century. They also developed major industries for the production of glass and ceramics, including the brilliant decorative tiles that still adorn palaces and mosques from Spain's Islamic period. From fields and shops all over al-Andalus merchants exported goods to markets in the western Mediterranean and beyond. Integrating Spain into the wider Islamic world did not happen overnight, but, by the ninth century, the connections and trade routes were in place and fully functional.

Economic expansion under the Romans, Visigoths, and the Muslims and their Christian counterparts undoubtedly took a toll on Spain's natural resources, though historians have not accorded that story the attention it deserves. Building construction, mining, shipbuilding, and – above all – glass- and tile-making all consume large amounts of wood. How did Spain's primordial forests fare over the course of a millennium of economic development? Here the evidence is murky and the interpretations widely divergent. Some scholars suggest that the Muslims expanded timber production and carefully managed the forests, while others argue that deforestation and the start of environmental degradation began in the Islamic period. Until scholars have time to examine this issue in more detail, it remains an open question. There is no doubt, however, that the Islamic period saw the expansion of artisan production and the growth of cities, both of which required the exploitation of forests.

Along with economic expansion, the rate of conversions to Islam increased during the heyday of the caliphate of

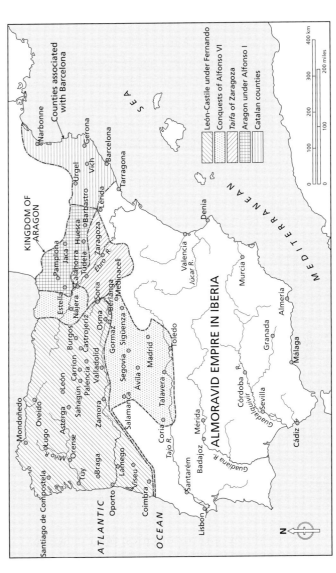

MAP 3.1 Iberia, late eleventh century. In contrast to the unity of the peninsula under Roman rule, the political divisions in the late eleventh century show the separation between Christian and Muslim areas during the medieval period.

Córdoba, troubling as it was to Christian and Jewish leaders. Even for the Christians and Jews who stayed within their ancestral religions, their material culture inexorably absorbed elements from the dominant Islamic forms that surrounded them. This included distinctive features of housing design, cuisine, and dress. Language changed as well, with the common use of Arabic by members of all three religious groups in Islamic Spain. The transmission of knowledge from Arabic scholarship and Arabic translations of the classical heritage of Rome, and especially Greece, to Latin Christendom was thus facilitated, and it would gather momentum in subsequent centuries.

The eleventh century marked the beginning of an important change in the relations between Christian and Muslim territories in Spain. As the caliphate collapsed, local rulers pursued independent courses in the *taifa* kingdoms, some of which controlled only a principal city and its immediate surroundings, while others controlled large regions. The most important *taifas* were Zaragoza, Toledo, Badajoz, and Seville, ruled by Arabs; Granada, ruled by Berbers; and Valencia, with kings of Slavic origins, descendants of the military slaves. The *taifa* period produced a brilliant cultural flowering, as the *taifa* kings prided themselves on maintaining glittering courts in contention with their rivals. They built palaces and civic buildings, amassed large libraries as testimony to their real or pretended intellectual attainments, and recruited and supported distinguished scholars.

Politically, no single *taifa* was a match for the emerging Christian kingdoms of the north, though Christian Spain was not yet strong enough to reconquer and repopulate extensive territories. Instead, Christian leaders intervened in the squabbles among the *taifas*, forming alliances with some *taifas* against others, or launching independent attacks to sack cities and capture territories. Instead of attacking, they might threaten a vulnerable *taifa* into paying protection money in the form of tribute (*parias*). All of these activities, which included frequent raids (*algaras*), honed the military skills of the Christian warrior class and reinforced their loyalty to their leaders. Although Christianity and Islam defined the two sides of the cultural frontier, religious differences were decidedly secondary motivations in their conflicts during the eleventh century. Moreover, during peaceful intervals, a variety of cultural, commercial, social, and political exchanges occurred across the religious frontiers.

Although the Christian states in the north gradually increased in power at the expense of the *taifas* during the eleventh century, they also expended great effort in disputes among themselves. Moreover, Christian rulers had a tendency to divide their hard-won territories among their heirs, dissipating part of their power. Despite these disadvantages, a few powerful kings were able to amass considerable power and territory in their lifetimes. Sancho III, called "the Great" ("el Mayor"), king of Navarre (1000–35), was one the first of these powerful leaders. Sancho extended his authority into Cantabria, joined Castile to Navarre, and seized the Tierra de Campos (between the rivers Pisuerga and Cea) from the kingdom of León. He also gained control of the counties of Aragon and asserted a degree of overlordship in the counties of Catalonia. Having put together the largest Spanish Christian kingdom since the time of the Visigoths, Sancho the Great began to call himself "the king of all the kingdoms of

Spain." He brought the nobles into line and pacified his territories. Navarre was open to influences from Europe beyond the Pyrenees, and Sancho extended this by fostering pilgrim traffic on the road to Santiago de Compostela. The hegemony of greater Navarre did not outlive Sancho, however. On his death in 1035, his testament divided his estates among his sons, naming the three eldest as kings: García, king of Navarre; Fernando, king of Castile; and Ramiro, king of Aragon. Thus both Castile and Aragon owe their origins as kingdoms to the testament of Sancho the Great.

The first king of Castile, Fernando I (1035–65), made himself the most noteworthy of the sons of Sancho. When the king of León, Bermudo III, tried to retake the Tierra de Campos that Sancho the Great had annexed, Fernando I fought him at Támara. Bermudo died in the battle, allowing Fernando to claim and take his kingdom, thus temporarily unifying Castile and León. Fernando later defeated and killed his elder brother García of Navarre (1035–54) at the battle of Atapuerca, which allowed him to extend Castile's border with Navarre as far as the Ebro River. He also continued forays against the Muslims, extending his control over Muslim towns in the west, including Viseu and Coimbra in what would become Portugal, although the Muslims later regained them temporarily. As an indication of Fernando's power and reputation, he forced the Muslim rulers of Toledo, Seville, Badajoz, and Zaragoza to pay him tribute. In sum, Fernando I converted Castile into the most powerful of the Christian states, yet, when he died in 1065, he divided his holdings. His eldest son, Sancho, received Castile and ruled it as Sancho II; Alfonso got León; and García got

Galicia. He left cities to his daughters. Urraca received Zamora, Elvira got Toro, and both secured income from monasteries throughout their father's lands.

Sancho II (1065–72) embarked on an aggressive policy and seized Galicia and León from his brothers, but he died at the hands of an assassin while laying siege to his sister's town of Zamora. Alfonso, who had gone into exile in Muslim Toledo, then succeeded Sancho as Alfonso VI of Castile. The highlight of Alfonso VI's reign was the conquest of Toledo. After a long siege, Alfonso's forces entered the city in 1085 and made it part of Castile. Toledo's conquest meant that Castile had a powerful fortress-city to protect recently reconquered towns south of the Guadarrama Mountains. Toledo was the largest city that the Christians had taken from the Muslims to that point, and it retained a large Muslim population.

The Christian capture of Toledo marked the beginning of a new stage in Christian–Muslim relations. In 1086, a year after Toledo fell, the Muslim ruler of Seville called in the Almoravids (al-Murābitūn) from Morocco for help against expanding Christian power. The Almoravids, or Almorávides, as they were known in Spanish, arose in the western Sahara, where the Moroccan 'Abd Allāh ibn Yāsin preached a reformist Islamic message to the Berbers that demanded strict adherence to the tenets of Islam, coupled with less tolerance for non-Muslims. He formed a *ribat*, or religious community, on the Senegal River not far from the Atlantic coast and attracted followers.

The movement began to expand its political control northward through Morocco, and controlled most of it by 1080. Six years later, the Almoravid leader Yāsuf ibn-Tāshfīn crossed the strait with a large army, complete with camels and drums, and routed the Castilians at a battle near Badajoz. In 1090 he returned in another campaign and took over much of al-Andalus (with the major exception of Zaragoza), arousing fears on the part of some *taifa* rulers, notably those of Badajoz and Granada. He also made excursions into Christian territory but could not retake lands that Christian rulers had fully occupied and repopulated.

Yūsuf's successors continued to control much of al-Andalus for some fifty years. Given the less tolerant attitude of the Almoravids toward non-Muslims, many Jews began to think that Christian Spain offered a safer haven and moved north, where they were welcomed into Christian kingdoms. By about 1145, the Almoravid Empire had fallen apart. Nonetheless, during their ascendancy, religious hostility increased on both sides of the Muslim–Christian divide.

In response to the Almoravid invasions, more foreign knights and monks came into Iberia from across the Pyrenees from the end of the eleventh century onward, and they brought with them an implacable hostility toward the Muslims. The knights and corresponding naval forces from Northern Europe also brought advanced siege tactics and weaponry, as well as new techniques of naval warfare. On both land and sea, they provided significant help to the Spanish Christian forces on several occasions. Nonetheless, they often expressed dismay at the willingness of Spanish leaders to honor surrender treaties with the Muslims and to extend good terms to them. As their militant attitudes toward the Muslims penetrated Spain, successive popes offered spiritual benefits and financial support for campaigns against the Muslims. In this new atmosphere, campaigns of the Spanish Reconquest, as it came to be called, often received the same standing as crusades to Palestine and elsewhere.

Despite this increasing militancy, it was still possible for exchanges and mutual respect to cross religious frontiers in Spain. One example is the welcome that the exiled King Alfonso of León received from the Muslim ruler of Toledo during his exile. By far the clearest example of the permeable frontier between Christian and Muslim areas was the career of Rodrigo Díaz de Vivar, known as "El Cid," who became one of the emblematic figures of the Reconquest. Born to a minor noble family from the town of Vivar near Burgos in the mid 1040s, Rodrigo entered the court of Prince Sancho to receive his education while Fernando I was still alive. After Sancho knighted him, Rodrigo sometimes joined Sancho and Fernando I in battle. After Sancho became king, Rodrigo served as the king's standard bearer (*alférez*), head of the king's militia. His prowess eventually earned him two nicknames: El Cid (from the Arabic *sidi*, lord or leader) and "Campeador" (from the Latin *campi doctor*, or chief field instructor), though he gained the former nickname toward the end of his career, and later writers may have invented the Campeador nickname.

Rodrigo was one of Sancho's main advisers, and when the king died, Rodrigo joined the administration of Alfonso VI. After accumulating enemies in Alfonso's court, he went into exile, during which he served five years in the military forces of the Muslim king of Zaragoza. Rodrigo was back in Alfonso's court at the time of Toledo's capture and then was exiled again. This time he raised an army and campaigned from Castile eastward toward

Valencia, which he conquered and then succeeded in holding for the rest of his life. His widow Doña Ximena was able to hold Valencia for a few more years before Muslims retook it. In all of Rodrigo's campaigns he employed Muslims and received help from them. That is clear even in the fictionalized story preserved in the *Poema del Cid* ("The Poem of the Cid"), Castile's major medieval epic, and in the lavish 1950s Hollywood film with Charlton Heston as El Cid, and Sophia Loren as Doña Ximena. By contrast, *The Song of Roland*, the French national epic, depicts the battles between Christians and Muslims as wars to the death, and Muslims as the personification of evil. In other words, these two national epics, written at about the same time, nicely illustrate the differences in Christian depictions of Muslims north and south of the Pyrenees. As the twelfth and thirteenth centuries progressed, it remained possible in Spain for exchanges and cordial relations to exist across the religious divide, but they became increasingly more difficult.

In addition to sparking the increase in Muslim–Christian hostility, Alfonso VI's conquest of Toledo unintentionally set the stage for the emergence of an independent Portuguese kingdom. Numerous French knights had joined Alfonso's campaign and participated in the successful siege of Toledo. Alfonso rewarded them handsomely. One of them, Henry of Lorraine (known in Spain as Enrique de Lorena), married Alfonso's illegitimate daughter Teresa and received as dowry the county of Portugal, a small territory in today's Portugal, to the south of Galicia. When Henry died in 1112, Teresa acted as de facto queen in the name of their son, Afonso Henriques (Sp. Alfonso Enríquez). During his long reign, Afonso extended the area of Portugal by reconquering lands south to the Tagus River. In 1147 his troops, reinforced by contingents of northern crusaders on their way to Palestine, took and held the city of Lisbon. Afonso and his dowager mother worked to make Portugal independent of León-Castile. He declared himself king in 1143 and a vassal of the pope in 1144; he finally received papal recognition of his kingship in 1179.

A few years earlier, a new wave of invasions from North Africa had begun. A second Berber Empire had arisen in Morocco, founded by a scholar named Muhammad ibn Tūmart. Born in the Atlas Mountains in the 1080s, he studied in various intellectual centers of the Islamic world and developed a strict interpretation of Muslim belief. Ibn Tūmart attracted followers called the Almohads (Almohades in Spanish, Muwahhidūn in Arabic), and declared himself to be the Mahdī, a leader inspired by Allah, in 1121. Following Ibn Tūmart's death, 'Abd al-Mu'min became the leader and began to expand Almohad influence in Morocco. He made a brief excursion into Iberia in 1145 or 1146, but the real beginning of the Almohads' power was in 1147, when they drove the Almoravids from Marrakesh. They followed this success by expanding their power eastward across North Africa as far as Tripoli.

In 1172, the Almohads conducted a major campaign in Spain, first taking Seville and later a large portion of al-Andalus. They won a large victory over the forces of Alfonso VIII of Castile at the battle of Alarcos, near Ciudad Real, in 1195. This disastrous defeat – Alfonso VIII narrowly escaped capture or death – and the failure of coordination among the Christian forces when promised

Leonese troops never arrived, galvanized secular and clerical leaders. Responding to the appeal of Pope Innocent III, the Christian kingdoms resolved to combine forces and take the offensive against the Almohads. Contingents from Castile, Aragon, León, and Navarre, with the addition of some French knights, met the Almohad army at Las Navas de Tolosa in July 1212 and won an overwhelming victory. That battle marked the end of major Muslim power in the peninsula, although it took the Christian forces some time to recover from the strains, losses, and expenses that had brought them victory.

Many Spanish Muslims recognized the battle of Las Navas as the beginning of the end for Almohad power, and some local rulers rose against them, with aid from Christian kings. Fernando III of Castile collaborated with the Muslims and used their help in his successful campaigns in Andalusia and Murcia. He conquered Córdoba in 1236, Murcia in 1241-3, Jaén in 1246, and – the most important prize of all – Seville in 1248. He captured Seville with a joint land and naval campaign by Castilian forces, for which northern port cities provided the ships that were decisive in the victory. Thereafter, northern merchants, shipbuilders, and mariners took an active role in developing port facilities and commerce in the south.

During the conquest of Seville, the Muslim king of Granada actively supported Fernando III. The kingdom of Granada remained as a tributary to the Castilian kings thereafter, obliged to pay an annual sum in gold. The Granadan kings did not always honor their agreement with the Castilian rulers and often missed their tribute payments, but the arrangement suited both sides for more than two centuries. Granada remained in Muslim control until 1492. Its geography made it easy to defend and hard to attack, and it served as a refuge for dissident Muslims living under Christian rule, and therefore as a safety valve against dissent in Castile.

Fernando III brought about the definitive union of the kingdoms of León and Castile, both of which had had functioning parliaments (*cortes*) since the late twelfth century. Fernando was a unifier in other ways as well. He was a crusader and a contemporary of the French King Louis IX, canonized as St. Louis for his zeal in defense of the Catholic faith. Whereas Louis was a thoroughgoing crusader and an almost fanatical opponent of the Muslims, Fernando held rather different views. He fought long and successfully against the Muslims of Spain, and took great satisfaction in converting former mosques into churches in the areas he conquered. Nonetheless, when he conquered territories, he continued the policy of toleration toward Islam and Judaism, considering himself to be the king of all three religious communities. He, too, would eventually be canonized, as San Fernando, but less for his religious zeal alone than for his exemplary life and benevolent rule. Among his other achievements, Fernando III founded the University of Salamanca, one of the oldest and most distinguished universities in medieval Europe.

Fernando's son Alfonso X followed his father as king of León and Castile (1252–84). Known to history as Alfonso the Wise ("el Sabio"), he excelled as an intellectual leader and a patron of learning, but he failed badly as a political leader for Spain. Alfonso wasted time and money in a campaign to be elected as Holy Roman Emperor. Although he was able to bribe his way to winning the election, the Germans would not accept a foreign emperor, and the

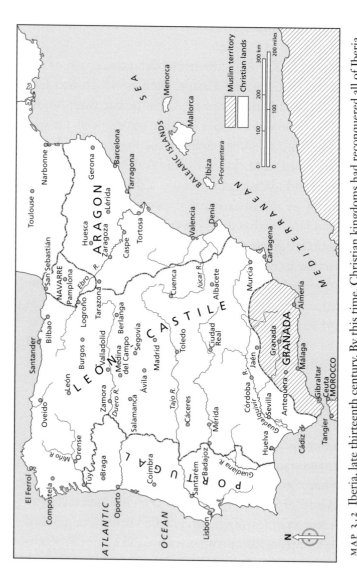

MAP 3.2 Iberia, late thirteenth century. By this time, Christian kingdoms had reconquered all of Iberia, except the Muslim kingdom of Granada.

Spanish nobility did not want their king to decamp to Central Europe while supporting himself with Castilian wealth. The position of emperor therefore remained open until 1273, when Rudolph of Habsburg was elected, the first in a long line of Habsburg emperors. Alfonso spent the last years of his life fending off efforts to depose him and dealing with rival claimants to the succession, contested by a son and by a grandson by another son.

Alfonso X's cultural contributions, by contrast, gained him deserved and lasting fame. They were part of a large movement of the transmission of knowledge from the Islamic world to the Latin West through the translation, often by Jewish scholars in Spain fluent in both Arabic and Latin, of Arabic scientific treatises and Arabic versions of Greek and Hellenistic scientific and philosophical works. Alfonso X himself translated or supervised the translation of Arabic works of science and chess, compiled law codes and historical works, and wrote poetry. As part of his efforts to centralize and rationalize royal authority, he sponsored the creation of a new law code for León and Castile, the *Siete Partidas* (lit., the Seven Divisions), which relied heavily on Roman law and, to a lesser extent, on traditional customary law. The first part dealt with religion; the second with kingship; the third with the administration of justice; the fourth with matrimony; the fifth with contracts; the sixth with testaments; and the seventh with infractions and punishments. Because the *Siete Partidas* is such a wide-ranging and thorough set of laws and customs, historians use it frequently as a window on thirteenth-century Spain. Ironically, it was not applied in Castile during his reign, because the nobles objected to its enhancement of royal power. Later jurists in Spain did make great use of the *Siete Partidas*, however, and it continues to form a component of the modern Spanish legal corpus.

King Alfonso also had a great regard for history and compiled a number of important works, employing a team of researchers and writers. The most significant works were a history of Spain, *La historia de España* – also known as the *Crónica general* – and a universal history, the *Grande e general historia*. The former was a compilation of earlier sources up to Alfonso's day and included all of Spain, not just the Leonese-Castilian portion. The latter was a compendium of historical knowledge from the beginning of Christian history to the late thirteenth century. Both histories were written in Castilian rather than Latin, because Castile was one of the first countries in Europe to use the vernacular for scholarly endeavors and public administration. In fact, the *Grande e general historia* was the first universal history of the European Middle Ages written in a vernacular language. Alfonso X was also a poet and wrote his verse in Galician instead of Castilian, because the softer sounds of Gallego seemed more appropriate for poetic discourse. Scholars attribute to him the *Cantigas de Santa María* ("Songs of Praise for the Virgin Mary"), a masterpiece of medieval poetry. The stories in the *Cantigas* are richly expressive and magnificently illustrated; modern scholars value them highly for their unparalleled window on thirteenth-century life.

Many scholars describe the thirteenth century in Spain as a sort of religious and cultural Golden Age, during which Christian, Islamic, and Jewish communities could live alongside one another in a harmonious relationship, or *convivencia*. This was not, however, what the modern world considers true toleration, with mutual respect and acceptance of diverse beliefs. Instead, we can best think of it as a wary civic harmony, fostered by the crown in the interests of social peace and punctuated from time to time by violent clashes. Nonetheless, given that three diverse religious communities shared a common space, and the numerous possibilities for constant strife and mutual hatreds among them, medieval Spanish *convivencia* was remarkable indeed.

As the events of the twelfth and thirteenth century unfolded in Castile, the Christian leaders in the eastern part of Spain also expanded the area under their control. The kingdom of Aragon, extending from the Pyrenees to the Ebro valley, had developed along lines similar to Castile. Catalonia, in the northeast corner of the peninsula, was a collection of counties, of which Barcelona was the most important. The union of Aragon and Catalonia took place in an extraordinary chain of events following the death of the king of Navarre and Aragon, Alfonso I "the Battler," in 1134. Because he had no heirs, Alfonso left his kingdom to the military orders dedicated to fighting the Muslims.

The Aragonese nobility decided that they could not honor this unprecedented bequest and therefore set it aside. They then chose a new king, Alfonso's brother Ramiro, who accepted the crown as Ramiro II. Unfortunately, Ramiro had become a monk, and his vows precluded marriage, which once again threatened the line with extinction. The nobles persuaded Ramiro to petition the pope for permission to leave the monastery and marry. When the pope granted his request, he married and sired a daughter, named Petronilla. The Aragonese nobles then arranged for the count of Barcelona, Ramón Berenguer, to become engaged to marry Petronilla, then still an infant, and to assume the kingship of Aragon. With the succession settled, Ramiro retired to his monastery again. All of these extraordinary events played out in a three-year period.

From 1137 on, Ramón Berenguer ruled a unified Aragon and Catalonia. When Petronilla came of age, the couple married. The king led a reconquest of frontier lands and offered generous terms to the Muslims, allowing them to live under Christian authority and to retain their religion. The rulers of Aragon and Catalonia also held possessions north of the Pyrenees in what is now France. Just as there was no medieval kingdom of Spain, medieval "France" was a collection of royal lands, counties, duchies, and quasi-independent cities. The French king ruled from Paris but had no authority over the Mediterranean region called by later scholars "Occitan" or "Languedoc," whose Provençal language is closely akin to Catalan. Trade and travel across the Pyrenees and along the sea-coast of the western Mediterranean linked the two areas. Ramón Berenguer began to extend his authority in Languedoc, and his son Alfonso II (1161–96) later enforced that authority, styling himself the "king of the Pyrenees."

Difficulties developed when the region became the focus of a heretical religion, that of the Cathars or Albigensians. Among other tenets, they held that a cosmic struggle between nearly equal forces of good and evil accounted for the unfolding of human history. The early Christian church had condemned this "dualism" as heresy, but echoes of such dualistic beliefs continued to crop up from time to time, especially in remote areas with a tenuous grasp of Christian orthodoxy. The Cathars of Languedoc gained many converts and much support, and, at their high point around 1200, they may have enjoyed the loyalty of a majority of the population in the region. Church officials were obviously concerned.

Pope Innocent III launched a military crusade against the Albigensians early in the thirteenth century, led by Simon de Montfort. King Pere II of Aragon, "the Catholic" (1196–1213), had vassals in the Cathar area who, while remaining Catholic themselves, favored the Albigensians because of their popularity among the peasants and townspeople. Law and custom obliged Pere II to support his vassals, but at the same time he was a very good Catholic and was also a vassal of the pope. Before the crusade, he tried to mediate between his vassals and the church officials and crusaders. When war became inevitable, Pere II ended up fighting against the crusaders, in support of his vassals. Pere had been one of the leaders of the great Christian victory at Las Navas de Tolosa against the Muslims in 1212. The following year, in an ironic turn of events, he lost his life fighting against the Catholic Church at the battle of Muret. Because of Pere's support for the Albigensians, the monarchs of Catalonia and Aragon lost all of their possessions north of the Pyrenees, which eventually came under the authority of the king of France.

Pere's son Jaume I, called the Conqueror (1213–76), became king at the age of twelve and worked for some fourteen years to end the disorder that had developed during his father's adventures outside the realm. By 1227 he had reestablished order, including a functioning parliament (*Corts*) in Catalonia. With relative stability at home, the king could look to expand. After the loss of their trans-Pyrenean lands, the monarchs of Catalonia and Aragon had to look elsewhere to enlarge their holdings. Muslim territory was the most obvious target. Eastward, in the Balearic Islands, the Muslims held Mallorca, Minorca, and Ibiza. Mallorca served as a major maritime base for Muslim corsairs who raided the Spanish coast for booty and slaves. Jaume I launched a campaign against Mallorca in 1227 and took the main city of Palma; by 1230 he had secured control of the whole island. Minorca remained in Muslim hands as a tributary state for fifty years. In 1277, forces led by the bishop of Tarragona took Ibiza, and Catalans began moving to the Balearic Islands in large numbers. By the end of the thirteenth century, they formed the majority of the population, and the islands became a separate kingdom.

Jaume I's major accomplishment was the conquest of the kingdom of Valencia, which was one of the principal *taifa* kingdoms and had grown rich from its Muslim agricultural heritage of terracing and irrigated agriculture. The *huerta* of Valencia was an extensive irrigated plain, heavily populated and highly productive. Jaume's conquest took thirteen years to complete. In 1238 he took the city of Valencia, and by 1248 he had conquered the entire kingdom. Many members of the Muslim elite left but others remained in the new Christian kingdom, as did many peasants and urban dwellers. Catalans were the major Christian settlers to the region, as they were in the Balearic Islands, and Catalan became its principal language.

Jaume I collaborated with his Castilian counterparts in the conquest of Murcia, and Castile secured control of the conquered kingdom, according to the terms of the Treaty of Almizra of 1244, which confirmed and slightly modified the Treaty of Cazorla (1179) designating then-unconquered Murcia as a future Castilian territory. That left nowhere in the peninsula for the Crown of Aragon to expand. To the north, Jaume I had made a treaty with the king of France at Corbeil in 1253, in which he recognized his father's losses north of the Pyrenees. In return, France gave up claims to the Spanish March, which dated from the time of the Carolingians. In modern times, the Republic of Andorra is the last remnant of the many small counties that once made up the Spanish March, and it remains under the joint sovereignty of the French President and the Catalan bishop of Urgel. With expansion by land closed off, the monarchs of Catalonia and Aragon looked eastward into the Mediterranean, beyond the Balearic Islands.

Pere III, "the Great" (1276–85), Jaume I's son, cast his glance toward Sicily, where he had dynastic claims based on his marriage in 1262 to Constance, daughter of Manfred Hohenstaufen, the illegitimate son of Emperor Frederick II Hohenstaufen and the last of the Sicilian rulers of that dynasty. In Pere III's time, the ruler of Sicily was Charles of Anjou, leader of a cadet branch of the French royal house, who defeated Manfred in 1266 and gained control of Sicily. Sicily had long been a crossroads where the diverse cultures of the Mediterranean met, and sometimes fought, but generally they coexisted well enough. Greek, Roman, Muslim, Jewish, and Norman

elements had made Sicily a place of relaxed accommodation among the diverse peoples of the Mediterranean.
Failing to appreciate the local culture, Charles tried to
impose rule in the French style, with new laws, new
taxes, and French officials. Smoldering popular discontent with the French administration broke into the open
in 1282, when a revolt erupted in Palermo after townspeople attacked French officers accused of raping a young
girl. The revolt broke out at vespers time, and thus the
long war that followed is called the War of the Sicilian
Vespers.

The Sicilian rebels asked for help from Pere III, who
conveniently had a large fleet assembled just two days'
sail from Sicily. The initial conquest was fairly easy for
Pere, but the subsequent war with France dragged on for
twenty years before the pope and the French monarch
recognized Sicily as belonging to Aragon. A new group of
mercenary soldiers formed in Catalonia during the long
war, recruited from subjects of the Crown of Aragon and
foreigners. These Almogávares were professional soldiers,
offering themselves for hire. A group of some 6,000 of
them, under the command of Roger de Flor, formed the
Catalan Grand Company, which contracted to support
the Byzantine Empire against the Turks. When their full
pay was not forthcoming, they began to conquer Byzantine territory on their own, ending up with two duchies
in Greece, including Athens. Their conquests were independent actions and not officially under the auspices of
the Aragonese kings, but they nonetheless had close ties
with the Crown of Aragon.

All told, as the thirteenth century ended, the various
Christian powers in Iberia were clearly in an expansive

mode. They had nearly completed their takeover of the peninsula from the Muslims, with the Leonese-Castilian conquest of much of Andalusia, the Catalan–Aragonese conquest of Valencia, and the Castilian–Aragonese conquest of Murcia. In the independent kingdom of Portugal, Christian forces completely drove the Muslims out, with the conquest of the Algarve by 1249. In the Spanish kingdoms, only Granada remained in Muslim hands. With the medieval reconquest of Iberia all but over, the notable political developments during the last centuries of the Middle Ages would play out in Christian lands.

FIGURE 3.1 The Great Mosque at Córdoba (Andalusia), built from the eighth to the tenth centuries, was one of the marvels of Islamic Spain. The characteristic keyhole arches of red and white defined a vast space for the daily prayers of the faithful.

FIGURE 3.2 The Torre del Oro (Tower of Gold) in Seville, a twelve-sided watchtower built in Almohad times (*c.* 1220), formed part of the city's walled fortress or *alcázar*. The lantern was added to the top in the mid eighteenth century.

FIGURE 3.3 The entry portico of the co-cathedral of Santa María in Guadalajara (Castile-La Mancha) shows the amalgam of Islamic and Christian architecture common in the period.

FIGURE 3.4 The graceful Romanesque bridge at Puente la Reina (Navarre) was built in the eleventh century to accommodate the growing number of pilgrims on the road to Santiago de Compostela.

FIGURE 3.5 Medieval convents typically included a colonnaded interior walkway around a garden or patio, which provided access to the outdoors for the cloistered residents. This cloister in the convent of Las Dueñas (Salamanca) is one of the finest examples.

4

The rise of Spain to international prominence

~

The modern geography of the Iberian Peninsula, which Spain shares with Portugal, seems so familiar that we might assume that the two countries were destined to evolve toward their modern borders. If we trace the late medieval history of the peninsula, however, there was no inevitability about the process. Castile might have amalgamated with Portugal, a possibility that informed the contingency plans of a succession of monarchs in both Spain and Portugal. And, instead of the amalgamation of Castile and Aragon in the late fifteenth century, those two kingdoms might have remained separate. In short, depending on the vagaries of dynastic politics and demographic realities, the Iberian Peninsula might have had a very different configuration from the familiar borders we recognize today.

To understand why events unfolded as they did requires recognition of the contingent nature of events in every aspect of the late medieval history of Spain. For example, in diplomacy, each of the Iberian kingdoms looked outward to strengthen diplomatic ties with various parts of Mediterranean and Atlantic Europe, as well as with North Africa, and those ties inevitably affected internal politics as well. Economically, growth in the Spanish kingdoms in the fourteenth and fifteenth centuries – based on stock-raising, agriculture, and manufacturing – supported an expanding export trade that benefited from Spain's location at the nexus of Mediterranean and Atlantic Europe. Over the course of the late Middle Ages, that economic growth prepared Spain to become the first world power.

Paradoxically, economic development took place against a background of enormous upheaval. The Black Death of the mid fourteenth century, in addition to causing a major demographic decline, also had widespread effects on Spanish economy and society. With a smaller population and fewer available workers, the herding industry, with low requirements for labor, could take advantage of the vast grazing lands available throughout the peninsula, at the same time that agricultural production declined. The Black Death also affected politics in ways both subtle and immediate. One of the most dramatic events was the death of King Alfonso XI of Castile in 1350, stricken by the epidemic as he besieged Muslim Gibraltar.

Alfonso was the only reigning monarch in Europe killed by the Black Death, and his demise set the stage for a struggle and eventually a long civil war between his legitimate heir and his bastard son, Enrique of Trastámara. The bastard won, and the emergence of the Trastámara dynasty in Castile was one of the most important political developments of the late medieval period. As we shall see, another Trastámara prince became king of Aragon in the early fifteenth century. Although the two branches of the line squabbled and occasionally fought, they finally came together with the marriage of Fernando of Aragon and Isabel of Castile in the late fifteenth century. With the two major Spanish kingdoms ruled by one dynasty, modern Spain as we know it began to take shape, not as an inevitable development, but as part of a historical process defined by contingency as much as by intent.

Of all the inhabitants of Spain, the Jewish communities probably experienced the worst effects of the upheavals in the late medieval period. Pressured by increasing restrictions from the dominant Christian society that surrounded them, many Jews chose to convert to Christianity, and many others were coerced into conversion during times of crisis. The net result was to reduce the number of Jews and to make them more vulnerable to increasing pressure from the Christian community. In 1492, the Spanish monarchs presented the remaining Jews with the bitter choice of converting or going into exile. The expulsion decree of 1492 meant that Jews could not legally reside in Christian Spain, and those who had converted to Christianity faced increasing scrutiny. Muslims, too, saw their position erode to nothing. In 1492, Christian forces conquered the last Muslim kingdom in Granada, followed by increasing demands for Muslims to convert to Christianity. To understand all of these contingent developments, we must enter into the complex history of late medieval Spain.

Reconquest and economic developments

In late medieval times, the various kingdoms of Spain had close connections with the outside world. The cities of Seville, Barcelona, and Valencia were important trading centers, the bases for merchants who traded throughout the Mediterranean basin. The Crown of

Aragon maintained commercial relations with the western Mediterranean and North Africa, and Castile had links with northwest Europe, as well as with Mediterranean lands. Scholars used to depict Castile as a backward hinterland uninterested in commerce. Just the opposite is true, both for the Castilian middle classes and for the nobility. The reconquest of Murcia and the Guadalquivir valley broke the Muslim hold on the Strait of Gibraltar and allowed more secure connections between Mediterranean and Atlantic coastal trading routes. Vessels from Italy and eastern Spain could sail unmolested through the strait and onward to Portugal and northwest Europe, especially to Flanders, where Bruges was one of Europe's chief banking and commercial centers.

The Christian presence near Gibraltar also set the stage for increased Italian commercial activities in southern Spain. Merchants from Italian cities were some of Europe's most successful traders in the later Middle Ages. The Genoese and the Venetians had resupplied the Christian crusader states in the eastern Mediterranean. In return, they received commercial privileges and portions of several cities in those states, which strengthened their already existing trade in that region. Italian merchants also traded with Muslims and continued to do so despite papal complaints.

After the crusader states fell at the end of the thirteenth century, ambitious Italians reassessed their commercial options. With the Venetians dominant in the eastern Mediterranean, the Genoese looked to the west. Following their existing practices, they established enclaves called *factoria* that negotiated for extraterritorial status from local rulers and officials. In each *factorium*, which included residences and warehouses, a commercial representative (the factor) managed the enclave and enforced the laws and commercial regulations of his home city. He also ensured that his compatriots obeyed local laws beyond the precincts of the *factorium*, to maintain cordial relations with local authorities.

In Spain, the Genoese had *factoria* in both Muslim and Christian ports. From the time of the Christian conquest of Seville in 1248, they were active in that city, where they managed trade to Genoa, mainly commerce in grain but also in wine and citrus products. In addition, they pursued opportunities to acquire gold from West Africa, where three important areas supplied the gold that reached Mediterranean markets. Muslim merchants had long-established caravan routes across the Sahara, exchanging horses and manufactured goods in sub-Saharan Africa for gold and slaves. The gold they acquired spread through the Muslim world and into Christian Spain, and the Genoese hoped to tap into that supply network.

The Genoese in Seville integrated into Spanish society through joint commercial ventures and intermarriages with local families. As a result, they helped to spread the techniques of capitalism learned from classical precedents and from contemporary practice in Italy and the Muslim world. Practically all modern techniques of capitalism – double-entry bookkeeping, drafts, bills of exchange, and maritime insurance – were already in use in the thirteenth century, and the Genoese were experts in all of those techniques. From Seville, they expanded first to Lisbon and, by the end of the thirteenth century, to Bruges – the center of commerce, banking, and wool-weaving in northwest Europe. They also established ties with England. Before long, Spaniards joined the Genoese and other Italians in Bruges, helping to spread the techniques of commercial capitalism.

The coastal towns in northern Spain – especially Santander, Laredo, Bilbao, and San Sebastián – produced mariners who ventured seaward, first for fishing and later for maritime trade. These northern ports grew prosperous in the late Middle Ages, providing a link between the various regions of Atlantic Europe. An extensive group of kingdoms and duchies bordering the Atlantic coast, including the Iberian Peninsula, western France, the British Isles, and the Low Countries, had important economic ties amongst themselves and, in the late Middle Ages, even wider connections toward the North Sea and the Baltic and into the Mediterranean. In the fifteenth century, several of these Atlantic states developed trade with Africa as well.

Close connections and extensive trade gave the Atlantic region the potential to form a complementary economic system. Within Atlantic Europe, the lands differed in their environmental characteristics, having wide variations in rainfall, sunlight, temperature, and coastal conditions. These characteristics interacted with the underlying geological structures of the land and their mineral deposits. Areas that could produce iron and precious metals had developed a trade in them from prehistoric times. Throughout the region, there were good agricultural lands, grasslands for pastures, and hilly lands with forests that still existed in the late Middle Ages. On the coasts, variations in sea currents, depths, and temperatures fostered variations in the numbers and species of fish available to coastal populations. Overall, Atlantic Europe held a wide range of natural resources.

The inhabitants of the various Atlantic regions took advantage of the conditions that nature handed them and tended to produce the crops and animals best suited for their region. They could augment what they got from local production with the acquisition of imported products, and they could pay for the imports with the profits they earned from exporting their own specialties. Thus, trade developed from early times along the Atlantic coasts, and by the thirteenth century there was a well-established network of commercial centers tied together by shipping lanes. Medieval and early modern roads and bridges did not permit the carriage of bulk goods for great distances, even without considering topography, so that most long-distance trade in this region was seaborne. Over centuries, the inhabitants of the Atlantic coasts had developed maritime skills in shipbuilding and sailing and commercial skills in marketing their agricultural products and manufactures. The evolution of ship design involved gradually changing small details that improved how vessels handled the conditions that local mariners faced. Sometimes they adapted features of foreign ships that they encountered; other times they developed improvements in their own ships independently. Because coastal inhabitants of the Iberian Peninsula commonly sailed in both the Atlantic and Mediterranean areas, they led the way in developing oceangoing ships that could handle a wide range of conditions at sea.

The items traded by sea constituted a long list. From Iberia to other parts of Atlantic Europe went Spanish and

Portuguese wines, including ordinary red and white, but more importantly fortified wines such as sherry and port. Other products of the vineyards – vinegar and raisins – also reached markets near and far. Orchard crops were popular as well: citrus fruits, apples, figs, dates, and nuts, especially almonds. Olive oil and the soap made from it were greatly in demand. Iron from the mines of Spain reached northern markets in the form of iron bars and manufactured iron products such as nails and needles, weapons and armor, anchors, fasteners, and ship fittings. Other exported mineral products included mercury and cinnabar, as well as salt. Animal products included fish – fresh and salted – and cured hides and leather goods. The greatest source of export income, however, was the fine wool produced from Spain's vast flocks of Merino sheep, which we will consider in more detail later on.

Imports to Iberia included various grains, primarily wheat and barley. Even though Castile produced large amounts of wheat, it was often cheaper in the Basque country to bring in wheat from France by ship rather than transport it from the northern plains over the Cantabrian Mountains. Castile produced a great amount of its own woolen cloth, enough to satisfy most local demand, but the finest types tended to come from England, and later from Flanders. Lead, tin, and silver were among the metals traded southward into Iberia. The luxury market in Spain also imported tapestries, ivory carvings, and paintings from Flanders. Mundane imports such as herring and hake from northern waters supplemented the harvesting of fish by Iberian seamen.

By the thirteenth century, trade between Castile and England followed a seasonal pattern. In the winter months, Castilian and English ships carried southern food products to Bristol. In summer, the northbound freight consisted of iron and manufactured goods: nails and combs; anchors and crossbows; olive oil and wine; soap and leather; alum for the cloth industries; and salt for northern fisheries. Some Spanish wool reached England in the later Middle Ages as well, but never in large amounts, because England produced a large amount of wool of its own. English exports to Spain included woolen cloth and the other products mentioned above, and English merchants were largely in control of the trade.

On the continent, Castilian merchants played more important roles. One important overland route ran from Burgos to Paris and Arras via Bayonne, Poitiers, and Orleans. Some trade goods from Castile, mainly alum, reached Toulouse in late medieval times, but the route was difficult and little used. The great expansion of Hispano-French trade occurred with the growth of maritime routes, and, by the thirteenth century, Basques had become prominent in the carrying trade between Spain and northern France, as well as in the trading circuit that connected Castile, France, England, and Flanders. For example, Basques and other northern Spanish shippers played a role in the trade of Gascon wine to England. Gascony, centered on Bordeaux in what is now southwestern France, was a famous wine-producing region, and it was under English rule until late in the Middle Ages. Gascony supplied a large proportion of the ordinary wine for English tables, but that wine was not carried in English ships. Instead, Gascon, Spanish Basque, and other Cantabrian shippers shared the trade, with the Spaniards carrying the bulk of it.

Perhaps Castile's most important bilateral trade along the Atlantic coast was with the county of Flanders in the Netherlands. Cantabrian and Basque shippers began to visit Flanders in the thirteenth century, and, in the fifteenth century, Castilian merchants began to establish colonies in the main Flemish weaving centers, principally in the city of Bruges. The main reason for their presence was to manage the sale of fine Spanish Merino wool to the weavers of Flanders. In return, the Flemings exported fine cloths, tapestries, paintings, and other luxury items, which testify not only to the luxury industries of Flanders, but also to the value of Spanish wool. Many of the churches in northern Castile acquired Flemish paintings in this way. Rather than remaining in separate commercial enclaves, over time the Castilians in Bruges intermarried with Flemish families and blended into local society, though they maintained ties with Spain.

Such merchant communities were important for facilitating trade all over Europe. There were English, Flemish, and some French merchants resident in various parts of Iberia, and there were important colonies of Spanish merchants in Brittany, Normandy, and other parts of France, as well as in Flanders. Spanish was one of the common languages in the trading towns of western France and Flanders, and it came to influence local dialects in cities such as Bruges. Even though trade helped to knit the Atlantic region together in a system that benefited all of the participants, the system suffered from frequent disruptions. For example, the Hundred Years War (on and off from 1337 to 1453) caused serious problems for the established seasonal trades, as did lesser conflicts.

The wool industry of Castile

Despite these periodic disruptions, the characteristic products of various regions continued to define their roles in international trade. In the kingdom of Castile, the production of, and trade in, fine wool provided income for a wide range of society, including shepherds, flock owners, merchants, and shippers. The royal government prospered, too, through taxes on the movement of sheep and raw wool. As we have seen, herding formed an important part of the rural economy in both Christian and Muslim areas. In the Christian areas of the north, most monasteries and towns raised large flocks of sheep, and they saw the expansion of lands to the south as an opportunity to increase their herding operations as well. As the Christian reconquest of territory pushed farther south, successive kings bestowed large blocs of land in Extremadura and La Mancha on the Castilian military orders of Santiago, Calatrava, and Alcántara. Because these areas faced a continuing threat of Muslim attack from the late eleventh to the early thirteenth century, it made little sense to populate the lands with farmers in settled towns and villages. Instead, the military orders used their lands primarily for grazing livestock, which they could simply herd elsewhere in case of attack. This allowed the military orders to gain economic benefit from the lands under their control, but without having to rely on a large civilian population.

The military successes of the thirteenth century brought a vast amount of additional land under Christian control. As a frontier area, the newly conquered land generally had a sparse population, which shrank even more after the Black Death in the mid fourteenth century. Given the sparse population, herding continued to be an ideal way to use the land, and the variable topography and climatic extremes in Spain favored the seasonal movement of flocks. In the north and in mountainous regions, grass grows abundantly in summer, but it dies off in winter, when, moreover, the weather is too severe for open grazing. By contrast, in the south and on the open plains, grass grows abundantly in winter, after the autumn rains, and dies back in the summer heat. To take advantage of this seasonal pattern, herding interests in Spain developed a pattern of long-distance flock movements called transhumance. Christian monarchs, well aware of the importance of herding, established *cañadas* or sheep paths for moving the migrant flocks through a mosaic of legal jurisdictions on their annual migrations.

Cities such as Cuenca and Béjar received royal charters at their foundation that defined their role in the herding economy. For example, Cuenca's charter mentioned that flocks owned by its citizens would graze during the spring near the town before being shorn and moved into the northern mountains for the summer. During the winter, they would be herded down to the plains of La Mancha to graze. As long as Granada remained in Muslim hands, the citizens of Cuenca had to provide soldiers to guard the sheep against Muslim attack during their winter pasture, even though at that point the flocks were far from Cuenca. Similar regulations applied to other Spanish towns and cities near the crucial *cañadas*.

As the pattern of transhumance developed, the annual migrations involved hundreds of thousands – even millions – of animals, and the routes of some flocks between summer and winter pastures could traverse hundreds of miles and last a month or more. Although herding formed part of the rural economy throughout Europe, the scope and scale of the Spanish migratory herding economy was unique. Not surprisingly, it required an elaborate network of laws and customs to function smoothly, and, even then, disputes between herding interests and representatives of other parts of the economy erupted frequently. Local organizations made and enforced rules regarding flock movements, and a kingdom-wide organization, the Mesta – El Honorado Consejo de la Mesta de los Pastores de Castilla, or The Honored Council of the Shepherds' Conclave of Castile – developed from an amalgamation of local associations in the thirteenth century. Although the owners of the principal flocks tended to dominate the Mesta, anyone who owned migratory sheep could belong. The Mesta served as a powerful advocate for the flock owners and promulgated rules for the proper management of the flocks, including rules to prevent the overgrazing of seasonal pastures. They also worked to limit disputes between shepherds and farmers, for example by insisting that shepherds keep their animals from harming crops and forests during migrations.

From the thirteenth century on, Castilian flock owners developed the Merino breed of sheep, probably from cross-breeding animals of Iberian and North African stock. Merino wool has long, curly, and extremely thin fibers, which can be spun into very fine yarn. Long the standard for fineness, pure Merino wool was produced only in Spain until the eighteenth century. Thereafter the breed spread around the world to appropriate locations, and in modern times huge flocks flourish, for example, in Australia, New Zealand, and the United States. Spain exported Merino wool to Northern Europe in huge quantities from the late Middle Ages, especially to Flanders. The Flemish centers of fine-cloth production used much more wool than local flocks could supply and relied heavily on English wool until the fourteenth century, when the Hundred Years War disrupted supply lines, and the English prevented exports in order to benefit their own cloth industry. The weavers of Flanders and elsewhere in the Netherlands or Low Countries then turned to Spanish wool, available in quantity and increasing in quality as the Merino breed developed. England imported some Spanish wool as well, but when the English tried to mix it with local wool, the resulting cloth was not of high quality, because Merino wool requires different techniques of cloth production.

Local merchants in Castile organized and controlled the wool export trade. Merchant associations in Burgos, Segovia, and other inland cities purchased the wool from flock owners, generally at the shearing, and arranged to have it graded, washed, and sacked for export. Then they had it transported overland to ports on the northern coast, where local shippers would take it aboard, on contracts with the merchants. A consortium of insurers, often also wool merchants, insured the cargoes, and once the wool reached Flanders, resident Castilian merchants took charge of the unloaded cargoes and sold them.

To manage the trade at the northern end, merchants from inland Castile and shippers from the north-coast towns established enclaves in Flanders similar to the *factoria* of the Mediterranean, with grants of extraterritoriality and the right to judge disputes among themselves by their own laws. The city of Bruges had merchant colonies of Italians from various cities, Castilians, Basques, and subjects of the Crown of Aragon. Because of their different interests, the shippers of the Biscayan coast and the merchants of Castile established separate colonies in Bruges. The Castilian merchants also established permanent colonies in Normandy and Brittany, and less enduring ones in England. Along with their goods and services, the merchant colonies transferred business techniques. For example, maritime insurance developed first in the Mediterranean, and Spanish merchants learned how to use it from Italian merchants in Iberia. Then the merchants from Burgos and Seville who went north introduced its techniques into northwest Europe.

Despite the importance of wool exports for the Spanish economy, from the late Middle Ages through the eighteenth century the amount of wool that remained in the peninsula was greater than the volume of exports in most years. Using that wool, a large number of manufacturing centers in the Spanish kingdoms produced a wide range of cloth, from coarse to fine. Only at the highest end of the cloth market did imports hold sway. By the thirteenth century, the kingdom of Castile had a number of textile centers – including Zamora, Palencia, Segovia, Burgos, Soria, Madrid, Alcalá de Henares, Toledo, Cuenca, Murcia, and Córdoba, among others. Each center specialized in making particular types of cloth, both to supply local demand

and for export to Portugal, Aragon, and elsewhere. The cities in the center and the south began to use newer techniques for weaving and dyeing and gained advantages over the older weaving cities and towns of the north. Castilian weaving interests benefited from a law in the mid fifteenth century that allowed them to claim up to a third of the wool destined for export, at market prices, allowing them access to the best-quality wool. With minor variations, this law remained in effect throughout the early modern period.

Cuenca, the best-studied of the late medieval textile cities, had a river to provide power for mills, and water for fulling and dyeing. Because the wool from some of the best Spanish flocks was shorn, washed, and sold in the vicinity, local cloth manufacturers secured a steady supply of high-quality wool. Entrepreneurs, called "lords of the cloth," directed textile production in Cuenca; they bought raw wool and maintained control over it throughout the manufacturing process. They employed a variety of skilled workers: wool sorters, washers, burlers (who removed the knots from the raw wool), carders, combers, and spinners, all of whom prepared the wool for weaving. In the fifteenth century, weavers used older methods as well as newer techniques based upon a narrower loom. Once woven, the cloth was finished by fullers and dyers, wool dressers, and cloth shearers. Workers in each specialty had guilds to regulate quality and prices and to manage the rules by which apprentices and journeymen rose to become master craftsmen. The guild officials also defended their collective interests before town officials and provided support for members' families and general charity in the city.

Over the course of the fifteenth century, some components of wool manufacturing moved into the Spanish countryside as well. Peasants who had traditionally produced homespun woolen cloth for their own use were now drawn into a broader productive network. Entrepreneurs distributed or "put out" their wool to household laborers, sometimes still in towns, but often in the countryside, to avoid urban guild regulations. The finishing and dyeing of woven cloths, the most specialized and technically complicated parts of cloth production, usually remained in the towns, but many other phases of the process could be done equally well in the countryside. As a result, the putting-out system became widespread and common in Castilian cloth manufacturing.

The trade of the Crown of Aragon

Late medieval trade boomed in the Mediterranean regions of the Crown of Aragon, with Barcelona, Mallorca, and Valencia the main hubs. Merchants and ship owners from those locations carried out a sophisticated trade that extended throughout the Mediterranean area and through the Strait of Gibraltar to northwest Europe. With royal support, they established *alfóndigos* or consulates in important trading ports from Alexandria in Egypt to Bruges in Flanders. The enclaves, with extraterritorial rights, offered temporary residential quarters and secure warehouses. Resident consuls supervised the affairs of merchants and shippers as they dealt with one another and with local merchants and officials. At home, the Consolat del Mar (Consulate of the Sea) supported the economic activities of merchants and shippers and resolved disputes among merchants, among shippers, and between merchants and shippers.

Within the extensive trading network they established, the merchants dealt in a variety of products and merchandise. They exported Catalan textiles and mid-range jewelry featuring coral they obtained in North Africa. They purchased spices from the Asian world in the markets of Egypt and redistributed them throughout the Christian Mediterranean. They bought slaves in North Africa and from the markets of the eastern Mediterranean and the Black Sea and acquired others by piracy. They exported wine and olive oil, fruits and nuts, honey and salt pork, rope and iron products for ship fittings. They imported raw wool from Castile and as far away as England, and exported the cloths they made from it. They secured grain in Sicily and transported it home and to markets in Italy and the south of France in times of scarcity there. Their well-regarded shipbuilding industry provided vessels for the use of their own shippers and for foreign buyers as well, at times to their competitive detriment. The enclosed medieval shipyard in Barcelona still exists, housing the city's impressive maritime museum. In the early fourteenth century, mariners from the Crown of Aragon were probing south along the Atlantic coast of Africa and to the Canary Islands.

A decline set in during the middle of the fourteenth century. It was especially acute for Barcelona; Valencia fared better but still endured rough times. In part, the decline was due to civil strife in the form of revolts at home and wars with Christian rivals. In larger part, it was due to the major upheavals that affected most of Europe and the wider Mediterranean world.

Economic crisis and recovery in late medieval Spain

Western Europe experienced a series of major crises in the fourteenth century. After two centuries of expansion, the population approached the maximum that could be sustained by existing agricultural technology. Famines and epidemics began to reduce the population and consequently lessened the demand for food. Farms on marginal lands, whose soils were by then depleted, were abandoned, in a process that left entire villages deserted in Northern Europe in the early fourteenth century. Then, at mid-century, the fearsome pandemic known as the Black Death hit Europe. In the course of less than four years, the disease killed between one-quarter and one-third of the entire European population. The initial wave of the Black Death was the greatest demographic disaster Europeans have ever experienced. Over the same period, the Muslim world of North Africa and the Middle East suffered roughly comparable losses. Following the acute decline of population, and in part because of it, Europe underwent economic changes and social alterations that in many cases led to mob violence and rebellion.

The pattern of famine and disease in Iberia in this period is not as clear as it is for northwestern Europe, where slightly cooler and wetter weather caused crop failures, subsequent famines, and the spread of diseases among humans and animals. Those climatic conditions, if they prevailed in Iberia, might have brought the more arid regions some improvement, rather than disaster. At mid-century, nonetheless, all of Western Europe experienced the Black Death. The first, and what turned out to be the worst, outbreak in the Iberian Peninsula began in March 1348 on the island of Mallorca, and in April spread to the northern frontier provinces of Rosellón and Cerdaña near the Pyrenees. Barcelona reported the sickness by early May, as did Tarragona and elsewhere in Catalonia. Almería, still a Muslim port in the mid fourteenth century, joined the ranks of stricken towns in the last days of May. By June, the epidemic struck the great pilgrimage center of Santiago de Compostela in the far northwest. Most, if not all, of the outbreaks in 1348 were presumably introduced from outside the peninsula, rather than spreading from one initial point of infection. Once established in port towns, however, the plague spread inland. From Barcelona and Valencia, it advanced along separate routes to the inland city of Zaragoza, arriving in September. By October, the city registered some 300 deaths each month. By 1349, the peninsula as a whole was infected, and the Black Death in its various forms reportedly claimed its largest number of victims in that year. All told, the first plague epidemic in Iberia lasted until March 1350.

As with the trajectory and overall mortality of the plague, the Iberian epidemic followed patterns well known in other areas of Europe. Coastal regions were, on average, hit harder than the interior. Larger towns and cities suffered more severe losses than smaller towns. Mountainous areas often escaped the infection altogether, while population centers on the plains seem to have been disproportionately afflicted, in part because they were connected by trade routes to one another and to coastal ports. While the epidemic raged, the overall death rates surged upward, but not all of the deaths can be attributed to bubonic plague – the classic candidate for the cause of the Black Death – and death rates varied considerably from place to place. There were also certain occupations that were at greater risk of infection. Members of the clergy, medical personnel, and notaries perished in huge numbers, placed in harm's way by the nature of their offices. Representatives of all three groups frequented the bedsides of clients stricken by the plague, attending to their spiritual concerns, attempting to cure their bodily ills, and recording their wills. In the course of their activities, they risked becoming infected themselves. Within towns, the poorer neighborhoods typically experienced the plague first and suffered more than wealthier neighborhoods.

Nevertheless, no class escaped the disease, and it was in Spain that the plague claimed its highest-ranking victims in all of Europe. Queen Leonor, wife of King Pere ("the Ceremonious") of Aragon and daughter of Afonso IV of Portugal, died at the end of October 1348. King Alfonso XI of Castile died from the plague in March 1350, while his army was besieging Gibraltar.

The Christian kingdoms of Iberia experienced profound consequences from the epidemic and the economic and social disruptions that followed. The responses varied region by region, however, and often followed different patterns from their neighbors across the Pyrenees. In Catalonia, farmers often abandoned individual farmsteads, especially in areas of marginal productivity, but villages remained inhabited. Some surviving peasants left marginal holdings and moved to ones that were more productive. Other peasant families simply absorbed deserted farms into their holdings. Consequently, few if any villages disappeared. The situation was different in Old Castile, where many of the villages in existence in the thirteenth century were ghost towns by the fifteenth. The question, however, is to what extent the Black Death caused the desertions. The answer, based on most studies, is that the Black Death provoked an acute phase within a chronic problem. The abandonment of villages in Old Castile was part of a process that began in the thirteenth century and probably was exacerbated by the plague.

In the aftermath of the Black Death, throughout the Iberian Peninsula, monarchs heard complaints from elite members of society, similar to those we know were common elsewhere in Western Europe. At the base of the complaints there were noticeable alterations in the ways society and the economy functioned, which, in the immediate term, increased the opportunities open to the laboring classes and reduced the control exercised by the elite. Working people moved from place to place, seeking and often securing better conditions and higher wages because of shortages of labor. With rising wages came higher prices. In response to such complaints, throughout the peninsula, the elite sought ordinances and regulations that would restore conditions prevailing before the plague. These generally fell into three categories. One was designed to place restrictions on freedom of movement, often phrased as measures to end vagabondage but really designed to keep workers in the fields or in their towns of origin. The other two categories were more straightforward: they aimed to cap both prices and wages at pre-plague levels.

In Aragon, the Cortes of Zaragoza of 1350 attempted to thwart the market pressures on both wages and prices caused by plague mortality. Detailed regulations for artisans specified their wages and their conditions of work, and threatened those who violated the regulations with fines. Similarly, the government fixed prices for artisan goods. King Pedro I of Castile, responding to the demands of the Cortes of 1351, issued restrictions on personal movement, wages, and prices. Conditions of work were also established for artisans and farm workers of various kinds, including plowmen, harvesters, vineyard workers, and day laborers. Among the provisions was a prohibition on the formation of workers' confraternities, presumably feared as a source of unrest. Although Pedro I acted in the face of an acute crisis, most of his provisions invented nothing new. Monarchs had long found occasions to intervene in the economy; the plague merely added greater urgency to those interventions.

Throughout the peninsula, the post-plague period witnessed a series of fundamental shifts in the relations between town and countryside and between proprietors and workers, both urban and rural. Just as certainly, many of those shifts had been in progress before the plague and continued long after its acute phase. Plague survivors could afford to abandon marginal lands and concentrate on the most productive ones, and to shift to the production of crops that would produce the highest returns in urban markets. The Castilian livestock industry, especially sheep herding, rose in the two centuries following the plague. It is not clear, however, whether the demographic decline freed more marginal land for pasture or whether sufficient pasture had always been available, and stock raising, especially for the production of fine Merino wool, simply offered better market returns in the aftermath of the Black Death.

Throughout Europe, popular revolts followed as seeming consequences of the Black Death. The Peasants' Revolt in England, various rural revolts or *Jacqueries* in France, and the rebellion (called the *Ciompi*) of urban artisans in Florence have all been characterized as reactions to government attempts to thwart the gains made by peasants and urban workers following the Black Death. In Iberia, some incidents of anti-Jewish popular violence erupted in Barcelona and other eastern cities in the late 1340s, but large-scale revolts only arose in the 1390s, two generations after the great epidemics. Those later revolts present problems of interpretation, and there is no consensus on whether they were primarily anti-Jewish in origin or were instead motivated more by socioeconomic aims. In either case, or in a combination of both (which seems more likely), the rebellions in late medieval Spain were responses to conditions that were longstanding by the late fourteenth century and that continued to spark unrest throughout the fifteenth.

Crisis and decline of Spain's Jewish communities

Medieval Spain had always been among the most tolerant areas of Europe. In Islamic Spain, as we saw in earlier chapters, Muslim authorities tolerated Christian and Jewish communities as "People of the Book." This continued in Christian Spain, with the authorities tolerating Jewish communities in the cities and larger towns and Muslim communities in Valencia and elsewhere. Under the strains of the late medieval period, this toleration declined. Elsewhere in Europe, England expelled its Jews in 1290, and

France did the same from 1306 in decrees restated at least twice later in the same century.

Widespread popular hostility against Jews did not develop in Aragon and Castile until the 1390s. How much of the anti-Jewish feeling sprang from religious animosity and how much resulted from economic causes is open to question. Whatever the reasons, the growing animosity led to anti-Jewish mob violence in a number of places in Spain, which often led to a wave of mass conversions, many of them coerced. Many Jews had no choice but to convert to save their lives. Popes, kings, and local bishops condemned both the violence and the forced conversions, but there was a catch. Catholic doctrine held that any baptism, even one forced by fear of death, was binding. Anyone baptized had to live a Christian life, regardless of the circumstances of the baptism. One could not renounce conversion or baptism or revert to one's previous religion without being labeled an apostate, a very serious charge. Involuntary converts were thus placed in an impossible situation, knowing they faced persecution if they went back on their conversions.

After several years of unrest, the anti-Jewish riots dwindled, but they left in their wake a large number of converts, both coerced and voluntary, known collectively as *conversos*. Not all converts had come to Christianity through force or coercion. Some, perhaps many, had converted voluntarily and thereafter sincerely tried to assimilate into Christian society. Yet they, too, faced a difficult situation. In the fifteenth century, sporadic anti-Jewish riots coincided with extensive anti-*converso* feeling, as so-called Old Christians often viewed all converts as suspect. In the 1440s and the 1460s, anti-Jewish laws were enacted in various Spanish cities, and some of those laws applied to *conversos* as well. In Toledo in 1449, the city council passed laws prohibiting Jews from holding public offices or exercising occupations that placed them in positions of authority over Christians. For example, Jewish doctors could no longer treat Christian patients. This was a local decision, but it had widespread ramifications. The crown condemned such measures and took action to rescind local laws in Toledo and elsewhere that targeted Jews. Nonetheless, in the 1460s, riots against Jews occurred in several Andalusian towns that had enacted laws similar to those in Toledo, and it was clear that anti-Jewish sentiment was rising.

In the same period, calls for some sort of religious investigation began to appear widely, with citizens asking for some formal means – in short, an inquisition – of judging who was a sincere convert, and who was not. Ironically, some of the most fervent calls for an inquisition came from some members of the *converso* community, anxious to prove their Christian orthodoxy. The Catholic Church always took seriously its right to judge the faith and morals of Christians. Bishops usually acted as the investigators, and in individual cases the local bishop would judge whether a person was a heretic or not. By the early thirteenth century, several heretical movements had surfaced in Europe, prominent among them the Cathars or Albigensians in southern France, as we have seen. To deal with the Albigensians, whom papal authorities considered a serious threat, in the early thirteenth century the popes established a new institution, the inquisition. Thereafter, investigators or inquisitors sent from Rome took the investigation of heresy out of the hands of local bishops in many areas of Europe. The new papal inquisition relied upon many of the procedures and processes of Roman law, just then being revived in Western Europe, among them the use of torture in interrogations. Neither Aragon nor Castile permitted the papal inquisition to operate in their territory. King Enrique IV of Castile sought and received papal approval to establish an independent inquisition in Castile, but he did not actually institute it. That dubious distinction was left to his half-sister and successor, Isabel of Castile, who, with her husband, Fernando of Aragon, would institute a religious inquisition in Castile in 1478 and expel Spain's unconverted Jews in 1492.

Political patterns in late medieval Spain

The inquisition and the expulsion of the Jews were far in the future as the late medieval period began, yet they had their genesis in the successive crises that rocked the Spanish kingdoms in the fourteenth and fifteenth centuries. Many of those crises involved noble unrest to one degree or another. The highest levels of Spanish political life witnessed a series of generally inconclusive struggles between the nobles and successive kings, largely over the issue of how much power each side could claim and enforce. The nobles as a group were content to have a monarch as ruler, but, individually and collectively, they wanted to have considerable influence in the affairs of state. Strong monarchs were averse to sharing their power, and factions among the nobility guaranteed that a monarch who was canny as well as strong could play the factions off against one another. One sure way to do this was through the manipulation of patronage in exchange for loyalty. A monarch would reward loyal nobles with grants of jurisdictions or royal offices that gave them a monetary income or the ability to collect fees. He or she would also award grants of land. Skillfully applied, a monarch's patronage powers could keep noble pretensions directed toward material rather than political gains.

Rulers also had to maintain mutually supportive relations with the urban network of cities (*ciudades*), towns (*villas*), villages (*aldeas*), and tiny settlements (*lugares*), each able to tax its citizens to one degree or another. The urban network held particular importance in Castile, as there was a legacy of rights granted to municipalities and their citizens during the centuries of the reconquest. Legal citizenship (*vecindad*) in a municipality gave each citizen (*vecino*) certain rights and privileges, including voting rights in the case of male heads of household. Many municipalities owed duties to an overlord, usually paid in monetary form. Members of the nobility and the church controlled some municipalities directly, often because of royal grants during the early reconquest. As time went on, successive monarchs granted other royal towns or villages to the church or the nobility, which gave the grantee access to income and jurisdictional rights.

Villages and small settlements generally fell under the jurisdiction of a town or city, which had varying degrees of local autonomy, regardless of their overlord. A typical town in Castile would have a council elected by the citizens eligible to vote, composed of a set number of councilors (*regidores*) and aldermen (*jurados*). The council was obliged to help the king in time of war and to apportion and collect taxes. In the fourteenth century, as monarchs realized that they were losing control of the municipal network, they appointed an agent called a *corregidor* to sit with each town council as the crown's representative. These royal agents became more powerful over time, and by the end of the fifteenth century were formidable forces in municipal government. Nonetheless, the towns retained considerable autonomy in partnership with the crown.

The wild card – literally and figuratively – in the game of late medieval politics was the nobility. In pursuit of power and financial advantage, the nobility made successive kings pay for their continued loyalty and support. In periods when a minor inherited the throne, individual nobles would take advantage of the crown's temporary weakness to extract benefits in return for loyalty. Even under established monarchs, factions of the nobility would contend with one another for royal favor, or passively disobey the royal will until they were rewarded for obedience. At times, factions of the nobility would even threaten civil war to get what they wanted. One ploy was to stage a coup by setting up a rival claimant to the throne. Even when the monarch countered the coup with loyalist factions, he would still have to provide benefits to the dissident faction to bring them back into the fold. The series of Spanish civil wars in the fourteenth and fifteenth centuries largely fit this mold. They seldom went too far and were rarely decisive. Instead, they defined a pattern of testing the monarchical authority in Spain, similar to the struggles going on elsewhere in Europe at the same time. War and civil war were extensions of politics. The political narrative of fourteenth- and fifteenth-century Spain illustrates this pattern of behavior very clearly.

Politics and personalities in late medieval Spain

Alfonso XI of Castile came of age in 1325. After having waited out a long minority, he seemed determined to build monarchical power by curbing the nobility, one of whose leaders was his own uncle, Juan Manuel, one of Castile's most prominent writers. The king ordered many unsanctioned noble castles to be destroyed and enrolled the most recalcitrant nobles forcibly into the military orders. Other nobles got the message and refrained from challenging him. Alfonso XI began the policy, frequently followed by his successors, of employing the nobility in campaigns against Muslim Granada. In these endeavors, nobles would be fighting under the king's banner against an outside enemy. If successful, they won land and booty for themselves, and the king would get his royal fifth. Even if they were unsuccessful, the campaigns against the Muslims kept the nobility out of mischief. In 1340 Alfonso and his forces were able to turn back the last Moroccan invasion of the peninsula by the Benemerines (Marinids) who landed near Tarifa. He died ten years later.

Alfonso XI left one legitimate son, who became Pedro I. He also left ten illegitimate children by his lover Leonor de Guzmán. Their leader was Enrique of Trastámara, who received his surname because of his exploits against the Muslims at the town of Trastámara. Pedro I and Enrique contested the kingship for nineteen years in a civil war that divided Castile. Both sides invited mercenary companies into the conflict. Enrique brought in the White Company from France under Bernard de Guesclin, while Pedro called in English mercenaries. In 1369, Guesclin arranged to meet with Pedro to discuss changing sides, but he remained loyal to Enrique and told him of the meeting. Enrique then confronted his half-brother and stabbed him to death, a political act, of course, but also an act of personal revenge, as Pedro had executed Enrique's mother and several of his siblings. Thus, Enrique of Trastámara took the throne of Castile as Enrique II, the first king of the dynasty that would rule Spain until 1516.

Enrique II faced the possibility of foreign war after gaining power, with potential adversaries in Portugal, France, England, and Aragon. To counter his rivals, he had to maintain a strong defensive posture and keep the nobility loyal, in case he needed them for war. Enrique's successors continued to support the nobility for the same reasons. Juan I devoted himself to foreign concerns and at one point tried to take over Portugal by asserting his Portuguese wife's claims. His invasion failed after his defeat at the battle of Aljubarrota in 1385, against Portuguese forces led by João de Avis. João took the Portuguese throne and founded the Avis dynasty, which continued to be a major rival for Castilian kings thereafter.

Despite the defeat in Portugal, Castilian power continued to build. When Juan I died in 1390, he left behind a fairly stable kingdom. His son Enrique III died in 1406, leaving as his heir a minor son, Juan II, who reigned until 1454, providing stability at the top of the political pyramid. While he was still a child, a regency council ruled Castile, including his mother Catalina and his uncle Fernando. The uncle, extremely powerful and ambitious, engaged in vigorous campaigning against Granada and gained the soubriquet "de Antequera" after a successful foray against that town in the kingdom of Granada.

He accumulated wide territories and many holdings in Castile and was favorably positioned to take advantage of a momentous political change in the Crown of Aragon.

In 1410 the king of Aragon, Martín I, died without heirs. For two years the throne remained vacant while a committee of arbiters met to sort things out in the town of Caspe, conveniently located for Aragon, Catalonia, and Valencia. In 1412, they agreed to the Compromise of Caspe, by which they offered the throne to Fernando de Antequera. He accepted and became Fernando I, king of Aragon and Sicily, ruling from 1412 until his death in 1416. That is how two branches of the Trastámara family came to occupy the thrones of Castile and Aragon. Though historians have often viewed this coincidence of power as foreshadowing the consolidation of the two kingdoms, it was certainly not a foregone conclusion.

To be sure, Fernando I kept his eye on Castile, even while occupied with his new responsibilities. He was, after all, the son, brother, and uncle of Castilian kings. Moreover, his wife was one of the richest women in Castile, and, through her holdings and his own, he held numerous towns and large territories in that kingdom. He used his position and his family connections to cement his influence in Castile. His children, called the *infantes* of Aragon, lived in Castile and held towns and property there; for a generation, they also stirred up great political trouble in Castile.

When Fernando I of Aragon died in 1416, the crown first passed to the eldest of the *infantes* of Aragon, Alfonso V, who later earned the title "the Magnanimous." His major concern was the Mediterranean portion of his scattered holdings. From his position as king of Sicily, he secured control of Naples, thus achieving his desire for imperial influence in the central Mediterranean. Alfonso V was also interested in the Balkan territories held by the Catalan Grand Company, principally the duchy of Athens. Alfonso V, as a flamboyant Renaissance ruler, maintained a beautiful and splendid court in Naples and essentially abandoned his Iberian possessions, leaving them in the control of his brother Juan. True to his birth as one of the *infantes*, Juan worked against the kings of Castile, his cousins. The other *infantes* also remained in Spain and followed Juan's lead. At that time, the king of Castile was Juan II (1419–54). His marriage to María of Aragon brought a sister of the fractious *infantes* into the royal bedchamber. The marriage did not pacify the *infantes*, however, and Juan II had to spend much of his time and energy in a series of struggles against their attempts to increase their power in Castile. Juan II of Castile was a learned man, without much taste for governing, let alone fighting difficult relatives. Consequently, he delegated much of the day-to-day business of governing to Álvaro de Luna, a Castilian nobleman. Luna enriched himself while in office and supposedly acquired nearly complete control over the king. By necessity, he was the adversary of the *infantes* of Aragon.

María of Aragon and King Juan II of Castile had a son, Enrique, who, early on as prince, inclined toward his mother's Aragonese heritage. At the age of fifteen, he married Blanca of Navarre, but he had the marriage dissolved after eleven years of childlessness. In a clerical hearing to investigate the grounds for annulment, Enrique testified that he had never had sex with his wife. He maintained that he was unable to have sex with her, though he produced women at the hearing who swore that he had had sex easily with them. Prince Enrique won the annulment of the marriage, but his enemies would later use his testimony to question his sexual orientation. Blanca did not contest the annulment and went back to Navarre. In her final testament, she left all of her possessions to Enrique.

Through most of Juan II's reign, there was periodic fighting between his Castilian forces and the *infantes* of Aragon. Finally, at the battle of Olmedo in 1445, the *infantes* suffered such a crushing defeat that they had to give up many of their possessions in Castile. Nonetheless, the king spared their lives and barely punished their followers, a typical end to yet another indecisive military campaign. María of Aragon died in 1445, and in 1447 Juan II was married again, to Isabel of Portugal, whose grandfathers were King João I of Portugal and Afonso, first duke of Braganza. Before he died, seven years later, Juan II had sired two more children, Isabel and Alfonso, who took their places in line for the succession in Castile behind Prince Enrique. When Juan II died in 1454, Enrique ascended the throne of Castile as Enrique IV.

In Aragon, Alfonso the Magnanimous died in 1458 without an heir, and his younger brother ascended the throne as Joan II, ruling over Aragon and its empire in Italy and the eastern Mediterranean. Joan II had been working to rebuild the power of the *infantes* of Aragon in Castile ever since the defeat at Olmedo in 1445. As king, he strengthened his campaign against Castile and its new king, Enrique IV. Joan II of Aragon and his followers believed that the Castilian king was incapable of producing an heir and, arguably, saw an opportunity to take over all of Castile. Back in Castile, Enrique IV was married a second time the same year he ascended the throne, to Juana of Portugal. For years, their marriage was childless, which helped to fuel speculation about the king's impotence. At last, in 1462, the queen produced a daughter, baptized Juana. The Castilian nobility and the representatives to the Cortes at the time all recognized Juana as princess of Castile and as first in line to the throne.

Enrique IV ruled successfully during the first half of his reign, working out political agreements with prominent nobles and bringing university-educated men into bureaucratic offices to professionalize the royal administration. To further strengthen his government, the king organized a rural police force called "the Brotherhood" (*Hermandad*), based in principal towns, and extended the use of *corregidores* in town councils. The king also showed favor to the woolen textile industry, which benefited many of the principal towns. All of these actions enhanced the ties between the crown and Castile's urban network, as a counterbalance to the power of the nobility. On the religious front, the king sought and obtained papal permission to begin an inquisition in Castile, a move favored by many town councils, though events precluded its introduction.

After the birth of Princess Juana, political pressure grew from Enrique IV's enemies. Supporters of the Aragonese contingent in Castile wanted someone on the throne more malleable than the king and thought that they could manipulate his young half-siblings Alfonso and Isabel. They began to claim that Juana was not the daughter of Enrique IV, but instead of the king's friend and confidant Beltrán de la Cueva, who coincidentally received a ducal title shortly after Juana was born. Consequently, the fractious nobles gave Juana the insulting nickname of "La Beltraneja" (lit., she of Beltrán). The propaganda campaign intensified, aiming to discredit Enrique in all ways possible. Rumors even circulated that the king was not a good Christian and favored Jews and Muslims in his court.

At a ceremony staged in Ávila, rebels symbolically dethroned Enrique in the name of Prince Alfonso and, on June 5, 1465, crowned the eleven-year-old Alfonso in his stead. Unfortunately for the rebels, Alfonso died of an intestinal disorder in July 1468, leaving his supporters temporarily without a figurehead. Its leaders then approached the young Isabel. In turn, she and her supporters approached the king and offered to help to stop the revolt against him, in return for his recognition of Isabel as heir to the throne. By implication, this meant that Enrique IV would disown Juana, but he agreed on the pragmatic grounds that ending the revolt justified his recognition of Isabel and his rejection of Juana. In exchange, he secured a clear agreement from Isabel that she could not and would not marry without his permission.

Viewing the early stages of Isabel's political career, it is difficult to know whether she or her supporters were in charge of her actions, but it soon became clear that she was making clever decisions that reflected her control. Isabel began to organize her own court and avoided Enrique's efforts to marry her off to one of his supporters. And, in a stunning political coup, in 1469 she decided to marry her cousin, Fernando, son and heir of Joan II of Aragon. They eloped and married in Valladolid, without the permission of King Enrique, who thereupon revoked his agreement naming her his heir. Strong evidence suggests that Enrique IV and his half-sister got along very well personally, but this conflict was political and deadly serious.

The dispute between the newlywed princess and King Enrique added a new source of factional strife to the political landscape. Both Prince Fernando and his father maintained close ties with the *infantes* of Aragon in Castile, and they continued those ties after Fernando married Isabel, forming the basis of support for the newlyweds against Enrique. Other nobles in Castile hoped to take advantage of the dispute by bartering their support for favors from one side or the other. In 1473, Isabel invited Enrique IV to meet Fernando and patch up their disagreements. After a preliminary meeting, Enrique accepted their invitation to lunch, sitting between the couple. Soon after the meal, the king suffered a debilitating pain in his stomach, and some scholars have suggested that the symptoms resembled those of arsenic poisoning. Whatever the truth of that accusation, Enrique IV never fully recovered his health and died the following year, 1474, triggering a crisis of succession.

To succeed him, the king's daughter Juana initially enjoyed a significant amount of support in Castile and from the king of Portugal, to whom she was betrothed. Isabel had also amassed considerable support in Castile, added to the weight of Aragonese power that Fernando brought into their marriage. It is ironic that Isabel had to fight Portugal to secure her throne, because her heritage included significant Portuguese connections, starting with her mother. Her husband, Fernando of Aragon, had two Castilian parents and grew up in an atmosphere closely associated with Castile, though he represented the Aragonese faction in Castilian politics. By contrast, Isabel grew up in a strongly Portuguese atmosphere. When her father, Juan II, died in 1454 and his son Enrique took the throne, the royal widow established her household in Arévalo on the plains of Old Castile to raise her children, Isabel and Alfonso. Soon Isabel's grandmother, Isabel of Barcelos, joined her daughter to help with running the household. In her youth, Isabel of Barcelos had married Prince João of Portugal, son of King João I. They were related, as her father, Afonso, was a bastard son of the same King João I and became count of Barcelos and the first duke of Braganza. The Braganza dynasty thereafter played a pivotal role in Portuguese high politics.

Isabel of Barcelos's brother-in-law was Prince Henrique, known in English-language historiography as Prince Henry the Navigator, and she lived in King João I's court as the Portuguese extended the frontiers of European knowledge about Africa and the Atlantic. At court, she observed the bitter in-fighting among Portugal's high nobility. She also witnessed the glory and gold that flowed into Portugal during the first phase of Atlantic exploration, conquest, and trade. Following the early death of her husband, Prince João, in 1442, Isabel of Barcelos remained a widow, but her public life was far from over. After 1447, she moved to Castile to join her daughter, and King Juan II made her a member of his royal council. In 1454, Isabel of Barcelos helped to negotiate the terms of the marriage between Prince Enrique of Castile and Princess Juana of Portugal. Following Juan II's death and Enrique's ascension to the throne, she settled in Arévalo with her widowed daughter and her two young grandchildren. She remained there until her death in 1466.

Thus, Isabel of Castile, between the age of three and ten, grew up in the Arévalo household run by her grandmother, Isabel of Barcelos, and her mother, Isabel of Portugal, surrounded by Portuguese influences. Attending the young princess was another Portuguese woman, Clara Alvarnáez, wife of Gonzalo Chacón, *comendador* of Montiel, who administered the dowager queen's household. Another Portuguese woman in the household, Beatriz de Silva, later founded the Order of the Immaculate Conception. Given these circumstances, Isabel's first language was probably Portuguese. In later years, she presumably conversed from time to time in Portuguese after she joined her brother Enrique IV's court in 1461, because his second wife, Queen Juana, had an entourage of Portuguese noblewomen and servitors. Later, as queen, Isabel of Castile would continue to have prominent Portuguese noblemen, including her kinsmen, as members of her court.

For the five years following Enrique's death, Castile faced a civil struggle complicated by two Portuguese invasions. In the course of that struggle, Isabel of Castile gradually won over many nobles who initially opposed her by offering them amnesty; new grants of lands, titles, and royal offices; and the confirmation of old grants. She also secured the backing of a majority of Castilian cities. The number of defections from Princess Juana's camp increased as time went on, and, in the end, Isabel and Fernando crushed their opponents on the field of battle. Juana decamped to Portugal, and her proposed marriage to the king of Portugal evaporated when she lost all hope of reigning in Castile. She lived out the rest of her long life in Portuguese exile. Thus, the Castilian succession crisis ended with a treaty between Castile and Portugal in 1479 that acknowledged Isabel as the undisputed queen of Castile. In that same year, Fernando became the king of Aragon when his father Joan II died.

With both of their thrones secured, Fernando and Isabel could begin their ambitious program of consolidating royal authority. Long before she had secured her succession in Castile, Isabel made an agreement with her husband about how to share in its governance. In that 1475 agreement, he acknowledged her position as heir to the Castilian throne and her exclusive right to grant gifts and favors to nobles and municipalities in Castile. Moreover, she was the only one who could name governors for fortresses in Castile and the only person who could administer domains of the crown. She had no real authority outside Castile and its dominions, but that, as it turned out, would be an impressive collection of territories. As Isabel's husband, Fernando could exercise certain restricted rights in Castile, in concert with the queen, but he could not act on his own. Moreover, he could only exercise such powers during Isabel's lifetime. Nonetheless, Isabel realized that it would be difficult to rule as a woman, particularly in such unsettled times, so that it would not be wise to restrict Fernando's role to ceremonial functions alone. The perception was that they ruled Castile jointly, and history knows them as the "Catholic Monarchs" (Sp. Reyes Católicos). By contrast, Fernando did not face a disputed succession or any serious opposition in the Crown of Aragon. Thus, he had no reason to concede any real powers to Isabel in Aragon, and he did not do so.

By 1480, Castile had achieved peace with its neighboring kingdoms for the first time in decades. Aragon's long border war with France continued but entered a quiescent period in 1493. From that war, the two provinces in the eastern Pyrenees, Rosellón and Cerdaña (Fr. Roussillon and Cerdagne), again came under the sway of Catalonia. Isabel and Fernando maintained close relations with the papacy but retained extensive control over the Spanish church in their domains. Among other things, they persuaded the pope to confirm their right to appoint bishops and archbishops, and secured the income from the bulls of crusade authorized by the pope, in recognition of the expenses of Castile's continuing confrontation with Muslim Granada.

The final conquest of Granada was undoubtedly the most important war fought by the Catholic Monarchs, and it occupied them on and off for ten years, from 1482 to 1492. A final assault on Muslim Granada represented both a challenge and an opportunity for Isabel and Fernando. Although it would be costly, a full-scale war offered them the prospect of adding the whole of the kingdom of Granada to their realms, as well as harnessing noble ambitions and energies to the royal agenda, against an external enemy. Thus, they began what turned out to be a long and arduous war against the last outpost of Islamic civilization in Spain. The mountainous terrain of southern Iberia favored the defenders and daunted the attackers, but Castilian forces eventually prevailed. By 1491, the royal armies had conquered a considerable amount of territory, and the monarchs had exploited internal divisions in Granadan politics to force King Boabdil to terms. He signed a treaty with Isabel and Fernando in late

November 1491, allowing them to enter the city of Granada, where he would hand over his kingdom.

Boabdil's final surrender of Granada occurred in January 1492. Isabel and Fernando received the Alhambra Palace on January 1 and 2, and staged a formal entry into the city on the 6th, thus ending more than seven centuries of Islamic rule in the Iberian Peninsula. At first glance, the terms of surrender for Granada's Muslims seem quite generous. They could freely leave for North Africa if they desired. Those who chose to stay were told they could keep their property and religion if they obeyed the laws of Castile, but the promise to tolerate their religion was short-lived. In 1499, citing continuing unrest, the Catholic Monarchs ordered all Muslims in Castile and Aragon, with the major exception of those in Valencia, to convert to Christianity or leave Spain. The converted Muslims, known as Moriscos, remained in Spain for another century in an uneasy relationship with the Old Christian community.

The Spanish inquisition and the expulsion of the Jews

A few months after taking over Granada, Isabel and Fernando decreed that Spain's remaining Jews had to choose between conversion and expulsion. That decree was the final act in a centuries-long drama that isolated Spain's Jewish communities. In 1478, even before the war over her succession ended, Isabel of Castile, together with her husband Fernando of Aragon, established a Spanish inquisition, under royal authority but with papal approval. As the administrative structure for the inquisition took shape, the papacy recognized that it had made a mistake in letting inquisitorial authority pass from its control to the Spanish monarchs, but it was too late to undo the error. The Spanish inquisition began first in Castile, and later in Aragon, with authority to inquire into the faith and morals of Christians in the Spanish kingdoms. It is worth emphasizing that the inquisition had no authority over Jews or Muslims, but only over baptized Christians. Many of the early examinations, however, involved converts or the descendants of converts from Judaism to Christianity. Such converts, called New Christians as well as *conversos*, continued to arouse suspicion on the part of Old Christians in the tense social atmosphere of the late fifteenth century.

The Spanish inquisition began first in Toledo and then in other towns, with a limited number of personnel but with the cooperation of local authorities. Inquisitors would first visit a town and post notices asking people to seek reconciliation if they had violated religious norms. After dealing with those who came forward voluntarily, the inquisitors turned to those whom their neighbors had denounced. Minor transgressors received minor penances and punishments. The more serious offenders included New Christians accused of secretly practicing Judaism or encouraging others to do so. A majority of the cases investigated in the inquisition's early decades dealt with accusations along these lines. Some of the accused had done very little to arouse the suspicion of their neighbors, such as never eating pork or practicing other customs associated with Judaism but often not even recognized as such by recent converts. They were simply following family traditions regarding diet, dress, and other aspects of their daily lives. Others accused had in fact secretly practiced the religion of their ancestors. It was the inquisitors' job to separate the real converts from the false, and the valid accusations from the invalid.

Inquisitorial procedure called for the accused to be held incommunicado as the process unfolded. Notaries attended every phase of an inquisitorial process to provide detailed accounts of what transpired. The ultimate aim was to have the accused recognize his or her transgressions and seek forgiveness and reconciliation. If the inquisitors were satisfied that they were dealing with sincere Christians, guilty only of minor lapses in social customs, they released the accused. The inquisitors also asked accused persons to name their enemies. If the names matched those of the accusers, the inquisitors would frequently dismiss the case. If the list of enemies failed to include the accuser, the pressure on the accused to recognize their transgressions would escalate, and at some point the inquisitors could resort to torture. According to Roman law, torture was intended to elicit a confession but not to permanently cripple an individual. Those who confessed would be "reconciled" to the community of believers, with varying degrees of punishment. Those who refused to confess in the face of persuasive evidence against them could be sentenced to severe punishment, including death, because, as heretics, they jeopardized not only their own salvation, but also that of the whole Christian community.

Inquisitorial campaigns ended with a solemn ceremony, called an *auto de fe* or Act of Faith. Citizens came together in the town's main plaza for the solemn religious rite. A procession would enter the plaza in the presence of the bishop, inquisitors, and local secular magistrates, and assemble at a stage built at one end of the plaza. Those who had been sentenced by the inquisitors would form the main body of the procession. As they entered the plaza, a crier would announce each person's crime and punishment, including fines that helped support the inquisition, and varying periods of public penance. People accused of minor crimes would come first, and the more serious cases came later. Those who had been reconciled would then attend a solemn mass in a nearby church. At the very end of the procession came the convicted heretics, condemned to death and a confiscation of all their property. Following the ceremony, soldiers led them away from the plaza to a place of execution.

Local employees of the town government would carry out the grim sentences, for members of the clergy were not supposed to take the lives of others. This was known euphemistically as "relaxing" the convicted to the secular arm of government for execution, usually by being burned alive. With the executioners standing by, a cleric would ask the convicted person one last time to confess. Those who did so could not escape death, but they would be strangled before being thrown into the flames. Statistically, there were relatively few burnings of people in person, but there were thousands burned in effigy, representing people who had been condemned *in absentia*, because they had fled before being arrested. According to a rigorous study of the voluminous inquisitorial records, as many as 15,000–20,000 people were tried by the inquisition in the first few decades of its existence, of whom about a third were convicted of heresy and executed, either in person or in effigy. In the early stages of the Spanish inquisition, nearly all of those who faced death were convicted of continuing to practice Judaism, or Judaizing, despite their baptism as Christians. As time went on, few Judaizers remained, and the inquisition thereafter spent most of its time and resources dealing with the Old Christian community. For the early period, however, there is no question that suspected Judaizers were the inquisition's principal targets.

Once the inquisition began to function as a check on false conversions, the remaining Jews in Spain came under increasing scrutiny, because Old Christians viewed them as a constant threat to the Christian orthodoxy of the converts. In 1492, responding to the increasing stridency of Old Christians and largely sharing their misgivings about the converts, Queen Isabel and King Fernando gave the remaining Jews in their kingdoms three months to convert or leave. At the time of the expulsion order, scholars generally agree that there were some 250,000 Jews living in scattered communities throughout the Spanish kingdoms. Faced with the choice of conversion or expulsion, about half of them converted, and the other half left. Those who left had the right to take moveable property with them, but they had to sell any real estate they owned, and buyers had no incentive to pay much for it.

In exile, Spanish Jews went to a variety of new homes, including North Africa, Portugal (before that kingdom expelled them as well), Italy, Anatolia, and the Netherlands. Their descendants are the Sephardic Jews of modern times. Many of the exiled communities prospered, and some maintained their distinctive Hispano-Judaic culture over the centuries. In Turkey, the Balkans, and even in California, there are Sephardic communities still using a language – Ladino – that their ancestors spoke in Spain at the time of their expulsion, and maintaining their rich cultural heritage. Small numbers of Jews began returning to Spain in the eighteenth century, though the expulsion order remained on the books until the dictator Francisco Franco revoked it in 1968. Since then, Jewish communities have grown in several places in Spain, most notably Madrid.

Consolidation of royal power under Isabel and Fernando

In moving farther toward religious uniformity than their predecessors, Isabel and Fernando signaled their aim to bring society as a whole under their control. Overall, their internal policies consolidated royal authority by following precedents set by previous monarchs, as well as by introducing new initiatives. At the end of the war of succession in 1479, Isabel and Fernando had achieved a high degree of noble solidarity with the crown of Castile for the first time in nearly two centuries. Keeping all segments of the nobility loyal to the crown was a pressing priority for the monarchs, given their direct experience of the disruptive effects of noble factionalism and challenges to royal authority. One tactic they adopted to avoid a resurgence of those challenges was to harness the military orders by securing Fernando's appointment as grand master of each of them when that office fell vacant. In that way, the crown took control of the Order of Santiago in 1476, Calatrava in 1487, and Alcántara in 1494.

Although historians often consider Isabel and Fernando the architects of a unified Spain, it is more accurate to say that they consolidated royal authority but maintained many of the laws and traditions of their various kingdoms and duchies. Their titles reflect the complexity of the lands they governed. Unquestionably, however, they took steps to make governance more consistent and effective in each of their territories. One important example was Isabel's commissioning of Alfonso Díaz de Montalvo to produce a reconciliation and codification of Castilian laws then in force. He began in 1480 and completed the work in 1484. His compilation was printed the next year. This formed a foundation for the issuance of the Laws of Toro in 1505, which superseded many contradictory ordinances in Castilian law with a set of consistent principles regarding inheritance and other matters.

Another example of their approach was the expansion of the role of royal agents (*corregidores*) in the municipal councils of Castile. From their inception in the fourteenth century, *corregidores* had sat with the municipal councilors in many Castilian cities, monitoring their work, reporting their decisions to the crown, and trying to ensure that the councils followed royal policies. Fernando and Isabel took care to place *corregidores* in every important town in Castile, and gradually extended their competence to act within the municipal councils. In royal government, they also valued the use of councils for discussion and advice on policies for each kingdom. Expanding upon the precedents set by Juan II and Enrique IV, the monarchs appointed many men to these councils who had post-baccalaureate university training in laws – known as *letrados* – as well as appointing nobles. The conciliar system of government was already well developed in Aragon. In Castile, the monarchs inherited a royal council (the Consejo Real), and created three new ones: the Council of the Inquisition in 1483, the Council of Aragon in 1494, and the short-lived Council of the Hermandad (1476–98). Another, the Council of the Indies, may well have been in existence by 1509 to discuss matters relating to the new lands claimed by Castile in the Americas, but it was not formally established until 1522–4.

Isabel's actions as queen of Castile show that she supported her subjects' long-established activities in the Atlantic. Moreover, throughout her reign she made efforts to gain control over the Atlantic ports of Andalusia, especially those in the region of the lower Guadalquivir River valley and around the Bay of Cádiz. In 1483 Isabel and Fernando built a totally new port, Puerto Real, on the part of the Bay of Cádiz controlled by Jerez de la Frontera, a royal city. In June 1492, the queen purchased the port and half the town of Palos de la Frontera. Isabel's interest in the ports of Andalusia illustrated her resolve to strengthen the seafaring vocation of Castile and to link her kingdom with trade to the Canary Islands as well as the ports of the rest of Atlantic Europe. In January 1493, Isabel and Fernando took over Cádiz and its ancient port upon the death of Rodrigo Ponce de León, compensating his family with the town of Casares, near Ronda, and a payment of 10 million maravedís. With the conquest of Granada in 1492, the monarchs had won Almería, Málaga, and the other ports on the Mediterranean side of the Strait of Gibraltar formerly controlled by the Muslim kingdom. By all of these actions, Isabel and Fernando made clear their resolve to support Castile's maritime commerce and to secure the kingdom's coastal defenses under royal control.

Looking toward the Atlantic Ocean, Queen Isabel was keenly interested in her subjects' actions in the

Canary Islands and beyond. Europeans first entered the uncharted portions of the Atlantic in the thirteenth and fourteenth centuries, landing in the Canaries and the Madeiras. Portuguese and Castilian ship captains initially visited the islands for easily obtainable items such as wood and the red dye called "dragon's blood," the resin of the dragon tree. Late medieval European visitors found the islands inhabited by natives related to the Berbers of northwest Africa and living at a Neolithic level of culture. Primarily herders, the natives had developed an agricultural economy only on the island of Gran Canaria. Throughout the islands, they organized politically as separate and often rival bands. When Castilian-sponsored expeditions began to conquer parts of the islands in the early fifteenth century, they made treaties with some of the bands and conquered others. By the end of the fifteenth century, Europeans had developed agriculture in the islands, with sugar cane as the principal crop.

When Isabel became queen, four of the Canary Islands (Lanzarote, Fuerteventura, La Gomera, and Hierro) had been conquered by Castilian-authorized expeditions, and three were yet to be conquered (Tenerife, La Palma, and Gran Canaria). Isabel reasserted prior Castilian claims to the islands, based ultimately on the assertion that they had been part of the Visigothic inheritance, though there is no evidence that the Visigoths had been concerned with the islands, or indeed had even known about them. On a practical level, Isabel reached an agreement by which Castilian noble families recognized her sovereignty over the four islands they controlled; in addition, she bought the rights they claimed over the three unconquered islands. Thus, her actions established solid juridical standing for Castilian royal control over the Canaries.

Through the same period, Portuguese explorers concentrated on the Madeiras and the Azores. There is one major difference between the experience of Castile in the Canaries and that of Portugal in Madeira, the Azores, and elsewhere: the Canaries were inhabited and the Portuguese islands were not. As Castilian expeditions proceeded with the conquest of the Canary Islands, Castilian monarchs, and Isabel in particular, grappled with what it meant to have Canary Islanders as subjects of the Castilian crown and how such subjects should be treated. One crucial part of this vexing question regarded slavery. Slavery has been a constant part of human history. In medieval Europe and in the Islamic world, it continued to be fed both by the enslavement of prisoners of war and by the trade in enslaved people from Central and Eastern Europe and sub-Saharan Africa. The Portuguese began exploring and trading with Atlantic Africa in the fifteenth century, bringing sub-Saharan African slaves to Europe. That trade led to a resurgence of slavery in Portugal and Spain, as did Spain's final conquest of the kingdom of Granada. The numbers of slaves grew in Andalusian cities, especially Seville, and in Valencia and other eastern cities on the Mediterranean coast.

At the end of the war with Portugal in 1479, Isabel had signed a treaty granting undisputed control over the Canary Islands to Castile in return for her prohibiting activities by her subjects along the African coast south of the Canaries without Portuguese permission. That deprived Castilians of what was becoming a lucrative trade in African products and the expanding trade in slaves from south of the Sahara. It also kept Castilians from participating in another desirable goal shared by Southern Europeans for some 200 years: finding a sea route around Africa to Asia.

As Portuguese expeditions probed farther and farther down the African coast in the fifteenth century, it was becoming clear that they would likely reach Africa's southernmost point and find a passage into the Indian Ocean. In fact, Bartolomew Dias did just that in 1486. The attractions of sailing directly to Asia and tapping into its lucrative trade were known in Europe thanks to the accounts of merchants such as Marco Polo in the late thirteenth century, and of Western Christian missionaries who traveled to China during the Mongol period of the twelfth and thirteenth centuries. Isabel and Fernando were also well aware that the 1479 treaty with Portugal barred Castilians from participating in the growing trade with Africa and in whatever trade might develop with Asia. That meant that the crown would also forgo the royal share of profits from those trades. Keen to pursue profitable opportunities overseas without risking another war with Portugal, Isabel's court was receptive to alternative schemes for reaching Asia.

Christopher Columbus's scheme to sail west toward Asia provided an intriguing possibility. Columbus, probably born in Genoa, arrived in Castile in the mid 1480s after a number of years in Portugal, where he had acted as a merchant, married a noblewoman, and gained an extensive understanding of Portuguese high seas ventures and their ultimate Asian goal. He had also learned much about the pattern of Atlantic winds and currents. He gained that knowledge through voyaging widely in the eastern Atlantic, at least as far north as England and possibly Ireland, and as far south as São Jorge da Mina, a Portuguese *factoria* on the African coast. He also learned about Atlantic sailing trajectories from the papers and maps assembled by his wife's late father, who held the captaincy of the island of Porto Santo near Madeira. Because of his own experiences and his wife's connections at the Portuguese court, Columbus was well placed to learn from conversations with mariners in venues as diverse as taverns in port cities and the royal court in Lisbon.

Although he failed to gain royal backing in Portugal, Columbus's Portuguese connections served him well when he moved to Castile, helping him to gain an audience with Isabel and Fernando. The monarchs expressed interest in his proposal, because a westward voyage to Asia would avoid the Portuguese monopoly on the eastward route around Africa. In the event, however, they had fully committed their resources to the war against Granada and could not commit to any new initiatives until that war was over. To avoid having Columbus take his proposal elsewhere, they nonetheless subsidized his expenses in Castile until such time as they could decide whether or not to back a voyage westward.

After the end of the war with Granada in January 1492, Isabel and Fernando were in a position to fund the venture proposed by Columbus. Experts associated with the royal court seem to have urged the monarchs to reject Columbus's scheme to reach Asia by sailing west, because they found his reasoning and geographical knowledge seriously flawed. They were correct. No one knows the full details of his proposal to the Catholic Monarchs. He might have formed his image of the world and his conjectural path to Asia in full before he spoke to the monarchs in the mid 1480s, or he might have modified and refined both elements after his first two voyages across the Atlantic. It would seem, however, that he believed the earth to be about 25 per cent smaller in circumference than it actually is, and that he believed Japan to lie some 1,500 miles off the coast of China. Taken together, Columbus's miscalculations made the westward voyage to Asia look plausible. In any case, whether he was wrong or not, the Spanish monarchs decided to back Columbus's scheme, making a fairly small investment for potentially large returns. Under the terms of their contract with him, contained in the "Capitulations of Santa Fe," Columbus agreed to share the expenses of the voyage and any profits with the crown. In exchange, if successful, he would gain noble status and bear the titles of admiral, governor-general, and viceroy over any lands he might claim for Castile.

Columbus realized that, at the latitude of the Canary Islands, the prevailing winds blew from east to west. Thus, he planned to stop in the Canaries on the outward voyage. Backed by private investors for about seven-eighths of the cost of the voyage, and by the crown for the rest, Columbus fitted out three vessels in Palos de la Frontera, with the help of the local shipmaster Martín Alonso Pinzón, and sailed from Spain on August 2, 1492. His choice of the Canaries was fortuitous, for they are still the preferred starting point for transatlantic sailing from Europe. After refitting and provisioning, he began the ocean crossing on September 9, 1492. By October 12, the small fleet had reached an island in the Bahamas, though Columbus was certain that they had traveled far enough to be near Japan.

After the first landfall, the fleet began to explore more widely. Pinzón took one of the smaller ships, nicknamed *Pinta*, and went off to explore on his own; he did not rejoin Columbus for months. Columbus took the two remaining vessels and explored part of the eastern end of Cuba before going on to the island he dubbed "La Española" (Hispaniola, now divided between Haiti and the Dominican Republic). He failed to find the rich ports and commerce of China, as described by Marco Polo and others, but he was still convinced he was in Asia. After his flagship, the *nao Santa María*, went aground and foundered on Christmas Day of 1492, Columbus built an improvised settlement for part of his crew, while he made plans to return to Spain in the smallest of the three original ships, nicknamed *Niña*. Pinzón rejoined Columbus, and they sailed together back toward Spain. At first, Columbus tried to retrace his outward path directly toward the Canaries, a decision suggesting that he still lacked full knowledge of the ocean's wind patterns. When the ships made no headway on that initial course, Columbus was forced to sail farther and farther to the north before he found strong and stormy winds blowing from west to east that took him first to the Azores and then to Iberia.

Columbus's return to Spain, on March 15, 1493, marked the highpoint of his career. Isabel and Fernando sent for him to report to them in Barcelona, where they confirmed his contract, ratified his titles, and gave him permission for a second voyage. He assembled a large fleet of seventeen vessels, with settlers, animals, tools, and seeds to found a colony. The fleet reached Hispaniola on November 22, 1493, only to discover that the men Columbus had left behind on his first voyage were all dead, killed in disputes with the native inhabitants.

From then on, Columbus's career headed downhill, as his forceful personality and his undoubted skills as an entrepreneur and a mariner failed to prepare him for founding and governing a colony. He chose a poor location on the north coast of Hispaniola for the settlers and left his brother Bartolomé in charge while he explored Cuba. The colonists became ill and their supplies ran low, and they disagreed with the Columbus brothers about how the settlement should be run. Columbus intended to follow Portuguese precedent and have the settlers serve as paid royal employees to gather gold and other presumed riches. They, on the contrary, wanted to follow the pattern familiar from Spain's reconquest of Muslim territory and conquest in the Canaries – the establishment of self-governing municipalities. When Columbus returned to Spain, a bitterly disillusioned stream of colonists had preceded him, spreading stories about his incompetence and high-handed management style.

By 1496, Fernando and Isabel had abandoned hope of short-term profits from Columbus's ventures. Only hard work and time would make the colonies pay. Despite reports about Columbus's failings as an administrator, he persuaded the monarchs to confirm his previous grants and give him permission for a third voyage, with a ship and two caravels to use for exploration, plus three other caravels to carry provisions to Hispaniola. He would transport three hundred men and thirty women as additional colonists, including ten pardoned murderers.

Departing from Spain together in May 1498, the fleet divided at Gomera in the Canaries. Three vessels sailed directly for Hispaniola. Columbus took the other three ships far south to the Cape Verde Islands before heading westward on July 7 and reaching the island of Trinidad on the 31st. He then sailed north and west to the mainland of South America, realizing from the vast flow of water at the mouths of the Orinoco River that he had encountered an enormous land mass, which he speculated might be near the Garden of Eden described in the Bible. After briefly exploring the coast of Venezuela, in the region known as Paria, Columbus sailed on to Hispaniola.

There he found the situation in crisis. Some of the colonists had mutinied, because they wanted greater freedom of action than Columbus's policies allowed. The Indians were increasingly hostile, and neither Bartolomé nor another Columbus brother, Diego, had been able to maintain order. Columbus himself scarcely had better luck. Forewarned by Columbus's own reports and news from others on Hispaniola, Fernando and Isabel sent out Francisco de Bobadilla to investigate, empowering him, if necessary, to take extraordinary measures to restore authority. Quickly sizing up the situation, Bobadilla arrested the three Columbus brothers for their failure to keep order in the colony, seized their money, and sent them home ignominiously in chains in December 1500. The monarchs told Columbus they had never ordered him to be put in chains, but they delayed granting his request for reinstatement to his official posts until September 1501.

Eventually Isabel and Fernando allowed Columbus to keep some of his titles and all of his property, but his titles would thereafter be empty of authority. Never again would the king and queen allow him to serve as viceroy or governor-general, and they also delayed granting him permission for another voyage. Instead, they began to provide their new colonies with a bureaucratic structure outside Columbus's control, appointing Nicolás de Ovando as governor of Hispaniola. Ovando sailed for the Caribbean in February 1502 with thirty ships and a large group of settlers. A month later, Isabel and Fernando finally granted Columbus permission for a new exploratory fleet under his command.

In the aftermath of the early voyages of discovery in the Atlantic, the ports of western Andalusia were well placed to take advantage of new trading opportunities, and, with surprising speed, Spain began to create a functioning colonial empire. To protect royal interests and extend some vestige of law and order in their overseas colonies, Isabel and Fernando sent a stream of royal governors and bureaucrats across the ocean. In 1503 they established the Casa de Contratación (House of Trade) in Seville to supervise emigration, transport, and trade with what Europeans would continue to call the Indies. In setting up a colonial administration, the government drew on centuries of European experience in dealing with lands conquered, settled, and brought under the rule of law. They also followed more recent precedents, set during the reconquest of Spain from the Muslims and the Castilian conquest of the Canary Islands. Aragonese experience in ruling southern Italy, and Portuguese experience in its outposts in Africa, the Azores, and the Madeiras also provided precedents for the colonial government of Castile in the Caribbean.

Without being aware of the centuries of European history that had prepared Spain for ruling and settling new lands, it would be easy to see the American empire as an improvisation, unplanned and almost accidentally created. There is a grain of truth in that observation. Isabel and Fernando had not planned to found a huge land-based empire; they had planned to find and establish ties with the fabled empires of Asia. Nonetheless, when China and its neighbors proved elusive, they moved quickly to organize and exploit the lands Columbus had claimed, with all the tools of bureaucracy and military organization available to them. Not far into the sixteenth century, what had begun as a search for a new trade route to Asia had turned into the Spanish Empire. Nonetheless, the American venture remained a sideshow for Spain well into the sixteenth century, although voyages of exploration continued to claim new territories for the crown of Castile.

To secure recognition for their territorial gains, Isabel and Fernando developed a grand diplomatic strategy of arranging marriages between their children and their most important allies and potential allies in Europe. The ultimate aim of that strategy was to construct a diplomatic wall around France, the traditional enemy of the Crown of Aragon, and now the enemy of the joint monarchy. As a foundation for developing alliances outside Iberia, the monarchs first worked to cement continued good relations with Portugal. In 1490 their daughter Isabel married a Portuguese prince, Afonso, but he soon died in a hunting accident. Princess Isabel, now a widow, married Afonso's uncle, Manoel, in 1497. The next year she died in childbirth, and the couple's son, Miguel, became first in line to inherit Castile and Aragon, as well as Portugal. The infant prince survived only two years, but the Catholic Monarchs continued to value the alliance with Portugal. They would later arrange a marriage between yet another of their daughters, María, and the aging King Manoel. As queen of Portugal, María bore eight children, the eldest of whom inherited the Portuguese throne as João III.

Isabel and Fernando intended their daughter Catalina to cement ties with England, another traditional enemy of France. The princess, known in England as Catherine of Aragon, was sent to marry Arthur, prince of Wales and son of Henry VII, in 1501, when she was fifteen. Whether the young couple consummated their marriage remains controversial, however, and Arthur died within a few months. Catherine remained in England, and in 1509 married Henry, Arthur's brother, who ascended the throne as Henry VIII. Catherine suffered several miscarriages but produced one living daughter, Princess Mary.

The most important area of Spain's matrimonial diplomacy lay in northwestern and Central Europe, where the Holy Roman Emperor Maximilian I Habsburg and his wife Mary of Burgundy controlled territories stretching from the coast of the North Sea to the plains of Hungary. For Juan, the eldest son of Ferdinand and Isabel, and Juana, their eldest daughter, the monarchs arranged marriages in 1497 that would ally the Spanish kingdoms with the Habsburg dynasty. Ideally, Juan's wife, Margaret of Austria, would rule with him in Spain, and Juana would go off to the Germanies with her husband, Philip "the Handsome." Death intervened to change those plans. Prince Juan died scarcely six months after his marriage to the "Imperial Margaret," and their child was stillborn.

The other Habsburg marriage had far better luck, at least in terms of fertility. Princess Juana would have six viable children with Philip, the third of whom was Charles of Ghent, born with the new century in 1500. By the time he was four years old, a string of deaths and the rules of dynastic succession meant that Charles would inherit a stunning collection of realms. His mother Juana of Castile was by then first in line for Castile and Aragon, along with Aragon's connections in the Mediterranean and the possessions overseas that Columbus and others had claimed for Castile. Charles's father, Philip the Handsome, was first in line to inherit all the Habsburg family lands in Central Europe and to be the likely choice as Holy Roman Emperor when his father Maximilian I died. From his mother, the late Mary of Burgundy, Philip was also slated to inherit the Netherlands and the Free County of Burgundy – perhaps the richest area in Northern Europe.

Upon the death of Queen Isabel in 1504, Juana became queen of Castile, and her husband became its king as Felipe I. Fernando of Aragon, who had only held power in Castile through his wife, returned to his Aragonese realms. Juana and her Habsburg consort arrived in Spain in 1506 and were recognized as rulers of Castile, but Philip the Handsome died later in the same year, leaving his widow so distraught that she was incapable of assuming her duties as queen. Indeed, she had shown so many signs of mental instability since her teenage years that Queen Isabel had provided in her will for Fernando to serve as regent for their grandson Charles, should Juana be "unwilling or unable to govern." Castilian officials decided that Juana was incompetent to rule and asked

Fernando to return as regent for his daughter. Forced out of power by temperament and circumstance, Queen Juana lived out the rest of her life in protective custody in the town of Tordesillas in Old Castile.

Back in power as regent, Fernando continued the territorial expansion that he and Queen Isabel had pursued throughout their marriage, including campaigns across the Strait of Gibraltar into North Africa. Castilian forces had conquered the fortress of Melilla in 1497, which remains a Spanish enclave to this day. In 1506, they captured Oran in a famous campaign that included Cardinal Francisco Ximénez de Cisneros, archbishop of Toledo. Both the cardinal and the Catholic Monarchs had long viewed the North African campaigns as an extension of Christian crusading, as well as an extension of Castile's political reach. After the successful campaign for Oran, Castilian forces made further gains in North Africa, establishing garrisons at several strong points.

Fernando's ambitions did not end with Isabel's death and the strategic marriages of their children. In 1505 he was married again, to Germaine de Foix, niece of King Louis XII of France and granddaughter of Queen Eleanor of Navarre and Gaston de Foix. Because of that marriage and a stout defense against a French army, Fernando was able to add the part of Navarre south of the Pyrenees to Castile in 1513. For Aragon, he won back two disputed border provinces, Roussillon and Cerdagne, which the French had taken a half-century before. The Aragonese faction at Fernando's court was intent on ventures in Italy, and the king also gained lands there in a series of wars against the French, both before and after Queen Isabel's death. Key elements in those victories were formidable

Spanish infantry units called *tercios* supported by cavalry and artillery, an important innovation at that time, and the distinguished leadership of Fernando González de Córdoba, known as the "Great Captain."

It seems clear that Fernando had hoped to engender a separate heir to the Crown of Aragon by his second marriage. In other words, he did not view the union of Castile and Aragon as an accomplishment to preserve. Circumstances intervened, however, to allow that union to continue. After the birth of a short-lived prince, Fernando and Germaine had no other children. By the time of Fernando's death in January 1516, the legacy of conscious diplomatic planning and a series of unplanned and untimely deaths combined to make Charles of Ghent heir to both Castile and Aragon, plus their lands outside Spain. Moreover, Charles would also inherit the Burgundian and Habsburg lands ruled by his other grandparents in Northern and Central Europe. Thus, he would control one of the largest collections of European territories ever held by one person, plus the expanding Spanish holdings in the Americas. With Charles of Ghent's accession as Carlos I of Castile and Aragon, Spain entered a new imperial era.

FIGURE 4.1 The Alhambra Palace in Muslim Granada was built between the thirteenth and fifteenth centuries with exquisite tiles, carved plaster, and stone decorations, all brightly colored.

FIGURE 4.2 With the reconquest proceeding to the south, frontier castles such as this one at Peñafiel (Castile-León), overlooking the Duero River valley, consolidated Christian control of the north.

FIGURE 4.3 Typical towns in the Christian part of medieval Spain featured timber frames, tile roofs, and wattle-and-daub walls with plaster exteriors. La Alberca near Salamanca (Castile-León) preserves its medieval character, as this view of the stone-colonnaded town square illustrates.

FIGURE 4.4 The city of Burgos was the major political, commercial, and religious center in Castile-León throughout the Middle Ages, serving as a major stop on the pilgrimage road to Santiago de Compostela. Wealth flowed into Burgos from all directions, enabling the city to build the magnificent cathedral of Santa María between the thirteenth and fifteenth centuries.

FIGURE 4.5 The city of Valladolid (Castile-León) rivaled Burgos for supremacy in the late medieval and Renaissance periods, becoming a major center for royal government, religion, and culture for all of northern Spain. The façade of the church of San Pablo (fifteenth-century) is a fine example of the Spanish architectural style known as plateresque.

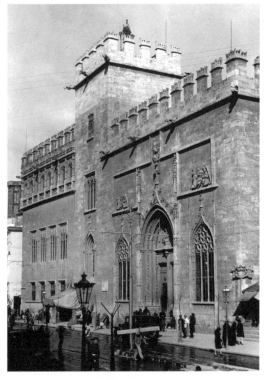

FIGURE 4.6 Built between 1482 and 1498, the Lonja de los Mercaderes (Merchants' Exchange) in Valencia is a unique example of late Gothic commercial architecture, indicating the power and wealth of the merchant community. Modern tourists are either charmed or shocked by its collection of bawdy gargoyles, ostensibly created to show the carnal weakness that good Christian merchants should avoid.

FIGURE 4.7 The palace of Infantado in Guadalajara (Castile-La Mancha) was built in the late fifteenth century by the second duke of Infantado to enhance the glory of his powerful clan. Although the building has undergone many changes in fortune over the centuries, its façade remains one of the best examples of Gothic civic architecture from the period.

5

Spain as the first global empire

~

The administrative structure that the Catholic Monarchs implanted across the Atlantic Ocean laid the basis for the empire that Spain created in the sixteenth century. They improvised that structure from past precedents, responding to the changing situation as Spaniards explored the new lands across the sea. For several centuries Spain also held an empire in Europe, though Spaniards more often referred to the whole collection of diverse territories as a monarchy – lands ruled by a single person. Ironically, Spain's European empire was even more accidental than its American one – the product of bad luck more than conscious planning, as we have seen.

Carlos I was proclaimed king of Spain in Brussels in 1516, ignoring the traditions and prerogatives of the various Spanish kingdoms, and prepared to take up his inheritance. In Spain Cardinal Francisco Ximénez de Cisneros, the driving force behind the reformation of the Spanish church and many aspects of the Spanish Renaissance, performed one last service for the crown by keeping the political situation stable until Carlos arrived in 1517.

Fernando's regency had allowed a generation of explorers to continue tracing the outlines of Castile's New World across the ocean, and Spanish settlers had founded colonies on Hispaniola, Cuba, and various small outposts of the mainland of Central and South America. Whether the embryonic empire would turn out to be profitable remained to be seen. In the meantime, the crown simply gave permission for lands to be explored and settled in its name, but invested little money in the enterprise.

The seventeen-year-old Carlos took great interest in Castile's overseas ventures. Shortly after arriving in Spain, he personally approved a proposal by the Portuguese explorer Ferdinand Magellan to sail westward to Asia to establish a Spanish presence on the far side of the globe. Magellan departed from Spain in 1519 on what would turn out to be the first voyage around the world, but that was not its original aim. Magellan was killed in the Philippines while intervening in a local conflict, and the survivors of the expedition could not find the winds and currents to take them back across the Pacific. Instead, they were forced to return to Spain by sailing around Africa through the half of the world that the Portuguese claimed as their sphere of influence. When the Basque Juan Sebastián del Cano returned with the remnant of Magellan's expedition in 1522, he wrote to the king that "we have discovered and encircled the entire world; going to the west, we have returned from the east."

By the time King Carlos arrived in Spain in 1517, young and untested, two of the three main preoccupations of his long reign were already well established: the ongoing struggle with the Islamic world; and Castile's commitment to global exploration, colonization, and empire-building. The third preoccupation that would mark Carlos's reign – the challenge posed to a unified Christian Europe by the Protestant revolution – had begun in 1517, though it was not immediately clear how serious or extensive it would become.

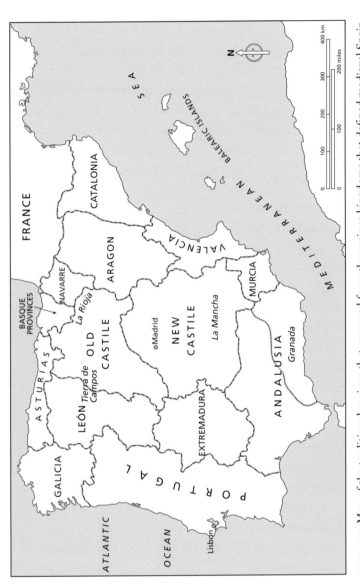

MAP 5.1 Map of the traditional regions that emerged from the various kingdoms that defined medieval Spain. Even when those kingdoms were amalgamated under one crown during the Habsburg and Bourbon periods, the traditional designations continued to hold great importance.

In his first years as king of Spain, Carlos made a series of tactical errors, including appointing members of his entourage in the Netherlands to lucrative Spanish posts in church and state even before he arrived. He also failed to realize the importance of Cardinal Cisneros's role in marshalling support for him in the crucial period after Fernando's death, and neglected even to pay his respects as Cisneros lay dying in a town near Carlos's route through Castile. Raised in the Netherlands, with the concerns of the Holy Roman Empire foremost in his mind, Carlos seemed to view his Spanish kingdoms and their overseas extensions as no more than a cash cow to serve imperial needs. Ironically, the only way that he could secure that aim was to gain the loyalty of his Spanish subjects. It took a hard lesson to bring that point home.

When Emperor Maximilian I died in 1519, Carlos and his advisers launched an all-out effort to have Carlos elected as the new Holy Roman Emperor, out-bribing his major rival Francis I of France by relying on loans from bankers in Central Europe loyal to the Habsburgs, including the Fuggers. Carlos left Spain hurriedly in 1520 after securing the imperial crown, barely stopping long enough to take his oath as king before the Cortes of Castile and its counterpart in Aragon. Having secured pledges of tax revenues from them, he departed, leaving behind kingdoms seething with resentment at his disregard for their dignity and ancient rights.

A serious rebellion soon erupted in Castile, sparked by a consortium of the most important cities and towns in the realm, which demanded in essence that he behave like a proper resident king rather than an absentee landowner. Because it was concentrated in urban areas, the rebellion and its proponents gained the name of the Comuneros. Many prominent local notables, and even members of the nobility, joined with the rebels, fearful that Carlos's imperial ties would rob them of political as well as economic power. It was left to Bishop Adrian of Utrecht, Carlos's old tutor, to coordinate the royal response to the rebellion, which lasted from 1519 to 1521 and involved major sieges and battles. Only when the rebellion began to turn toward a general social revolution did the elite come back to the royal side and suppress their former allies. A separate rebellion in the kingdom of Aragon in 1520–21, known as the Germanías (slang, gangs of ruffians) because of its links with the criminal underworld, had a social revolutionary character from the beginning and was put down swiftly by royal forces in concert with members of the local elite.

When Carlos returned to Spain in 1522, he exacted harsh and exemplary punishment on several of the rebel leaders, but his advisers persuaded him to be lenient with most of the formerly rebellious towns, to remind them of the benefits of loyalty. They learned that lesson well, but Carlos also learned from the experience. Though the Comunero rebels failed on the battlefield, they arguably won most of their demands. For the most part, Carlos conducted the rest of his reign in Spain with respect for local rights and traditions and appointed Spaniards to offices in Spain and the Indies – the designation for Castile's American empire.

Carlos remained in Spain from 1522 to 1529, his longest sojourn in Iberia. He married his first cousin Isabel of Portugal in Seville in 1526 and moved their court periodically around Spain to other important venues.

Their son and heir, Felipe, was born in Valladolid in 1527, their daughters María (1528) and Juana (1535) in Madrid. All of them would play important roles in Habsburg dynastic strategies, just as Carlos and his siblings were doing.

The emperor's sisters sealed alliances with various European states as the wives of reigning monarchs or heirs to the throne: Leonor with Portugal and then France after the death of her first husband; Isabel with Denmark; María with Hungary; and Catalina with Portugal. Carlos's brother Fernando, raised in Spain, was sent to the Germanies once Carlos arrived, married Anne of Hungary, and eventually succeeded Carlos as emperor. The Habsburg women became famous for producing viable heirs, a crucial characteristic for queens and consorts. In a century that saw both the English Tudor dynasty and the French Valois dynasty die out – in the Valois case with help from an assassin's dagger – the Habsburgs continued an unbroken line. That helps to explain why the Spanish and Austrian branches of the Habsburg dynasty regularly intermarried, despite the need for dispensations from religious prohibitions against incest and the dangers of inbreeding. The need for an unbroken succession outweighed most other considerations.

During Carlos's seven-year residence in Spain, he was able to follow the expansion of his empire in the Americas closely. Hernán Cortés, a member of the lower nobility from western Castile, left Cuba for the mainland of Mexico in 1519 and conquered the Aztec Empire in Carlos's name, while defying the direct instructions of the governor of Cuba. Cortés's five letters to the emperor in the aftermath of that conquest justified his actions with partial truths and derogatory remarks about his rivals. There is no question, however, that the conquest was one of the defining moments of the sixteenth century and one of the most dramatic events in the history of world exploration. Cortés traveled to Spain in 1524 with several "Indians" in his entourage. They all spent many months at the emperor's court, dazzling everyone, just as Columbus had done a generation earlier.

Cortés returned to Mexico in the summer of 1530 as the marquis of the Valley of Oaxaca and presided over the vast estates that the emperor had given him. At his own expense, Cortés had fitted out a small fleet and sent it across the Pacific in 1527, led by his cousin Álvaro de Saavedra. In addition to carrying messages and supplies for the ill-fated expedition of García Jofre de Loaísa that had followed Magellan's route to Asia in 1524, Saavedra was supposed to reconnoiter Portuguese strongholds in Asia and verify that they were not in Castile's sphere of influence. The Treaty of Tordesillas in 1494 had defined Portuguese and Spanish areas for exploration in the Ocean Sea (Atlantic Ocean), but where the Tordesillas line cut through the other side of the globe remained a matter of speculation and contention. Through the 1520s, Spanish and Portuguese diplomats continued to advance the claims of their respective monarchs to the Moluccas or Spice Islands. In the meantime, men from successive Spanish expeditions remained in Asia, stranded for lack of a return route to Mexico and serving as placeholders for Spanish claims. Carlos left Spain in 1529, the same year that he relinquished those claims in Asia to the Portuguese for 350,000 ducats. When the news finally reached them, Spanish mariners from three successive westward expeditions to Asia returned home via the Portuguese hemisphere, because they were unable to find a route back across the Pacific. In other words, like Sebastián del Cano and his crew from Magellan's first voyage, they circumnavigated the globe by necessity, arriving back in Spain in 1536.

By then, Emperor Carlos V was fully engaged in the struggle against the Islamic world. He sponsored the relocation of the Knights of St. John to the island of Malta in 1530, seven years after an Ottoman attack had driven them from the island of Rhodes. From their base on Malta, for several centuries the knights served as an international Christian force fighting against Islam – Christian corsairs to counterbalance the Muslim corsairs of North Africa. The Ottoman Empire, under the powerful Sultan Suleiman I ("the Magnificent"), sponsored the North African corsairs at sea and also waged war against the Holy Roman Empire in Central Europe – the heart of Carlos's Habsburg inheritance. In 1526 at the battle of Mohács, the Ottoman army had defeated imperial forces under Carlos's cousin and brother-in-law Louis of Hungary, who was married to Carlos's sister María. Louis died in the conflict, adding a personal dimension to Carlos's quarrel with Islam.

When the thirty-year-old emperor arrived in the Germanies after his official coronation in Rome in 1530, he worked to rally the diverse states and peoples of his empire into a united front against the Ottomans. His imperial Chancellor, Mercurino Gattinara, a brilliant political theoretician from Piedmont of northern Italy, helped Carlos to craft an overall strategy for his polyglot, multicultural empire, which has been summarized and simplified as "peace among Christians and war against the infidel." For the rest of his reign he followed that strategy, facing endless frustration as Christian forces often seemed more interested in fighting one another – and the Habsburg emperor – than in confronting the Ottomans and their client states in North Africa. Catholic France under Francis I posed a more or less continuous challenge to Carlos's vision of Christian unity. Carlos scored a triumph over the French at the battle of Pavia in 1525, capturing Francis himself, whose lavish campaign tent still resides in the Royal Armory in Madrid.

In 1529, Ottoman forces attacked Vienna, the Habsburg capital of the empire, but imperial forces were able to turn them back. When Suleiman launched another assault toward Vienna in 1532, Carlos raised a huge army to defend his empire. Spaniards followed news of the Ottoman threat with great interest, anxiety, and ultimately joy when the Ottomans gave up, buying into the imperial vision more wholeheartedly than many of Carlos's other subjects. Meanwhile, across the Atlantic, bureaucrats sent from Castile consolidated Spanish administration in New Spain (Mexico), and a series of expeditions explored in Carlos's name, from North America to the Andean highlands of South America, in search of other empires to conquer and bring into the Christian fold. Francisco Pizarro and a force of 163 Spaniards and their Indian allies defeated the Inca emperor in 1532–3, adding another huge swath of territory to the area claimed for Castile's American empire.

Carlos resided in Spain from 1533 to 1535, and again from 1536 to 1539, reinforcing the country's imperial identity. During a new war against French challenges in

1535–9, the French king allied with the Ottomans to stem the power of his Habsburg rival and even aided Ottoman attacks in the western Mediterranean, an act that scandalized all of Christendom. Carlos responded to raids by North African Muslim states against Spanish shipping and Iberian coastal areas by attacking La Goleta and Tunis in 1535, a military success commemorated by a famous series of tapestries that can still be seen in the Reales Alcázares of Seville.

He also followed news of the religious and political contention in the Germanies, where several decades of colloquies and negotiations failed to produce a solution to the breach opened by Martin Luther's challenge to the Roman Catholic Church. As Holy Roman Emperor, Carlos was duty-bound to defend Roman Catholicism as the only true version of Christianity, and he never wavered in that duty. Of necessity, Carlos could be in only one place at a time. During his absences from Spain, members of his family acted in his stead: first his wife, the Empress Isabel, and then, after her death in 1539, one after another of their children. In the Netherlands and the Germanies respectively, Carlos's widowed sister María of Hungary and his brother Fernando acted in his name. The many capable members of the Habsburg dynasty, supported by able and loyal bureaucrats everywhere, made it possible for Carlos to maintain a royal presence in the farthest reaches of his European realms.

In New Spain and Peru, a series of extraordinary viceroys brought administrative order out of the chaos of conquest and shaped a well-structured hierarchy of power that relied on the loyalty of soldiers, clerics, nobles, bureaucrats, and ordinary citizens – Spaniards, Indians,

Africans, and those of mixed ancestry – to create stable societies. Some areas in the Americas continued to resist Spanish control, but overall the empire functioned as an evolving fusion of Spanish and New World laws, peoples, institutions, and social structures.

By the 1540s, the situation in the Germanies had descended into open warfare, with coalitions of princes and other local authorities allied against their emperor. More often than not, the battle lines were drawn between Protestant and Catholic, though occasionally the two sides could still come together against their common Ottoman enemy. Carlos was back in Spain in 1541–3, during which time he presided over a crucial debate about the treatment of Indians in Spanish America. Spurred by Friar Bartolomé de las Casas's generalized charges of brutality against Spanish colonists, Carlos instituted the New Laws of the Indies (1542) that were designed to curb the worst abuses, protect the Indians, and tighten royal control of the colonies.

Spanish mining of extraordinarily rich veins of silver at Potosí (in today's Bolivia) after 1545 produced a huge flow of bullion that helped to finance growth in the economies of Europe and around the globe, as well as the emperor's wars. In the Germanies, Carlos continued to pursue his aim of reuniting Christendom, disregarding the entreaties of advisers in Spain who urged him to concentrate on the Ottoman threat in the Mediterranean. His victory at the siege of Mühlberg in 1547, immortalized in a famous equestrian portrait by Titian, caused Carlos to incur huge debts to his German bankers, which even the flow of silver from the Indies could not erase. Forced to accept that he could not reunite the Germanies, Carlos agreed to the

Peace of Augsburg in 1555, which acknowledged that the sovereign power in each of the several hundred polities in the Holy Roman Empire could define its own religious affiliation ("cuius regio, eius religio").

The defeat of his dream for a reunited Christian republic, and the death of his mother Juana the same year, seem to have persuaded the emperor to abandon his worldly titles and honors. He abdicated the imperial crown in 1555, along with the Habsburg lands in the Germanies, in favor of his brother Fernando; the German electors obliged by ratifying his choice, his brother becoming Ferdinand I. In Spain, Carlos had reigned jointly with his mother in legal terms, though she had remained in seclusion since 1508 on the grounds of her mental instability. Her death left Carlos undisputed title to Spain and its overseas empire. In 1556, he abdicated his Spanish and American titles to his son Felipe, along with his titles in the Netherlands, the Free County of Burgundy, and northern Italy. Thereafter, the Spanish and Austrian branches of the Habsburg dynasty would remain separate, though closely linked through affection, intermarriage, and shared international policies.

On his long, slow, painful journey in 1556 from Brussels to the heart of the Spanish monarchy, Carlos – crippled by gout – was accompanied by his sisters María, the widowed queen of Hungary, and Leonor, the widowed queen of Portugal and of France. After decades as the most powerful prince in Christendom, Carlos V of the Holy Roman Empire retired to a modest set of apartments at the monastery of Yuste in the Gredos Mountains northwest of Madrid. There he lived quietly until his death in 1558, keeping in touch with his wide political network throughout Europe, but no longer focused solely on the concerns of the world.

Carlos's son and heir, Felipe II, was not in Spain when he assumed the throne in 1556. Instead, he was in England as the consort of Queen Mary I, the daughter of Henry VIII and his first wife Catherine of Aragon, Carlos's aunt. In other words, Felipe II of Spain and Mary I of England were cousins; his father had urged the marriage upon Felipe, to reinforce the diplomatic alliance between the Spanish kingdoms and England. Felipe was twenty-seven years old and a widower when they married. His bride was forty-three and, like Felipe, a fervent Catholic, though her father Henry VIII had broken with the papacy in 1534 in order to divorce her mother and marry Anne Boleyn. King Henry's marriage with Anne produced Princess Elizabeth, but the king subsequently had Anne executed for infidelity. Subsequent marriages produced a son, who reigned briefly as Edward VI (1547–53), whom Mary succeeded.

England, like Northern Europe as a whole, went through decades of religious instability after the break with Rome, and the marriage of Queen Mary to Felipe of Spain, a committed defender of the Roman Catholic cause in Europe, filled many English Protestant subjects with dread. Contrary to their worst fears, however, Felipe played a circumspect role in England with regard to religion and tried to temper Mary's instincts to mete out exemplary punishment to English Protestants. He also saw to the improvement of English coastal defenses on the Channel facing France and the Netherlands – an accomplishment that would come back to haunt him.

When his father abdicated his official responsibilities and left the Netherlands for Spain in 1556, Felipe traveled across the Channel to assume command of the Habsburg forces that had been fighting France since 1551. Mary remained in England, supposedly pregnant with their first child. In fact, she had a stomach tumor that would take her life in 1558, leaving the English throne to her half-sister Elizabeth. Carlos V died that same year at Yuste. Felipe's sister Juana, the widowed princess of Portugal, had become regent of Spain in 1554, taking up that daunting responsibility at the age of nineteen, just months after her husband, prince João of Portugal, had unexpectedly died, and having given birth to their son Sebastian while in the deepest mourning. When called by her father and brother, Juana left her infant son in Lisbon and traveled to the Spanish court to assume the regency. She would serve in that capacity for five years, overseeing the complex interests of the Spanish Habsburgs in Iberia, elsewhere in Europe, and around the globe. She would also maintain her contacts with the Portuguese court during her son's infancy, planning to return to Lisbon as soon as her brother relieved her of duty at court.

Felipe acquitted himself well as the head of the Habsburg armies in the north and participated in the successful siege of Saint-Quentin in 1557 that put his forces in a position to attack Paris. Instead of pursuing that advantage, however, Felipe made peace with the French monarch Henri II in 1559 and returned to Spain. By then, both France and Spain were on the verge of bankruptcy after decades of warfare, during which time the radical

Protestant movement in France led by Jean Calvin had made enormous gains.

The peace agreement between Spain and France included a marriage contract between Felipe II and the French princess Isabel of Valois. She arrived in Spain in 1560 as Felipe's third wife, and by all accounts his most beloved. Felipe had married his cousin María Manuela of Portugal in 1543, when they were both in their teens, but she had died giving birth to their son Carlos less than two years later. His marriage to Mary Tudor had failed to produce an heir. His third marriage to the young French princess would produce two daughters, Isabel Clara Eugenia and Catalina Micaela. Felipe, after so many years in his father's shadow as a dutiful, hardworking prince, had come into his majority.

Felipe established his capital in Madrid in 1561 and gave the court a permanent home for the first time. Madrid – a relatively small and unimportant town at the time, though it had a royal fortress – was centrally located and had great potential to be developed into a proper setting for a world empire. The older centers of the Castilian monarchy – for example Burgos, Valladolid, Toledo, and Seville – had old and cramped central districts that would not easily lend themselves to restructuring. Each of them, moreover, had a long and proud municipal history and served as the base of power for various aristocratic clans. By choosing Madrid as his capital, Felipe could establish its identity as the royal court and avoid some of the factional strife that might have challenged his authority in more prestigious cities. Secure on his throne at the apex of a global monarchy, Felipe of Spain was the most powerful sovereign in Europe. Not surprisingly, the fashions and amusements of his court would influence styles all over Europe, whether the countries that adopted those styles were friends or foes.

Once the war with France was settled in 1559, the major personal worry of Felipe's middle years was the increasingly erratic behavior of his son and heir, Prince Carlos. Despite having a succession of capable and dedicated tutors and mentors, Don Carlos showed signs of extreme mental instability that did not augur well for his future rule. Nonetheless, Spain remained stable politically in the 1560s, as France descended into the so-called "Wars of Religion," a series of struggles for reasons that were far broader and deeper than religious loyalties alone. The unexpected collapse of the threat from France eased one burden that Felipe had inherited from his father, but it nonetheless made political as well as religious sense for him to support the Catholic factions in the French civil wars.

In Spain itself, the few Protestant enclaves had been driven out of existence by the Spanish inquisition in earlier times. To ensure that heresy did not taint his subjects, Felipe II worked hard to limit possible contamination from Protestants visiting the peninsula; he also greatly restricted the opportunities for Spaniards to study in Protestant lands. Although his uncle, the Emperor Ferdinand I, was forced to accommodate the reality of a mixed religious landscape in the Germanies after the Peace of Augsburg in 1555, Felipe II did not face the need for any such accommodation. Spain remained militantly Roman Catholic, and the king would use Spanish resources to fight for the Catholic cause in the Mediterranean and the rest of Europe. He also continued to bar Protestants, Jews, and Muslims from his American empire, so as to protect the souls of Catholic converts from jeopardy. He would also support Catholic reformers such as Teresa of Ávila, founder of the Discalced Carmelites, and Ignatius of Loyola, founder of the Society of Jesus (a.k.a. Jesuits).

Felipe II famously remarked that he would "prefer not to rule than to rule over heretics." His uncompromising religious stance would help to drive his subjects in the Netherlands into rebellion, as well as drawing Spain into a series of expensive wars and fueling anti-Spanish propaganda. Modern historians rightly point out that the king's religious policies were costly for Spain, but, for Felipe, that was a price worth paying in the fight for religious orthodoxy. He was not alone in that fight, though the combatants differed greatly in how they defined the one true religion. The shattering of Christian unity in sixteenth-century Europe produced a variety of new orthodoxies and claims to religious certainty. The voices arguing for tolerance and multiple truths were in the minority. Among heads of state, those who could enforce adherence to a single version of belief did so and considered that they had defeated a dangerous enemy. Rulers who had to accept a plurality of beliefs in return for political stability eventually made a virtue of necessity. In the long run, state-sanctioned religious plurality would pay dividends, but that was not apparent in the late sixteenth century. Moreover, Felipe's battles were not solely motivated by religion. He had ample political and dynastic reasons to defend the lands he had inherited in Europe and the Americas and to support his Habsburg kin in the Germanies.

Once he assumed the full burden of the Spanish kingship, Felipe turned his immediate attention to the struggle with the Ottoman Empire and its client states in the Mediterranean. The first serious test came in 1565, when corsairs of the aged Sultan Suleiman I launched a huge amphibious operation to force the Knights of St. John from their island stronghold on Malta. Besieged by a force reportedly numbering 38,000 men, the 600 knights and a few thousand armed civilians held out against all odds until reinforcements sent by Felipe from Spanish Sicily broke the siege. In the next several years, virtually every summer saw a major Christian campaign in the Mediterranean against fleets launched by the Ottomans and their clients in North Africa.

Far from the Mediterranean, the year 1565 saw another major advance in Spain's oceanic empire. The Augustinian monk Andrés de Urdaneta finally solved the puzzle of the return route across the Pacific from Asia to New Spain, after several decades studying the problem on land and sea. Once Urdaneta returned from Spain's outpost in the Philippines, named for Felipe II, merchants in New Spain began a regular trading venture between Acapulco and Manila. Known popularly as the "Manila galleon," this trade would directly link the silver from Spanish mines in Mexico and Peru with the huge Asian market, enriching merchants in Spanish America and adding to Felipe's international stature, if not to the royal coffers in Spain. Mining output climbed higher and higher during Felipe's reign, not only providing funds for the continued growth of the American colonies and their trade with Europe and Asia, but also enabling the king to continue his father's struggles against political rivals and in favor of Roman Catholicism in Europe.

In 1568, events in Northern Europe challenged the Mediterranean for Felipe's attention. A long series of confrontations between the local elite in the Netherlands and the Habsburg government, led by Margaret of Parma, Felipe's half-sister, escalated into open rebellion that year, ending hopes for a compromise. To deal with the rebels, Felipe dispatched the duke of Alba, one of his most experienced generals, to the Netherlands with orders to do whatever was necessary to put down the rebellion.

Adding to the political challenges of 1568, the death of Isabel of Valois in October dealt a horrible personal blow to Felipe, especially coming just three months after the death of his heir Don Carlos. The prince was under guard in the Alcázar Palace in Madrid when he died, placed there by his father for plotting, it seems, to join the rebels in the Netherlands and proclaim himself king. Don Carlos in his derangement disclosed his plans to one of his father's most trusted advisers! Despite the summer heat in his rooms in the palace, the prince reportedly indulged in "excesses of food and drink" and slept on bags of ice to cool off. He died in July of a fever, presumably made worse by his behavior. King Felipe wrote anguished letters to the pope and to many heads of state in Europe, accepting that the prince's disabilities and death were God's punishment for the king's own sinfulness, and clearly hoping to persuade them that otherwise he had nothing to do with his son's death. Despite these efforts and the evidence from many witnesses, Don Carlos's death became one of the central elements that Spain's enemies would use to attack Felipe's kingship. Immortalized in a play by

Heinrich Schiller in nineteenth-century Germany, and set to music in Giuseppe Verdi's opera *Don Carlo*, both the hapless prince and his demonized father live on in the collective culture of the Western world.

The horrors of 1568 were balanced in part, a few years later, by one of the most dramatic Christian victories in the long struggle with the Ottomans. Spain, the Republic of Venice, and the papacy put together a huge fleet in 1571 under the overall leadership of Felipe's half-brother Don Juan of Austria. Juan was Carlos V's illegitimate son by a German woman, Barbara Blomberg. Raised in Spain in a humble family loyal to the emperor, and acknowledged by Carlos as his son, Don Juan grew into a bright and capable young man eager to serve the Habsburgs. He was just twenty-four when he led the Christian fleet to a decisive victory over the Turkish admiral Ali Pasha near Lepanto in the Gulf of Corinth in 1571. Hundreds of vessels and tens of thousands of men participated in the battle, which included many distinguished soldiers and sailors on both sides. All of Christian Europe celebrated the great victory at Lepanto, even monarchs who had every reason to fear Habsburg power. Felipe himself commemorated the victory with a portrait showing him with his infant son, born of his fourth wife (and niece) Ann of Austria, whom he married in 1570. Ann was true to her Habsburg genes. After giving birth to several more children, she died in 1580, leaving Felipe a widower for the fourth time, but with the succession assured.

In another of the poignant coincidences that so often marked Felipe's life, in the same year that his fourth wife died he would reach the pinnacle of his power by acquiring the Portuguese throne. Sebastian I of Portugal, child of Felipe's sister Juana, had grown into a troubled young man under the strong and conflicted influence of a coterie of Jesuits and his Spanish grandmother Catalina. In 1578, still a teenager and having refused to consider any and all plans to marry, he went off to North Africa on a Christian crusade and got himself killed. Although Felipe had tried to dissuade his nephew from his foolhardy adventure, when Sebastian died Felipe had one of the strongest dynastic claims to the Portuguese throne and the resources to make his claim succeed. After Spanish troops overcame token resistance from rivals, Felipe entered Portugal and took his oath at the Cortes of Tomar in 1581, promising to rule the country well, to favor Portuguese officials for posts at home and in the Portuguese Empire, and to keep the two Iberian empires bureaucratically and financially distinct.

The king kept his word, though he tried to persuade his Spanish and Portuguese subjects to cooperate with one another in their various outposts around the globe. The English corsair Francis Drake had replicated Magellan's route into the Pacific during his voyage around the world (1577–80), attacking largely defenseless Spanish settlements along the way, though Spain and England were not at war. The unsettled Portuguese situation after King Sebastian's death suggested that Portuguese Brazil was open to takeover as well.

Alarmed that the American empires of Portugal and Spain were no longer protected by distance or by the conventions of international law, King Felipe and his ministers launched efforts to bolster their defenses. One of the earliest of these efforts – an expedition to the south Atlantic in 1581–4 – met with considerable success. The expedition sought to end long-standing French incursions into the brazil-wood areas of northeastern Brazil; to bolster the Spanish presence around the Rio de la Plata; to fortify the Strait of Magellan; and to plant a colony in Patagonia. The expedition as a whole, under the command of Diego Flores de Valdés, ousted the French, at least temporarily, from northeastern Brazil and dealt cordially with Portuguese colonial officials in Brazil grateful for their help. Flores also reinforced Spain's tenuous settlements in southern Patagonia north of the strait. The effort to fortify and colonize the area around the strait itself – an ill-conceived dream of Pedro Sarmiento de Gamboa – failed miserably, but at least demonstrated the Iberian powers' commitment to defending their exclusive claims to the whole of South America. An English fleet under Edward Fenton, aiming to replicate Drake's exploits, instead returned to England, discouraged by the mere presence of Flores's fleet along the Brazilian coast and points south.

At the same time, back in Europe, the French civil wars and the anti-Habsburg rebellion in the Netherlands claimed more and more Spanish resources. These financial strains forced the king to suspend payments to his creditors and renegotiate terms of repayment several times in the course of his reign, despite record levels of treasure coming from Peru. The royal share of that treasure – collected as taxes, assay and minting fees, and other assessments on the colonies and their trade – generally accounted for no more than one-fifth of the total. Nonetheless, together with taxes from Castile, American treasure allowed the king to continue a foreign policy nearly as ambitious as that of his father.

The development of Madrid and its environs as a proper capital for the monarchy required subsidies from the royal coffers. In addition, Felipe built a summer palace in the foothills of the Gredos Mountains just northwest of the capital, to avoid the summer heat in Madrid. More or less completed in 1584, the Escorial Palace housed a pantheon for the burial of the Spanish Habsburgs, a monastery, and an important library of books and manuscripts, many of them in Arabic. By the 1580s, however, there were ominous signs that the Castilian economy had entered a critical period, with population growth outstripping meager natural resources. Then, just as the internal economy of Castile faltered, Felipe's monarchy had to face an array of mounting expenses abroad.

The Ottoman Empire and the rest of the Muslim world continued to form part of Spain's foreign policy concerns after Lepanto, but Felipe's most pressing challenges and expenditures shifted to Northern Europe. Efforts to arrange a marriage between Queen Elizabeth I of England and her former brother-in-law Felipe II had failed, and the international political and religious situation combined to chill relations between the two states. After decades of wary peace between Spain and England following the death of Mary Tudor, war came to seem inevitable to both parties. In the 1560s and 1570s, Queen Elizabeth more or less openly supported anti-Habsburg rebels in the Netherlands and anti-Catholic factions in the French civil wars; she also eagerly shared in the booty that English corsairs captured from Spanish settlements and merchant vessels. King Felipe, for his part, supported Catholics in England and Ireland as much as he dared, and also supported Mary, the Catholic queen of Scotland and a rival claimant to the English throne. Elizabeth had Mary imprisoned. Held captive for nineteen years, she was executed in 1587. That, and repeated attacks on Spanish colonies by English corsairs, persuaded Felipe to move against Elizabeth.

The king planned an invasion of England, drawing together a fleet of 130 ships and nearly 30,000 men, which entailed enormous expense and bureaucratic coordination. It was impossible to keep the preparations for such a huge undertaking secret, and by the time the armada left Lisbon in May 1588, the English were on the alert with a comparable fleet of their own, which had the advantage of defending homeports from which it could be resupplied. The "great armada," as Spanish authorities called it, was unable to embark land forces from the Netherlands – a crucial component of the invasion plan. Battered by storms and harassed by the English fleet, the Spanish armada never attempted an invasion of English soil. Instead, the remnant of the fleet continued to sail northward and then around Scotland and Ireland before returning to Iberia. Overall, the armada lost about half of its ships and three-quarters of its men, most of them to storms and shipwrecks on the return voyage. Although all of the large Spanish-built warships survived, the losses were nonetheless devastating. When the remnant of the armada straggled into port in northwestern Spain, the king famously reacted with great calm and returned to his ever-present paperwork, but the failure of the invasion no doubt represented a serious setback for his international policy and caused a huge expenditure and loss of life – all for nothing.

Felipe rebuilt the country's naval capacity in a few years but did not launch another direct assault on England, although the two countries remained at war for the rest of his reign. He also continued to support Irish unrest against English rule, in the hope that an open rebellion would weaken England's ability to wage war on Spain in Europe and abroad. A force of English privateers, including Francis Drake and John Hawkins, attacked Spanish America in 1595–6 but met insurmountable resistance from local populations and the fortifications that Felipe II had ordered. Both Drake and Hawkins died during that campaign.

In Europe, Elizabeth of England continued to aid anti-Spanish and anti-Catholic forces in France and the Netherlands, and an English raid inflicted considerable damage on the city of Cádiz in 1596. As an adjunct to the English war effort, a vitriolic pamphlet campaign against Felipe II, Spain, and all things Catholic influenced public opinion in England and added to the anti-Spanish rhetoric emanating from other areas in Europe that considered Spain a rival or a threat. This rhetoric later became known as "the Black Legend," and many historians think that it continues to influence public opinion about Spain in the modern world.

Felipe II spent his last years crippled by gout and other ailments, even as he continued to oversee a multinational effort in defense of the Catholic faith and his dual patrimonies in Spain and Portugal. He died in November 1598 at the Escorial Palace, having been too ill to return to Madrid at the end of the summer season. His modest apartments in the palace, situated so that he could view the main altar of the monastery's church from his bedroom, belied his power and that of his monarchy in the late sixteenth century. For much of his adult life he had presided over the first global empire, with responsibilities for the well-being of subjects from Madrid to Mexico to Manila, and from Lisbon to Goa to the Moluccas. Felipe II took those responsibilities quite seriously, once describing kingship as a "form of slavery that bears with it a crown." Felipe II's successor would inherit his vast responsibilities, but without his determination to deal with all of them personally.

Felipe III was born in 1578, the child of his father's fourth marriage. Barely twenty-one years of age when he came to the throne in 1598, he married his Habsburg cousin Margaret of Austria in 1599 to secure the succession. They would have eight children before her death in 1611, five of whom survived to adulthood. Unlike the other Spanish Habsburg monarchs, Felipe III would die at the relatively young age of forty-two, in 1621. Moreover, instead of waging nearly continuous warfare as his precursors had done, his administration negotiated a series of peace agreements that settled ongoing conflicts, at least temporarily. Perhaps for those reasons, historians long neglected Felipe III's reign and wrote the king off as a lazy and feckless placeholder whose only notable aspects were his piety and devotion to his wife. Historians are finally beginning to recognize the importance of the reign for structural changes in the way that government functioned, both internally and internationally.

A peace agreement with France was already in the works when Felipe III inherited the throne. Once the French Bourbon King Henri IV returned to the Catholic fold, Felipe II had no compelling reason to continue fighting him, and Henri was anxious to turn his energies to rebuilding France, after four decades of civil wars, and building support for his rule. The Peace of Vervins in 1598 ended the open warfare between Spain and France, but diplomatically their mutual hostility continued into the new century. The government of Felipe III negotiated the Peace of Dover with the government of James I of England in 1604, a year after the death of Elizabeth I. A new century, and the accession of two young monarchs signaled a fresh beginning in Spanish–English relations. King James admired Spanish power and worked to model his monarchy on the successful example of the Spanish Habsburg kings. Moreover, although he had been raised as a Protestant, he was the son of Mary Queen of Scots from the French Catholic Guise family and was more open toward Catholic Europe than many of his English subjects, among whom "the Black Legend" remained influential.

The only remaining conflict draining Spanish resources after 1604 was the rebellion in the Netherlands, then entering its fourth decade. With unofficial French hostility still posing a threat in Northern Europe, Felipe III's government worked to arrange some sort of deal with rebels in the northern Netherlands, brokered by the king's half-sister Isabel Clara Eugenia and her Austrian Habsburg cousin and husband Albert, the archdukes of the southern Netherlands.

Isabel Clara Eugenia had remained in Spain long after the age when she might have married and left to serve her country's interests elsewhere. Her father Felipe II reportedly could not bear to part with her; he had already lost too many members of his immediate family to death and political needs. When her younger sister Catalina Micaela left to marry the duke of Savoy, Isabel Clara Eugenia remained at the Spanish court. That is why she and her much younger half-brother, the future Felipe III, were able to know one another. Her future husband Albert of Austria spent many years at the Spanish court and he later served Felipe II abroad, testimony to the continuing solidarity of the Habsburg dynasty. When Isabel Clara Eugenia and Albert took up their responsibilities in the Netherlands, they made Brussels into the hub of the dynasty's diplomatic and communications networks. At the same time, they tried to create an independent monarchy in the southern Netherlands, defined by Catholicism and Habsburg rule, even as the northern Netherlands moved closer to independence from the Habsburgs and a state dedicated to the Dutch Reformed version of Calvinism.

The Twelve Years Truce arranged in 1609 between Spain and the northern Netherlands gave both sides a needed respite from decades of warfare but settled nothing. Felipe III would not accept the idea that the rebels in the north, an area dominated politically by Protestantism, could succeed in throwing off Habsburg rule, and, by extension, Catholicism. By the early seventeenth century, two hostile power blocs existed in Europe, partly defined by religion. Spain was the dominant Catholic power, and other countries defined their foreign policies in alliance with, or opposition to, Catholic Spain. Religion was not the only ingredient in Spanish foreign policy, however. Instead, religious, political, and geographical considerations blended in defining the ways in which Spain related to the rest of the world. Above all, the

Habsburgs aimed to keep open lines of transport and communication linking the Iberian Peninsula with the Netherlands, and to maintain exclusive control over the overseas colonies of Spain and Portugal.

Felipe III also maintained close ties with his Habsburg relatives in the Holy Roman Empire and was prepared to assist in their defense against Ottoman incursions or internal threats, if need be. The Dowager Empress María, Felipe III's aunt, had returned to Spain from Austria after the death of her husband and resided in the convent of the Descalzas Reales in Madrid. She and her daughter Margaret, Felipe's queen, served as powerful advocates for the interests of the Austrian Habsburgs at the Spanish court. Ambassadors and other diplomats, allied rulers, and spies provided crucial information to king, court, and councils in Madrid, linked to the Habsburg information network that operated mostly from Brussels, coordinated by the archdukes Albert and Isabel Clara Eugenia.

From the point of view of Spain's rivals and enemies in Europe, whether or not they belonged to the Protestant bloc, Habsburg power always appeared threatening. Catholic France, for example, remained a hostile neighbor of Spain, until the unexpected death of Henri IV in 1610 at the hand of an assassin. Thereafter, French foreign policy became less overtly anti-Spanish, and the new French king Louis XIII would marry Ana of Austria, Felipe III's daughter. English foreign policy aimed to prevent either Spain or France from dominating Europe. Nonetheless, James I maintained cordial relations with Spain, and Felipe III's able ambassador to England, the count of Gondomar, saw to it that his sovereign received regular intelligence reports from London.

Internally, the Spain of Felipe III was the site of the adventures of Don Quixote de La Mancha, the fictional hero created by Miguel Cervantes de Saavedra. When the first part of the novel appeared in 1604, the domestic economy had entered a depression, and the government would later debase the money supply with a large issue of copper coinage. Nonetheless, until 1610, treasure and tax revenues from Spanish America climbed toward record heights. That paradox – a growing depression amid the continued increase in treasure from America – was neatly captured in the writings of an extraordinary group of intellectuals known as the *arbitristas*. So called because they projected remedies (*arbitrios*) for what ailed Spain in the new century, writers such as Martín González de Cellorigo and Sancho de Moncada captured in factual terms the same malaise that Cervantes captured in fiction. The most powerful country in Europe was internally weak and morally adrift; the fabled wealth of the New World passed through the Spanish economy without much effect, as far as they could see. And the Spanish government, a global power under the formidable Felipe II, had become an ineffectual assemblage of bureaucrats, manipulated by the king's favorite, the duke of Lerma.

That gloomy vision of Felipe III's reign went largely unchallenged until recently, but some scholars are now taking another look at the events and personalities at the court in Madrid in the first decades of the seventeenth century. The duke of Lerma, Don Francisco Sandoval y Rojas, once viewed solely as an influence-peddler and charming manipulator, now appears as an effective manager of the ambitious swarm of personalities who always gather around the centers of power. Nonetheless, there is no question that he often acted to further his own financial and social interests. For example, in 1601, he persuaded the king to move the court from Madrid to Valladolid, where he owned substantial property and which was nearer to his estates at Lerma in Old Castile. The price of land, food, lodgings, and a multitude of other items rose as a result, benefiting the duke and other owners of property and businesses in Valladolid. At the same time, the Royal Court of Appeals (Real Chancillería) moved from Valladolid to Burgos, a thriving commercial capital when the wool export trade with Northern Europe flourished, but which rapidly lost wealth and population when that trade declined in the late sixteenth century. In other words, although the court's move to Valladolid benefited the duke of Lerma, it can also be seen as a bold move to revitalize the economy of northern Spain.

At the same time, the early years of Felipe III's reign saw an extensive shift in the way that the central government carried out its business. After an initial period of transition, the king replaced many of the advisers who had served his father and put new men in their place. University graduates trained in law (*letrados*) continued to be the backbone of the government bureaucracy and formed a solid, stable middle group in Spanish society. During the reign of Felipe III, they would play an increasingly important role, not only in advising the king, but in crafting and implementing policy. The Council of State continued as the most important of the royal councils, debating recommendations from the other councils and dealing with matters of importance all over the globe.

The various territorial and thematic councils had subcommittees (juntas) to consider particular issues and as a way to manage the increasingly complex problems of administration. Each junta would meet – sometimes daily – to consider a problem, suggest a course of action, and carry it to the full council, which would deliberate further and then forward its recommendation to the king. Royal secretaries served as liaisons between the various councils and the king. Under Felipe II, the king normally made decisions himself and often sent detailed comments back to a given council for further consideration. Under Felipe III, the king more often accepted a council's recommendation without comment, simply noting that the council should implement the course of action suggested. That alone marked a major change in the way that the Spanish government functioned and serves as evidence of the growing complexity of the issues involved.

Felipe II had worn himself out trying to master every detail of his government. Felipe III showed little inclination even to make the attempt. Rather than faulting the king for laziness or a lack of character, historians are now more inclined to acknowledge that the burdens of the Spanish kingdoms had become too weighty for one individual to bear alone, and to recognize the value of delegating responsibility to competent bureaucrats.

What historians know about the government of Felipe III adds to the ongoing debate about the notion of "absolutism" in Europe. Historians used to think that kings and queens exercised absolute power and authority in strong centralized monarchies such as Spain. They now acknowledge that monarchs were restricted not only by the rule of law and the strictures of religious morality, but also by the practical requirements of governing. Monarchs could not simply issue decrees. They had to have well-articulated bureaucratic structures in place to persuade local officials to implement the decrees, laws, and directives emanating from the central government. Spaniards expected their kings to be just, to obey the laws of God, and to act in the best interests of their subjects, but they retained the right to disagree with their sovereign. When officials could not or would not carry out orders, they traditionally wrote to the crown that they would "obey but not comply," thus fulfilling the letter, but not the spirit, of their duties. In that milieu, the Spanish writer Juan de Mariana (1535–1624) could write a defense of regicide against tyrannical kings and dedicate it to Felipe III.

The government of Felipe III, with the duke of Lerma acting more or less as a chief of staff, if not a Prime Minister, carried out one major operation of considerable complexity: the expulsion of Spain's converted Muslims, or Moriscos. Although the Moriscos were nominally part of the Christian community, Old Christians often viewed them with distrust, particularly in Castile. Their Islamic styles of dress and culture, the linguistic usages that set them apart from Castilian speakers, and tendencies to live apart from Old Christians all made them suspect. In the kingdom of Valencia in eastern Spain, the huge Morisco population had assimilated no better, but powerful landowners protected them as skilled and quiescent agricultural workers.

In response to the government's attempt to force their assimilation, Morisco communities in the mountains south of Granada rebelled in 1568–71, resulting in their defeat and dispersal northward. Although the government of Felipe II had hoped that their dispersion and resettlement would accomplish their complete assimilation into the Christian community, the government of Felipe III realized that the effort had failed. Moreover, the relocation of the Moriscos northward had brought them closer to the center of the monarchy at a time when Spain was especially worried about potential attacks by client states of the Ottomans in North Africa. In fact, some Moriscos were in contact with the leader of Morocco, inviting him to invade Spain. Lobbying by various firebrand clerics against the Moriscos as false Christians added to the list of charges against them.

At precisely the same time as Felipe III's government negotiated the truce with the Dutch rebels in 1609, it decreed the expulsion of the Moriscos. The government implemented the decree from 1609 to 1614, which affected some 175,000 people. Lerma and the bureaucracy arranged for their escort to the coasts, where ships waited to take them to North Africa, though some later went to France or Portugal. Along their trek toward the coasts, their armed escorts arranged for their food and tried to guard against illegal returnees. Though thousands of people reportedly evaded the expulsion order or escaped along the way to the coasts, the expulsion nonetheless proved that Lerma's government could function efficiently in pursuit of a difficult and controversial goal.

Bullion imports from America reached a peak in 1608–10, perhaps encouraging the king and his advisers to think that the returns from overseas would continue to increase. To secure the Spanish coasts and maintain regular contact with the Spanish Empire, the government of Felipe III made plans to expand Spanish shipping, both for military purposes and for trade. The government issued three sets of rules for ship construction – in 1607, 1613, and 1618 – and collected expert testimony about the ideal configurations for ocean-going vessels as they refined the rules. The government sponsored a similar effort in Portugal, designed to produce regulations for ideal ships on the trajectory from Lisbon to the Far East. There was also government-sponsored debate about the naval chain of command and the definition of duties for the principal officers on board. Such debates and initiatives contributed substantially to the improvement and expansion of Spain's presence on the seas, even as revenues from the Indies entered a slump at the end of the reign.

In the cultural sphere, Felipe III and his court were major patrons of theatre, literature, and art. A large number of authors flourished in Spain during the reign, which fits squarely in the period that literary historians call "the Spanish Golden Age." In addition to Cervantes, the prolific writer Lope de Vega flourished in Felipe III's reign, as did Tirso de Molina and a long list of authors associated with the genre called "picaresque novels" – stories about clever rogues who lived by their wits and flouted society's rules. Theatre flourished too, in provincial capitals as well as in Madrid, although the rapid growth of the capital gradually attracted most of the best authors and performers. Felipe III and his court enjoyed theatrical performances and other leisure pursuits, tempered by piety and interspersed with religious observance.

In 1619 – just two years before he died – Felipe III traveled overland to Lisbon to bolster his identity as the king of Portugal as well as Spain. His retinue included some of the most important noblemen from Castile, as well as his son and heir. Once in Portugal, members of the most important noble families there joined his escort and contributed to his lodging and entertainment. Cities and towns along his route also vied with one another to provide an extravagant welcome. For the Portuguese, the royal visit offered a chance to persuade the king to shift the capital of the joint monarchy to Lisbon, and the lavish festivities in their capital made that case explicitly. Despite his pleasure at the warm reception afforded him in Portugal, Felipe III could not consider abandoning Madrid. Castilian taxpayers provided the bulk of royal revenues; he could not risk alienating the most solid tax base of his monarchy, given his vast global responsibilities.

While he was in Lisbon, the king received word that his cousin Matthias, the Habsburg emperor, was under attack by the Calvinist prince of the Palatinate along the River Rhine. King Felipe hurried back to Madrid to monitor the situation, but, when he reached Castile, he was already ill from the malady that would take his life two years later. Meanwhile, in the Germanies, although no one knew it then, the Thirty Years War had already begun. It would haunt the reign of Felipe III's successor and end Spain's tenure as the most powerful state in Europe.

Felipe IV had accompanied his father to Portugal in 1619, in part at least to demonstrate the Habsburg dynasty's commitment to both of the Iberian realms and their empires. When he unexpectedly inherited the two Iberian crowns in 1621, he was only sixteen years old – untried, but supported by one of the most energetic and effective bureaucrats in all of Europe: Gaspar de Guzmán, the count-duke of Olivares, who had been appointed to the prince's staff in 1615. That same year, Felipe was married to the French Princess Isabelle of Bourbon, a diplomatic event ratifying the end of the latest round of hostilities between Spain and France. Because both the bride and the groom were still children at the time, the consummation of the marriage would not take place for several years.

Felipe IV, known – among other nicknames – as "The Poet King," had a passion for the arts. He would preside over the last half of Spain's "Golden Century" (*siglo de oro*) of cultural brilliance, and over the course of his long reign would amass the largest private art collection in Europe. The paintings that he purchased, commissioned, or received as gifts would later form the basis of the famed Prado Museum in Madrid. Diego de Velázquez, Juan Bautista Maíno, Eugenio Caxés, and a host of other Spanish painters he favored would leave an artistic legacy that still inspires admiration nearly four centuries later. In addition, two of the other great painters of the seventeenth century – Peter Paul Rubens and his pupil Anton van Dyck – were natives of the southern part of the Netherlands that remained under Spanish rule. Rubens served as an artistic adviser to the Spanish Habsburgs, as well as carrying out diplomatic missions for Felipe IV.

Olivares supported the king's cultural pursuits as part of his larger aim to restore the monarchy to its former glory. Under his guidance, Madrid acquired the shape and embellishment necessary for the capital of the young king's global monarchy. If the Escorial Palace was the architectural legacy of Felipe II, the core area of Madrid, from the old Alcázar Palace in the west to the new Retiro Palace and gardens in the east, would become the architectural legacy of Felipe IV.

In Velázquez's numerous portraits of Felipe, we can follow his development from fresh-faced youth to jaded exhaustion in middle age. It is not clear whether the exhaustion resulted from the king's political and diplomatic battles or from his sensual excesses, though many historians have tended to emphasize the latter and to blame Olivares for aiding and abetting the king's many romantic adventures. Felipe IV reputedly fathered at least thirty bastard children from uncounted sexual liaisons, in addition to various children from his two marriages. The royal offspring from his marriage to Isabelle of Bourbon included the charming Prince Balthasar Carlos, heir to the throne until his untimely death at the age of seventeen, who appears in many portraits by Velázquez. The children from his second marriage to Mariana of Austria, his Habsburg niece, included Princess Margarita Teresa. This lovely child, the favorite of her father, was the focal point of Velázquez's *Las Meninas* ("The Ladies-in-Waiting") which some have lauded as the finest painting in all of European history. At the age of fifteen, she married her uncle, the Habsburg Emperor Leopold I, and bore six children before dying at the age of twenty-one.

The cultural brilliance of Felipe IV's reign deserves to be remembered, because most often the period is recalled only for its political and economic disasters. In the year that Felipe came to the throne – 1621 – the Twelve Years Truce with rebels in the northern Netherlands expired, and the conflict that became known as the Thirty Years War had already begun in the Germanies, where the king's close Habsburg relatives held the imperial crown. For three decades, war would rage all over Europe, pitting the Habsburgs and their allies against a range of adversaries in Europe and around the globe. Although religion often defined the battle lines, the situation was far more complex than confessional loyalties alone necessitated. Catholic France, under Louis XIII and his great minister Cardinal Richelieu, would go to war against Catholic Spain in 1635, and the Protestant ranks were often divided by the hatreds between Lutherans and Calvinists. Ironically, although few of the battles in the Thirty Years War were fought on Spanish soil, Felipe IV's global monarchy was arguably more involved in and affected by the war than any of his allies or enemies. Spanish resources, both human and material, would be stretched beyond breaking point by the constant need for money and men that the war entailed.

Those disasters were not on the horizon in 1621, however, and Felipe IV and Olivares could view the future with energy and the certainty that they would prevail against their enemies. Olivares gave direction to the monarchy's foreign affairs, and his grandiose aims, while easy to summarize, were very difficult to achieve. Above all, he worked to maintain and enhance the power and reputation of Spain. To achieve that goal, however, Spain had to contain the ambition of France; to make the Habsburg alliance the arbiter of all Christian Europe; and to keep other European powers out of the Spanish Empire overseas. Only with Spanish power restored and enhanced could Spain continue to defend the Catholic faith against its enemies and secure freedom of religion for Catholics in the United Netherlands and the Germanies. Olivares and his king deemed those aims important enough to justify an

extraordinary commitment of money, men, and bureaucratic energy.

As war progressed, Felipe's government would supply
money and troops in support of his Habsburg cousins in
Central Europe. His two brothers, the dim-witted Don
Carlos and the dashing Don Fernando, would both serve
in the imperial armies. Don Fernando, in particular, would
later distinguish himself in many battles, including the
battle of Nördlingen (1634) that cost the life of Sweden's
King Gustavus Adolphus.

Things went well for Spain and its allies until about
1625. That year, dubbed the "Year of Marvels" (*annus
mirabilis*), saw victories for the imperial forces at Breda
in the Netherlands, Genoa in Italy, Bahía in Brazil, and
Puerto Rico in the Caribbean. Spanish forces also held
off an English attack on the port of Cádiz in southwestern
Spain, though England and Spain were not technically at
war. All of the victories appear in a brilliant series of paintings commissioned by the king for his new Retiro Palace,
built at great expense and in record time in 1634–6.
Although the main palace no longer exists, the Retiro
Park in Madrid, together with its fountains and botani-
cal gardens, and several original structures near the Prado
Museum survive from Olivares's grand plan to display
the revived grandeur of the Spanish monarchy. The battle paintings survive as well and have a prominent place
in the newly renovated exhibition spaces of the Prado
Museum.

By the mid 1630s, however, the ongoing conflicts
in Europe and around the globe had placed increasing
strains on Spanish resources, even as the fortunes of war

turned against the Habsburgs. In 1628, the Dutch captured a small Spanish fleet off Matanzas in Cuba, for which the crown would later execute the hapless Spanish commander, Don Alonso de Benavides. The same year as the Matanzas disaster, Spain provoked the War of the Mantuan Succession in Italy (1628–31), gaining little and losing considerable goodwill. Moreover, after the death of Sweden's King Gustavus Adolphus in 1634, fear of a revived Habsburg hegemony led France to enter the war against Spain in 1635, despite the fact that Felipe IV was married to the Bourbon Princess Isabelle, sister of France's Louis XIII. In 1643, French forces defeated the Spanish at Rocroi in the Netherlands, the first time in 150 years that a Spanish army had lost a land battle.

During the 1640s, the Thirty Years War took an increasing toll on all of the participants, most of all Spain. In 1640, both Catalonia and Portugal rebelled against the Spanish Habsburg crown, in large part because of government demands for revenue and troops for the war effort. In both cases as well, members of local elites had decided that those demands outweighed the benefits derived from continued loyalty to Madrid. England descended into civil war in the 1640s, taking it out of active participation in the continental wars. Spain remained neutral regarding England's internal conflict, but Felipe IV took advantage of the English monarch's execution by purchasing many of the late king's collection of paintings. Despite that cultural coup, the 1640s arguably marked the low point of Felipe IV's reign. Distressed by the continued wars and the rebellions against his rule, the king allowed Olivares to resign in 1643. He was convinced that Spain's misfortunes were a direct punishment from God for his own failings, and he determined to take a more active role in governance to atone. For the rest of his tenure, Felipe IV would rule as well as reign over Spain and its empire, taking responsibility for the continued decline in Spanish power.

Louis XIII of France and his minister Richelieu both died in 1643, leaving the child Louis XIV to inherit the throne, under the guidance of his mother, Ana of Austria, sister of Felipe IV of Spain. Nonetheless, the Franco-Spanish war of attrition continued, as one of the threads in the network of conflicts that defined the Thirty Years War. As that war wound down, rebellions in the Netherlands, Catalonia, and Portugal continued in force, with the support of France, and a further rebellion in Spanish Naples in 1647 added to the strains on the Spanish monarchy. In 1648, the Peace of Westphalia finally ended many of the conflicts that comprised the Thirty Years War. Among other tradeoffs, Spain recognized the independence of the northern Netherlands in return for Dutch recognition of Spain's exclusive right to its overseas empire. Because Portugal had rebelled against Spanish Habsburg rule, Portuguese Brazil was not covered by that agreement, and the Dutch retained their hold on northeast Brazil until 1654.

Although Felipe IV and his government could hardly have viewed the regicide of Charles I of England in 1649 with anything but horror, they recognized Oliver Cromwell's republic as the government of England. If they had hoped thereby to deflect English interests in the Americas, however, they were disappointed. As part of Cromwell's "Western Design," England attacked the Spanish Indies in 1654 and joined France in war against

Spain from 1655 to 1659. In the latter year, the Peace of the Pyrenees finally ended Spain's war with France and England. To seal the bargain, Spain's Princess María Teresa was betrothed to the teenaged Louis XIV of France, the Spanish king's nephew, with whom he shared a common ancestor in Felipe II. Despite his Spanish connections, however, Louis XIV came of age in 1660 determined to make France the most powerful country in Europe, supplanting Spain.

Though Spain's foreign affairs spiraled from success to failure during Felipe IV's reign, the situation on the domestic front presented a more mixed picture. In addition to sponsoring the flourishing cultural scene, the king and Olivares hoped to continue the restructuring of government and the reversal of economic decline begun in the previous reign. They initiated various tax reforms and aimed to ensure an equitable sharing of the tax burden among all subjects of the Spanish monarchy. Castile traditionally had borne the heaviest share of that burden, and Olivares's scheme to create a "Union of Arms" (1626) aimed to spread the financial burdens of warfare more broadly. Predictably, the plan met determined resistance in parts of the monarchy whose contribution would rise, notably in Catalonia, Aragon, and Valencia. Similarly, a plan to tap into local resources by levying a salt tax in the Basque regions of northern Castile in 1631 led to open rebellion and a revocation of the tax the following year. The continued and escalating demands of warfare also led to the rebellions in Catalonia and Portugal mentioned above.

Contributing to the political upheavals, the government's attempts at structural reform coincided with a lengthy economic crisis in Spain, though many other parts of Europe also experienced economic distress at the same time. In Castile, the decline in agriculture that began in the late sixteenth century continued through most of the seventeenth. The population, already hit by the epidemics of 1597–1602, with 500,000 victims, and the Morisco expulsion of 1609–14, with estimated departures of 175,000 persons, faced a serious round of epidemics in 1647–52 that reportedly killed another 250,000 Spaniards. Migration to the Indies, on average, drained 4–5,000 people each year from the Spanish economy, and soldiers serving in European wars added a temporary drain of some 12,000 men each year. Overall, the Spanish population probably fell from 8.5 million to 7 million people during the seventeenth century, a large proportion of them during the reign of Felipe IV.

Because of the declining population, the prices for agrarian products slumped, and some landowners lost their lands to foreclosures for debts incurred in better times. In general, land lost value as a profitable investment in grain-producing regions, and flock owners faced lessened competition for grazing land. Some crops held their value – for example grapes, olives, and vegetables – if they grew near urban markets. Overall, however, we can view the first half of the seventeenth century as a period of agrarian distress in the Spanish countryside.

In urban areas, declines in industry and urban vitality followed on the heels of the agrarian crisis. The Segovian woolen cloth industry, one of the great success stories of the sixteenth century, declined precipitously during the seventeenth, along with the cloth industries in other large cities. Small cities and large towns surrounded by productive agricultural lands held up as the larger centers shrank, however. The production and consumption of cloth and other manufactured goods focused on local markets, and the Castilian economy, at least, seems to have turned inward, even as Spain's foreign entanglements drew the country's resources outward.

The great exception to urban decline under Felipe IV was the "town and court" of Madrid, which experienced enormous growth in the first half of the seventeenth century, spurred by its position as the national capital and the hub of Spain's European and global empire. The growth of Madrid coincided with the decline of many smaller cities, as urban workers and members of the social and economic elite moved to the capital. Such patterns of adjustment in the hierarchy of cities were common in early modern Europe, but it was particularly notable in the economic crisis of early seventeenth-century Spain.

Government policies worsened the crisis by aiming to reform royal finances and pay for incessant warfare at the same time. Notably, it proved impossible to spread the tax burden more equitably without alienating members of the elite who led the Spanish army, navy, bureaucracy, and diplomatic corps. The government's efforts to cut pensions and entitlements and redeem government bonds faced the same obstacle. Without the willing support of the elite, financial as well as professional, the Spanish war effort could not have continued. In the event, rather than implementing real tax reform, the government simply heaped additional excise taxes and other fees onto the ungainly array of levies that already existed, lurching from one fiscal crisis to another. The government of Spain was not unique in having financial difficulties in the early seventeenth century, but Spain was arguably more overextended than her allies and rivals, simply because of the larger political arena that she claimed to control.

Paradoxically, the economic disasters of the middle third of the seventeenth century seem to have laid the basis for recovery thereafter, though historians are just beginning to recognize that trend. For example, with the decline in population, farming in Castile retreated to better lands, abandoning some marginal lands that had been put to the plow because of population pressure in earlier generations. Consequently, crop yields seem to have improved, especially in areas that introduced new methods of cultivation and new crops, such as maize and turnips in the north.

In the final years of Felipe IV's reign, after Spain had made peace with its enemies and had settled reluctantly into the role of a secondary power in Europe, there were signs that the population and the economy were on the rise again. The reign of Felipe IV should therefore be seen not as a time of unmitigated disaster for Spain, but as a cautionary tale of overextended power, demonstrating the costs of cultural and political hegemony.

Felipe IV died in 1665, worn out and oppressed by the disasters that had afflicted Spain during his reign. The promise of renewal that had seemed so sure in the 1620s had lost out to the realities of the Thirty Years War abroad and economic crisis and rebellion at home. When the king died, Spain was at peace with her European rivals, and the only conflict left to resolve was the ongoing rebellion in Portugal. Felipe IV had refused to concede defeat in that struggle, though Portugal and its Braganza dynasty had been functioning as an independent nation since the start of the rebellion in 1640. Along with a worn-out Spain, Felipe IV would bequeath to his successor the need to recognize the end of Habsburg rule in Portugal and its empire.

Although no one knew it at the time, the end of Habsburg rule in Spain was not far off either. Felipe IV's successor was the four-year-old Carlos II, the child of Felipe's marriage to his Habsburg niece Mariana. We see her in Velázquez's portraits as a silly teenager in the early years of the marriage, and she did not improve much with age. Rather than entrusting her alone with the regency for their son, Felipe IV's will designated a regency council to guide Prince Carlos to maturity. Despite those legal strictures, Mariana and her chosen advisers exercised considerable influence, some of it arguably not in Spain's best interests. A constant stew of factional strife marked Carlos II's reign from the beginning, as one interest group or another vied for favor and power at court.

Taking advantage of Spanish weakness, Louis XIV of France launched the so-called "War of Devolution" in 1667, invading the southern Netherlands, controlled by Spain, on the pretext of unfulfilled dowry terms for his Spanish wife. John Everard Nithard, the queen mother's Austrian Jesuit confessor, took the lead in setting Spanish foreign policy at that point, much to the irritation of the Spanish nobility. Nithard bought off the French with a string of strategic towns in 1668, and, facing the inevitable, Spain recognized Portuguese independence that same year. Louis XIV precipitated another war in 1672–8, again aiming to gain territory in the Netherlands at Spain's expense. With the Peace of Nijmegen (1678) he succeeded.

Carlos II had officially come of age in 1675, a sickly fourteen-year-old who lived his whole life surrounded by rumors of his imminent demise. As the product of centuries of Habsburg inbreeding, Carlos inherited a range of family traits, including the prominent lower jaw that assumed grotesque proportions when he reached maturity. Unfortunately, he did not inherit the qualities of mind or statesmanship that had served the Habsburgs so well. As time went on, it became clear that he also lacked the ability to father an heir, despite two marriages and extraordinary efforts to do so. Rulers and diplomats all over Europe knew that the Spanish Habsburgs would die out with the unfortunate Carlos II. The only question was whether Spain's rivals and allies should wait for his demise to parcel out the spoils. The growing power and menace of France helped to make up their minds.

As Louis XIV grabbed for lands in the Netherlands and elsewhere, Spain's former adversaries, such as the Dutch and the English, became allies in order to curb French ambitions, which Spain was clearly unable to accomplish alone. Carlos II and his mother chose many of their advisers based on charm rather than ability, including Don Fernando de Valenzuela, a minor nobleman despised by the high nobility at court. With his wife, one of the queen mother's ladies-in-waiting, Valenzuela wielded great influence, until a rival faction forced him from power in 1676. Don Juan José, the king's half-brother, more or less ran the government for a few years thereafter, until his death in September 1679. He had no talent for government, his only asset being his birth to one of

Felipe IV's mistresses; because of that, he could serve as a useful pawn in the strife-ridden court.

With the latest war with France patched up in 1678, the following year Carlos II married the French Princess Marie Louise of Orléans, niece of Louis XIV. The marriage gave the French a greater presence at the Spanish court, though the unfortunate Marie Louise had to bear the blame for the failure to produce a viable heir. Within Spain, spiraling inflation created a crisis that the political factions were incapable of confronting. Almost miraculously, the king appointed a tough and capable minister to deal with the crisis. The eighth duke of Medinaceli, a nobleman of the highest social standing, became First Minister in 1680, instituting a revaluation of the currency that cut prices in half overnight and sent a shock through the whole economy. There is no doubt that the revaluation caused serious short-term distress at all levels of society, but Medinaceli managed to hold on to power until 1685, by which time the economic situation had stabilized. Another round of serious epidemics in 1677–85 made his tenure in office even more difficult, costing the lives of an estimated 250,000 people in Spain as a whole. Nonetheless, like earlier epidemics, the population losses lessened pressure on land use and created more opportunities for those who remained. From the 1680s on, there were unmistakable signs of economic growth all over Spain, especially on the Mediterranean coast of Catalonia and Valencia.

When the duke of Medinaceli's enemies caused his downfall, the count of Oropesa succeeded him as First Minister. Another member of the high nobility, and one of the richest men in Spain, Oropesa held power from 1685 to 1691, presiding over a rigorous program of tax reform and bureaucratic streamlining. Because his reforms undercut the incomes of many members of Spain's social and political elite, Oropesa made many enemies, especially at court. Queen Marie Louise died in 1689 without having produced an heir for the king. In 1690, Carlos II married Maria Ana of Neuberg, a German princess whose violent rages terrified her feeble husband. She and her entourage schemed in favor of German interests in the forthcoming sweepstakes that had Spain and its empire as the grand prize. Even if the royal couple had a child, which looked more doubtful by the month, Spain would hardly be in a position to prevent the dismantling of the empire.

Impatient at Carlos II's refusal to die, Louis XIV launched yet another war of aggression in 1688. Despite his attempts to cultivate English neutrality, this time Louis faced a coalition of European states determined to block his designs. In European history, the war goes by the name of that coalition – the "War of the League of Augsburg." It is sometimes known as the "Nine Years War" because it lasted until 1697, or in British America as "King William's War," referring to William III of the Netherlands who also reigned in England with his wife Mary. As the various names suggest, this confused struggle was global, and it ground on as a war of attrition that resolved nothing.

One of the issues at stake was the fate of Spain and its empire. After the Peace of Ryswick ended the war in 1698, Louis XIV made a secret partition treaty with other European powers to divide the Spanish Empire after Carlos's death, which seemed increasingly imminent. In addition, French, Bavarian, and Habsburg contenders vied for Carlos's favor to occupy the soon-to-be-vacant Spanish throne. The king himself, subject to his queen's rages and the machinations of all the factions, must have felt himself besieged in his own palace. He had few trusted advisers. Oropesa had been driven out in 1691, and the men who succeeded him, though competent, lacked his stature and vision. Nonetheless, even in the midst of war and factional politics, in 1693 the king's advisers devised a "Plan of Government" that proposed a thorough overhaul of the various councils and committees that defined the royal bureaucracy. Although those plans came to little at the time, they laid the groundwork for the reorganization carried out by Carlos's successor.

As the king entered his final agony late in 1700, he made a surprising choice. Persuaded by his confessor that France was the only power capable of preventing the disintegration of the Spanish Empire, Carlos II named as his heir Philip of Anjou, a grandson of Louis XIV. Two centuries of intermittent warfare between Spain and France had also provided opportunities for a succession of marriages between the Spanish Habsburgs and the French Valois and Bourbon dynasties. Because of those marriages, Louis XIV had one of the best dynastic claims to the Spanish throne, despite his decidedly unfriendly attitude toward Spain in the previous four decades. Although he could not claim the throne for himself without provoking another war, Louis could entertain the notion that one of his grandsons could be a placeholder for French interests in Spain and its empire. Once assured that the Spanish people would accept Carlos II's will, Louis gave his blessing to Philip of Anjou becoming Felipe V, the first Bourbon king of Spain.

Even though the terms of the will precluded the merging of France and Spain under the same sovereign, the Bavarian and Habsburg factions at the Spanish court reacted to the news with horror and anguish. England and the Netherlands were equally stunned and fearful of an absolute French hegemony in Europe and abroad. Even before Felipe V could settle into his new role, it was clear that he would have to fight to retain the throne of Spain. The War of the Spanish Succession would define that fight from 1701 to 1714, as most of the other powers in Europe came together in fear of French power. Although Spain was an active combatant in that war, the other powers continued to view France as their main adversary, with Spain and its empire seen more as the prize in the conflict. As the new century began, it was clearer than ever that Spain was no longer in the top ranks of the European powers, even though she still possessed Europe's largest collection of overseas territories.

Throughout the war, Louis XIV demanded full payment for the help he provided to his grandson, and, when things went badly in 1709, he suspended French help altogether, expecting an allied victory in favor of the Habsburg claimant. The situation changed drastically in 1711, however, when the Habsburg claimant to the Spanish throne became the heir apparent to the imperial crown in the Germanies. The prospect of a resurgent Habsburg hegemony cooled the ardor of the anti-Bourbon forces, even though Louis of France had reentered the war in aid of his grandson. The war wound down fairly quickly thereafter.

The treaties that settled the various aspects of the conflict (Utrecht, 1713; Rastadt, 1714) confirmed Felipe V as Spain's first Bourbon king and head of the Spanish Empire overseas. Spain lost its various possessions in Italy, however, a humiliation that the Spanish Bourbons would later work to reverse. It lost control of Gibraltar as well, which the British had captured in 1704 and successfully defended for the rest of the war. The British considered Gibraltar a poor substitute for Cádiz, which successive Anglo-Dutch fleets had failed to capture during the war, but, over time, the Rock of Gibraltar came to serve as a valuable toehold in the Mediterranean for successive British governments and as a constant source of irritation to their Spanish counterparts.

Although Felipe V came to Spain as a foreigner, he would become a Spaniard, just as his distant ancestor Carlos I had done two centuries earlier. By nature, he had a passive and melancholy disposition, though he could steel himself to acts of bravery and intellectual resolve when the situation demanded. Felipe V was the last king of Spain to participate personally in combat, and he distinguished himself in the Aragonese campaign during the War of Succession and earning the admiration and loyalty of his Spanish subjects in the process. He reigned longer than any other king in Spanish history, married twice, and fathered three subsequent kings of Spain. He also founded an offshoot Bourbon dynasty in Italy for another son to rule as king.

Despite these important markers, historians most often discuss Felipe V by proxy, through the individuals who surrounded him, both at court and in the government. He married his first wife María Luisa Gabriela of Savoy in 1701, just as he began his reign, when they were both teenagers. The princess d'Ursins, whom Louis XIV placed in their household as a personal adviser and spy, dominated the royal couple in the early years of their marriage and made sure that French interests remained at the forefront of Spanish policy. The young queen died in 1714, leaving two sons, Luis and Fernando. Even without that personal loss, Felipe V's melancholy nature had already taken a worrisome turn. For the rest of his long life, he would be subject to bouts of deep depression that often left him incapable of governing. Fortunately, Felipe developed a talent for selecting accomplished bureaucrats who could run the day-to-day business of government without close supervision.

Shortly after the queen's death, Felipe V banished the princess d'Ursins from his court and placed his trust in the cleric Giulio Alberoni, who had come to Madrid as ambassador for the duke of Parma. In addition to urging the king to direct his diplomatic efforts toward regaining Spain's lost Italian territories, Alberoni suggested a new marriage to Isabel Farnese, a daughter of the dukes of Parma. Intelligent, attractive, and cultured, Isabel Farnese became Felipe V's second wife and the dominant personality at court for the rest of her husband's reign. Her enemies called her a shrew and resented the power she held over her husband, but there is no question that he was devoted to her. The royal couple had six children together, and, by all reports, an active and passionate sexual life. Recognizing that her two stepsons led the line of succession for the Spanish throne, she worked competently and tirelessly to acquire other kingdoms for her two eldest sons, Carlos and Felipe.

Felipe V is often known as "the king who reigned twice," referring to a peculiar interlude. In 1720, the king wrote a secret document outlining his plan to abdicate the throne in favor of his eldest son, Luis, probably fearing that madness would make it impossible for him to continue his reign. Despite the strenuous objections of Queen Isabel, the king followed through on his plan in 1724, when Luis was just sixteen years old, though already married (unhappily) to a French princess, Luisa Isabel of Monpensier. Although the abdication came as a great surprise to the rest of Europe, the young couple took their places as the new sovereigns of Spain, seemingly destined for a long reign.

Then the unforeseen happened. Luis I died of smallpox just eight months after ascending the throne, plunging the court into crisis as well as mourning. For legal, moral, and ethical reasons, Felipe V argued that he could not rescind his abdication. Queen Isabel was determined that he should do just that and eventually persuaded her husband to take up the crown once again. He reigned until 1746, fighting a continual personal battle against the depression and madness that closed in around him. In this battle, Queen Isabel was his indispensable support and ally, presiding over a lively court culture and an ambitious building program for the Spanish monarchy, both architecturally and politically.

Felipe V's reign saw the start of "Frenchification" (*afrancesamiento*) in Spanish society and culture, including fashions in language, dress, and literary style, and mostly among the elite. This was not merely because Felipe V had been born in France. Just as the Spanish hegemony in earlier centuries had led to an adoption of Spanish cultural styles, so the dominance of France thereafter spawned imitators in the rest of Europe. The Spanish palaces built or remodeled during Felipe V's reign all borrowed from French forms of architecture and decorative norms, and all bore the personal stamp of Queen Isabel. La Granja near Segovia was a small and charming imitation of Versailles in the foothills of the Guadarrama Mountains, and Aranjuez, south of Madrid, provided a cheerful springtime venue for the court in the French style. The most ambitious project was the complete rebuilding of the royal palace in Madrid, after a fire in 1734 destroyed the old fortress palace that had served the crown during the Habsburg centuries. The queen's most personal project was the palace at Riofrío not far from La Granja, a relatively small country house set in a deer park.

Felipe V and his advisers began the Bourbon accession with the declared intention of effecting a profound transformation of the structure and functions of government, in order to augment Spain's power and wealth. Administrative reform provided the key to that transformation, in which the decision-making process would be centralized in Madrid, in the person of the king (when he felt up to the task), and of his ministers. With enhanced centralization, in the French style, the monarch and his ministers could implement laws and royal decrees more easily and uniformly at all levels, which the Habsburg monarchs had rarely achieved. Not surprisingly, local officials and members of the elite, the backbone of the Habsburg style of shared and negotiated authority, resented losing power to the central government. Whereas strong Habsburg kings had often been able to impose their will on recalcitrant members of the elite in one way or another, Bourbon centralization aimed to make that imposition permanent. That marked a change, and one that many Spaniards were loath to accept.

Under the Bourbons, the Council of Castile eclipsed the Council of State, which lost its primary function when Spain lost its European possessions. The Council of Castile eventually encompassed all major ministries for Castile, plus functions of the Council of Aragon after 1707, which the king abolished during the War of Succession. Administratively, the Council of Castile, with 140 minor functionaries, had a broad range of powers, including the appointment of teachers; the approval of university syllabi; the control of printing and archives; and the conduct of foreign affairs. The council also served as the supreme court of justice for cases of treason and insults to the crown. Legislatively, the redefined Council of Castile drew up decrees, convoked the Cortes, and defended crown rights against, for example, the Papal Curia. As a counterweight, however, the council could oppose the king if he tried to use ecclesiastical funds for state purposes. Councilors wore a grand official uniform featuring a black gown and cape, and a full-bottomed wig, and carried a long staff with a round gold top. Their Habsburg counterparts would have been amazed, not just by the uniform but by the enhanced powers that the uniform denoted.

Whether or not an area had supported the Bourbon accession, all Spaniards encountered strong pressure from Madrid for more centralized authority and administrative uniformity. That was the overarching goal of the Bourbon reforms. The first challenge came in Catalonia, which favored the Habsburg pretender during the war. Felipe

V began to establish centralized control in Catalonia as early as 1707, when he abolished the Council of Aragon and ordered the criminal courts to conform to Castilian norms. He allowed civil courts to remain under local control, because they posed no threat to the central government.

In 1714–15, the king issued a series of harsh decrees for Catalonia, which its inhabitants could only view as further punishment for their disloyalty. The Frenchmen Jean Orry and Jean Amelot, both trained by Louis XIV, came to Spain to serve Felipe V. Initially bent on effecting a thorough and rapid transformation of the Spanish state, Felipe and his ministers soon learned that regional privileges, history, and irregular borders demanded a more piecemeal approach, particularly in Catalonia. To blunt the power of regional opposition, Felipe V abolished the historic organ of government known as the Consell de Cent and the legislative Corts, merging them with Castilian institutions. He disbanded the University of Barcelona and moved it to the countryside, no doubt hoping to end its influence in politics. As a further move toward punitive uniformity, the king banned the use of the Catalan language in government, though he still allowed its use for legal and commercial purposes. He followed precedent in appointing Catalans to local offices, but only if they were loyal to Madrid. Similar changes applied on the island of Mallorca in the Mediterranean.

The Basque areas in the far north of the crown of Castile received milder treatment from the king, because they had backed the Bourbons in the war. Nonetheless, the government in Madrid determined to exercise more control in local governments in the northern Basque country. Navarre had also supported the Bourbon cause and benefited from that choice. The king appointed a viceroy for Navarre – essentially a political office – rather than a captain-general, whose powers combined military, administrative, and judicial functions. Felipe V's government favored the office of captain-general for the efficiency it represented, and the men appointed developed sufficient power to be able to thwart later royal attempts to dilute their authority. For example, when the king established the office of intendant in Spain in 1718 to manage local financial affairs, the captains-general succeeded in having the new office abolished.

In judicial affairs, Felipe V allowed only the cities of Valladolid and Granada to keep the courts of Chancillería, which combined the functions of provincial political councils and regional courts of appeal for northern and southern Spain, respectively. Other cities retained their function as regional judicial centers (*audiencias*). These administrative organs all had medieval roots in Castile, as did the *corregidores* – royal representatives on town councils. Because these officials held broad policing and legal powers at the municipal level, the Bourbons retained them for their obvious value in maintaining order and good government.

Legislatively, the Bourbon monarchy of Felipe V had little respect or use for the ancient Cortes of Castile and the Corts of Aragon. The king suppressed the Corts of Valencia and Aragon in 1707 and the Corts of Catalonia in 1714. As part of the Bourbon reorganization of government, he merged them with the Cortes of Castile as a national forum whose only function was to swear loyalty to successive sovereigns. There is little doubt that

such actions fed local resentment of Bourbon rule, especially in the Crown of Aragon. After Felipe V received the
pro forma oath of loyalty from the Cortes in 1725 for his
resumption of the throne, he never called them into session again.

Economically, the Bourbon monarchy intervened in the
economy according to mercantilist policies – as the Habsburgs had done – but much more extensively and more
efficiently. When Felipe V first came to the throne, his
grandfather Louis XIV seemed determined to make Spain
and its empire into economic colonies of France, but that
effort soon foundered, not only because of international
opposition, but also because even the bureaucrats whom
Louis had trained and hand-picked, such as Jean Orry and
Jean Amelot, came to favor Spanish interests over those
of France. After the War of Succession wound down, the
Bourbon monarchy in Spain, rather than private business
interests, took the lead in fostering growth.

The most contentious points in the Bourbon reforms
in Spain involved church–state relations. Because the
Roman Catholic Church had always played a central role
in Spanish politics, society, education, and the economy,
government attempts to exercise control in all of these
spheres inevitably caused a conflict with the ecclesiastical
establishment. Although the government and the church
hierarchy had not always seen eye-to-eye under the Habsburgs, under the Bourbons, for the first time, the role of
the church in Spain became a major issue in the conflict between those who defended traditional norms and
those who favored change. This was not a conflict of values, at least not in the eighteenth century; there was no
anti-Catholicism or atheism in Spain at the time. Instead,

it was a conflict over who should control the finances and administration of the Spanish Catholic Church and the Spanish inquisition. In the centuries to come, controversies surrounding the role of the church would largely define the split between what many call "the two Spains."

The internal debate intersected with the larger issue of papal power versus royal power, which affected every Catholic country in Europe to a greater or lesser extent. The Society of Jesus, often known as the Jesuits, played a key role in supporting papal claims, in Spain and elsewhere. Because of their intellectual accomplishments, close connections to the elite, and dedication to papal interests, the Jesuits were a force to be reckoned with – and often feared – wherever they worked. Those who favored papal authority were often dubbed "ultramontanes," because they looked beyond the mountains (i.e., to Rome) for their inspiration. Catholic monarchs, in Spain and elsewhere, held a variety of powers related to religious affairs in their countries. These generally included the use of certain taxes collected through church authority; the right to register papal decrees and order them disseminated (or not); and a role in selecting bishops. In Spain, the monarchs also included the Spanish inquisition as an organ of state, even though the papacy held the ultimate authority of appeal in individual cases, at least in theory. Each of these powers would come into question from time to time in the eighteenth century, as they had in the past, and would help to define the ongoing role of the church in Spanish society.

As important as these developments were to the new Bourbon monarchy, foreign policy occupied the central place in the aims of Felipe V and his advisers. Because the war over his succession had stripped Spain of many of its European possessions, Felipe's government determined to revise the terms of the Treaty of Utrecht in Spain's favor, especially in Italy. The aims of their revisionism focused on regaining lost territories in Italy, in part to earn prestige abroad and instill new self-confidence at home, and in part to provide realms outside Spain for the sons from Felipe V's marriage to Isabel Farnese. Like any ambitious mother, Queen Isabel wanted to assure the future of her children. Unlike ordinary mothers, however, her ambitions had international repercussions. Spain's aggressive stance throughout the long reign had paradoxical consequences. Whereas the repeated wars strained government finances, caused social instability, and undercut the program of internal economic reforms, they also stimulated economic growth and provided opportunities for capital accumulation.

Historians generally define three phases in the foreign policy of Felipe V's reign after the War of Succession ended. The first two phases occurred under foreign tutelage. From 1714 to 1719, Giulio Alberoni held sway. He had suggested the king's marriage to Isabel Farnese, and prospered under her patronage. Pope Clement XI named him a cardinal in 1717. Alberoni urged the king toward an anti-Austrian policy, to further Spain's Italian aims, but argued overall that Spain should remain independent, especially with regard to France. In the looming struggle for dominance between France and England, a minor power such as Spain had no hope of going it alone. She had to choose sides, but it was not initially clear which side would bring the most benefit for the least cost. Both

England and France had designs on the Spanish Empire. Under Alberoni's tenure, Spain fought a brief war against England but accomplished little.

When Alberoni fell out of favor, a most unlikely character replaced him. John William Ripperdá, baron of Ripperdá, was a Dutch adventurer with questionable ethical standards and no proven talent for public affairs. In the freewheeling atmosphere of the early eighteenth century, however, he charmed his way into the highest court circles and controlled Spanish foreign policy from 1719 to 1726. For most of that time, he supported an alliance with France, but he also engineered an alliance with England in 1721. In the confused period of Felipe V's abdication and Luis I's brief reign, negotiations with France for a royal marriage broke down, and Ripperdá developed a Spanish alliance with Austria instead. With Felipe V back on the throne, Ripperdá finally fell out of favor. True to his mercurial nature, he later converted to Islam and ended his career as an adviser to the Bey of Tunis.

For the remainder of Felipe V's reign, a distinguished succession of Spanish bureaucrats came into their own as directors of Spain's foreign policy, establishing a clear set of goals and a coherent pattern of alliances. José Patiño was first among them in the late 1720s and early 1730s. Born in Spanish Milan and briefly trained as a Jesuit, Patiño learned from the tutelage of Jean Orry and began his rise in the bureaucratic ranks. He eventually occupied the posts of Minister of Marine and Minister of the Indies, plus eight other positions – an astonishing combination of responsibilities. He was the equivalent of a Prime Minister, In fact, 'equal in power to his contemporaries Robert Walpole in England and Cardinal Fleury in France. Focusing on Spain's role in the Mediterranean, Patiño organized the recapture of Oran and Mers-el-Kebir in North Africa, helping to secure Spanish shipping. He also oversaw a rebuilding campaign for the Spanish navy, recognizing that Spanish designs on Italian territories would depend upon sea power.

Patiño died in 1736, having set a high standard for successors such as José Campillo. A poor Asturian orphan, Campillo rose through the bureaucratic ranks to become director of Spain's foreign policy near the end of Felipe V's reign. He favored free trade in Spain's American colonies, reduced customs duties, and supported private trading companies, all in aid of developing both the Spanish economy and the economies of the colonies in the Indies. After Campillo's death in 1743, an aristocrat – Don Ceñón de Somodevilla y Bengoechea, the marquis of La Ensenada – rose to prominence. He would remain in power well into the next reign.

This succession of highly competent ministers pursued a firm alliance with France as the best choice for both Spain and its empire. Two so-called "Bourbon Family Pacts" of alliance with France (1731, 1743) placed Spain firmly in the French camp in the struggle with England during the eighteenth century. Regardless of the Bourbon connection, Spain had little choice but to define England as the enemy, given England's naval strength and the growth of her colonies in the Americas. Confrontations between English and Spanish shipping in the Atlantic led to the so-called "War of Jenkins' Ear" in 1739, sparked by an assault on a British sea captain by Spanish coastguards. The conflict settled little, but both governments deemed it necessary as they jockeyed for position in the Americas.

As hostilities continued, the war merged with the larger War of the Austrian Succession in 1740.

In the Mediterranean, Spain's obsession with Italy finally paid off in the Treaty of Vienna (1735), in which the Spanish Prince Carlos, eldest son of Felipe V and Isabel Farnese, was confirmed as king of the Two Sicilies (Naples and Sicily), thus reversing the terms of the Treaty of Utrecht. Instead of being part of the Spanish Bourbon monarchy, however, the installation of Carlos marked the creation of an Italian Bourbon monarchy, albeit with close ties to Spain. In pursuit of further Italian gains, Spain entered the War of the Austrian Succession (1740–8), although ill-prepared to do so. The war proved expensive and very damaging to the navy that Patiño and his successors had worked so hard to build. Nonetheless, the war allowed Isabel Farnese to secure the duchies of Parma and Piacenza for her second son Felipe, in fulfillment of decades of foreign policy. Felipe V died in 1746, having spent his final years largely incapacitated by mental illness. His reign had begun and ended in warfare, but it had also seen a substantial restructuring of government, the start of economic revival, and a reassertion of Spain's role in European politics.

Fernando VI (1746–59) ascended to the throne at the age of thirty-three, mature and well trained in the business of government. As the second son of Felipe V and his first wife María Luisa Gabriela of Savoy, Fernando was not first in line for the throne, but upon the premature death of his older brother Luis I in 1724, he became the heir, ahead of his half-brothers Carlos and Felipe. Historians often consider Fernando VI as the first "Spanish Bourbon," not only because he was born in Madrid, but also because his government chose not to continue the reliance on France that had characterized the long reign of his father. Open to question is whether that was a useful strategy for Spain at the time.

In contrast with the active and warlike stance of Spain under his father and stepmother, Isabel Farnese, Fernando consciously chose the pursuit of peace as the best way to serve his people. He shared his father's ability to recognize talent among the pool of potential advisers at court; he appointed a series of competent men to the highest posts in his government and let them do their jobs without royal meddling. The king set the tone and direction of his administration, but he felt no need to try to control every aspect of government.

Fernando's wife Barbara of Braganza, the Portuguese ruling dynasty, set the tone for the cultured court life in Madrid and in the other palaces of the realm. Because both the king and queen had a passion for music, orchestral and vocal performances and multimedia spectacles occupied an important place in court entertainments. Domenico Scarlatti, the son of Alessandro Scarlatti, had served as the queen's music tutor in Portugal and came to the Spanish court with his royal patroness. He spent the rest of his life serving the royal couple and writing hundreds of compositions for them. The queen also patronized Father Antonio Soler, a notable Spanish composer who studied with Scarlatti. To organize the elaborate spectacles and outings that defined the life at court, the royal couple hired Carlo Broschi, the famous *castrato* singer better known as Farinelli. As the court traveled from palace to palace on a regular annual round, taking advantage of the seasonal attractions in each venue,

Farinelli made sure that they had sufficient amusements to distract them from the tedium of daily life and political responsibilities.

These distractions were of particular importance for the king, who lived under the same cloud of depression that had haunted his father. Also like his father, Fernando depended heavily on the loving support of his wife. In the arcane language that historians use to describe that dependence, he was uxorious, a characteristic often attributed to the Spanish Bourbon kings as a whole. When it became clear, after years of devoted marriage, that the royal couple would have no heir, both the king and queen felt the lack of children keenly. The lavish entertainments that they sponsored at court can be seen, at least in part, as an attempt to fill the emptiness in their lives.

Court culture included an affinity for the mathematical and scientific interests of the Jesuits as well as the early stirrings of the Spanish Enlightenment, most notably in the writings of the Benedictine monk Benito Feyjóo. Lamenting that Spain had fallen behind its European neighbors in intellectual pursuits, Feyjóo argued tirelessly for a new spirit of inquiry, particularly in the sciences. Although his writings met with strong criticism from traditionalists, Feyjóo enjoyed the steadfast support of the king.

Although Fernando sent his stepmother Isabel Farnese into retirement at the palace of La Granja, he did not entirely abandon her quest to recover territories in Italy lost in 1714. His half-brother Carlos had inherited the duchies of Parma and Piacenza in 1731, when the Farnese line died out. Carlos conquered Naples in 1735. That same year, the Habsburg emperor ceded the kingdom of the Two Sicilies (Sicily and Naples) to Spain, in exchange for Parma and Piacenza. Carlos reigned as king of the Two Sicilies from 1735 to 1759, and Fernando regained the duchies of Parma and Piacenza for his half-brother Felipe by allying with France in the War of the Austrian Succession (1740–8).

Thereafter, Italy ceased to be the major focus of Spanish foreign policy, and the Bourbon "Family pact" with France no longer defined Spain's relations with its European neighbors. The main proponent for this new posture was José de Carvajal y Lancaster, a Spaniard of Anglo-Portuguese origins on his mother's side and one of the king's foremost advisers on foreign affairs from 1746 to 1754. He held the posts of Secretary of State and president of the Junta de Comercio (Trade Committee), as well as serving as the head of the Council of the Indies. After the War of the Austrian Succession ended, Carvajal moved away from the pro-French policy of his precursors. Although England continued to pose the most serious threat to the Spanish Empire, Carvajal followed the Portuguese example by choosing cordiality rather than confrontation with England as the best way to protect Spain's interests abroad.

The king and Carvajal also worked to end friction with Portugal regarding the borders between Spanish territories in South America and Portuguese Brazil. By the Treaty of Limits in 1750, Spain and Portugal agreed to a frontier that many Spaniards branded as too favorable to the Portuguese. In effect, the treaty abandoned considerable territory in Uruguay to Portugal, bordering on the missions that the Society of Jesus had established in Paraguay among the Guaraní people. Despite the crown's support for missionary activities in the American empire, officials in Madrid faulted the Jesuits for managing their missions largely without regard to the crown's interests and supervision. The dramatic story of Portuguese harassment of the Jesuit missions and their eventual dismantling serves as the basis for the 1986 film *The Mission*.

Predictably, the Jesuits were angry about the terms of the treaty, and many members of the Spanish elite agreed with them. Among their supporters, the Jesuits could count the marquis of La Ensenada, who had continued as a key adviser to the crown during the reign of Fernando VI. Like José Patiño before him, Ensenada held responsibility for numerous government ministries, dealing with finance above all, as well as war, the navy, and the Indies. The responsibilities of Ensenada and Carvajal overlapped at several points, and they disagreed about many aspects of Spanish policy, both in Europe and abroad. For example, Ensenada was pro-French, as well as pro-Jesuit, whereas Carvajal remained wary of both of those positions.

Conspiracies at court swirled around Ensenada in the aftermath of the Treaty of Limits, and he encountered royal displeasure for corresponding about its terms with King Carlos of Naples, Fernando VI's half-brother. In 1754, Ensenada's enemies brought about his fall from favor, an outcome that the English ambassador Benjamin Keene claimed as his doing. Even though Ensenada's career ended in disgrace, he accomplished a great deal during his decade in power, including the negotiation of a new agreement with the Vatican: the Concordat of 1753. Settling a series of jurisdictional disputes between the papacy and the Spanish crown, the Concordat clarified and arguably increased the role of the crown in the religious life of Spain.

Perhaps the most important legacy of Ensenada's tenure in office was his focus on the need to strengthen the Spanish economy and rebuild Spanish shipping capacity for both military and mercantile needs. Like his rival Carvajal, he thought the crown should play a major role in building up all the resources of the state, both human and material. With a growing population and a strong economy, Spain could defend its interests in Europe and abroad. The government inquiry called the "Catastro de la Ensenada" set out to survey the landed wealth of the kingdom, preparatory to instituting a single tax ("Única Contribución") based on wealth. That inquiry, carried out by the system of intendants reinstalled in 1749, remains the most important source of information on the Spanish economy in the mid eighteenth century. Much as Ensenada had hoped, the Catastro suggested that both the population and the economy were indeed experiencing impressive growth. Tapping into that growth in the guise of tax reform met resistance, however, from the large landowners who would have paid most of the new tax. Faced with their resistance, the "Única Contribución" never came into effect.

Instead of general tax reform, Ensenada had to settle for piecemeal revisions of existing taxes. He also instituted other reforms that contributed to the goals of a stronger Spanish economy with an enhanced military capability. For example, he set up seed banks (*pósitos*) that helped poor farming families survive through lean times without depleting their seed for the next planting. As for the military, after years of preparatory work, in 1748 his office published a thoroughgoing new set of naval regulations for ship construction, manning, and general administration.

Key to Ensenada's naval reform was the creation of three large naval districts, with headquarters at Ferrol on the north coast, Cartagena on the Mediterranean, and Cádiz on the southern coast west of Gibraltar on the Atlantic. Moreover, Ensenada was able to install a marine registry (*matrícula*), based on economic incentives, which his precursors had planned but had not implemented. With the registry in place, the government could ensure a steady supply of crewmen for the navy, based on a strengthened merchant marine, and without relying on coercion or violence to enlist them. With the support of the king, Ensenada had been able to secure huge resources for the navy, even with the country at peace, and new ship construction up to the early 1750s aimed to make Spain into a formidable naval power once again. Jorge Juan y Santacilia pioneered the new science of hydrography to study how ships moved through water, and Spain's new warships took advantage of the best in modern design and the best materials available.

With both Carvajal and Ensenada out of power after 1754, government reforms lost their momentum in all spheres. Ricardo Wall, a mediocre bureaucrat of Irish ancestry, became the dominant adviser to the king. Although some historians consider him pro-English, he seems to have lacked any clear vision for the direction of Spanish foreign policy. Some of Ensenada's appointees stayed on in the government, presumably with their pro-French and anti-English sentiments intact. In the growing rivalry between France and England, the neutrality that

Wall and the king seemed to favor was not necessarily a bad choice. Even though England still posed the greatest threat to the empire, France had been an unsteady ally. Only through avoiding a renewal of warfare could Spain hope to concentrate on continued economic growth.

When warfare broke out in 1756, Fernando VI refused to participate, even though the stakes clearly included control of overseas territories. Most of Europe would know the conflict as the "Seven Years War," whereas North American historiography would call it the "French and Indian War." Spain would call it the "First Anglo-French Maritime War," denoting both its major antagonists and its global character. In the fluid diplomatic climate of the times, the war featured a "diplomatic revolution," in which France allied with Austria rather than Prussia, and England allied with Prussia rather than Austria. Although England wanted a Spanish alliance as well, Spain probably benefited from her neutrality in the short term, not least because the Spanish monarchy was in serious disarray in the late 1750s.

Queen Barbara of Braganza died in 1758, and her death afflicted the king beyond all reason. He soon sank into the same black depression that had claimed his father at the end of his life. By the time Fernando died in 1759, madness reigned. Both King Fernando and Queen Barbara are buried in the Convent of the Royal Salesians in Madrid, on the street that bears the queen's name near the National Library.

Although his reign lasted only fourteen years, Fernando VI continued the Bourbon reform program, as well as the royal building program begun in his father's reign. That was possible because the king appointed capable men loyal to the interests of the crown and of the Spanish state. Like other European monarchies at the time, Spain had developed an identity apart from that of its monarch, so that government business and the loyalty of the citizenry did not depend as heavily as they had in the past on the person of the king. That was fortunate, given the king's battles against mental illness. Despite those battles, however, Fernando worked hard to be an enlightened king to his people and to keep Spain out of the wars that dominated the mid eighteenth century and drained his neighbors' treasuries. That was a difficult posture to maintain, however, because Spain was a second-rank European power with a first-rank global empire, viewed by its rivals and allies alike as an attractive prize.

Though Fernando VI's reign saw the end of French tutelage, the latest intellectual currents from France and elsewhere circulated among the Spanish elite and characterized Spain's version of the Enlightenment. Spain adopted the enlightened passion for scientific investigation, governmental reform, and social justice that affected much of the rest of Europe. However, Spanish intellectuals rejected the anti-religious and anti-Spanish stance that marked the writings of Voltaire and others. These characteristics of the Spanish Enlightenment would continue into the reign of Fernando's successor, though Spain's foreign policy would change dramatically.

Fernando's half-brother Carlos had spent all of his adult life in Italy, first as duke of Parma and Piacenza (1731–5) and then as king of the Two Sicilies (1735–59). Nonetheless, it had been obvious for some time that he was the most likely successor to the Spanish throne, given that Fernando VI and Barbara of Braganza had no children.

Carlos and his queen, María Amalia of Saxony, whom he married in 1738, left Naples for Madrid with mixed feelings. The kingdom of the Two Sicilies boasted a huge and elegant capital city, a strong economy, and a manageable size. The Spanish capital at Madrid was presumably much less attractive – even though Carlos had been born and raised there – and carried with it the burdens of a global empire.

Groomed to be a ruler by his father Felipe V and his mother Isabel Farnese, Carlos had received an excellent education and knew Spain well because of the wide travels of his parents' court. He remained in close touch with the Spanish court after he moved to Italy, and he presumably did not agree with the neutral foreign policy that Fernando and his advisers pursued. From Carlos's point of view, England was the enemy. Quite apart from England's continued possession of Gibraltar and the island of Menorca, English forces posed the greatest threat to Bourbon interests in the Mediterranean and to Spanish interests in the Americas. When he left Naples to take up the crown of Spain in 1759 as Carlos III, he moved Spain away from neutrality and toward an active foreign policy aimed at thwarting English ambitions.

The world war that began in 1756 had seen Spain on the sidelines, anxious to avoid taking part. In 1761, however, Carlos's government signed a third so-called "Family Pact" of alliance with Bourbon France and entered the fray, in what Spaniards would call the First Maritime War against England. The timing could not have been worse. After more than a decade of relative inactivity, Spanish naval forces were not prepared to confront the English. They failed to regain Gibraltar at home and lost Havana and Manila overseas, two of the key ports of Spain's global empire. However, in the complicated negotiations that ended the war in 1763 with the Treaty of Paris, Spain regained Manila and Havana and gained Louisiana from France, while losing the colony of Sacramento in Uruguay to Portugal and Florida to England. The settlement of the war saw France defeated and left England in effective control of the eastern part of North America, but Spain's American empire remained largely intact. Analysts at the time and thereafter credited that outcome less to Spanish diplomatic efforts than to the bungling of the English Foreign Minister and to general misgivings about England's power. Carlos of Spain certainly shared those misgivings and spent the rest of his reign working to blunt English power, especially in the Americas.

At home in Spain once again, Carlos would continue the personal style and policies that had made him revered in Italy, extending the enlightened reforms of Fernando VI in Spain. Carlos was devoted to his wife and family, and did not remarry after María Amalia's premature death in 1760, just a year after they moved to Spain. Like many other monarchs, he was fond of hunting, both as exercise and to escape the formalities of court life. In his case, hunting also served a therapeutic purpose, helping to relieve the melancholy that ran in the family. The great Spanish artist Francisco Goya y Lucientes painted Carlos in a hunting pose early in his career, and it remains one of his most engaging portraits, with the king smiling shyly and guilelessly at the viewer. Despite the necessary trappings of monarchy, he seems to have been a man of modest and unpretentious demeanor, highly intelligent, pious, and hardworking.

Modern Spaniards continue to rank Carlos III as one of the best rulers that Spain has ever had – a king conscious of his power, but determined to use it to further the well-being of his subjects. Many historians agree with that assessment and consider him the most genuine and effective enlightened ruler in all of eighteenth-century Europe. When he took up the crown of Spain, Carlos announced to the president of the Council of Castile, "I want to apply the law so far as possible to favor the poor," and in many other ways he exemplified the movement of enlightened reform sponsored by a powerful monarchy. At the same time, the king's conservative habits and sincere piety helped to deflect criticism from Spaniards who feared reform as detrimental to their interests.

Among his other virtues, Carlos III was an excellent judge of character. He chose his ministers for their ability rather than their lineage or political connections, though several of his best appointees came from distinguished families. He brought the marquis of La Ensenada, who had already served the first two Spanish Bourbons, back into royal service. He retained Ricardo Wall as Secretary of State (1759–63), even as he shifted Spain's foreign policy away from Wall's pro-English stance. He also fostered the careers of a number of men who distinguished themselves in the various branches of government. An astute diplomat, the count of Aranda (Pedro Pablo Abarca de Bolea) became the architect of Spain's newly active foreign policy. The count of Campomanes (Pedro Rodríguez Campomanes) specialized in economic policy, tackling the difficult issue of agrarian reform. Perhaps the greatest among them, the count of Floridablanca (José Moñino) shaped overall domestic policy during the last half of the reign.

Carlos III and his ministers aimed at a thorough overhaul of Spain's economic structures, in order to foster a growth in production and trade that would support the rising population. All over Europe, the eighteenth century saw an increase in the number of inhabitants, both rural and urban, and every state faced the challenge of feeding them. To fail that challenge could easily lead to social unrest, as public officials well knew. The problem was particularly acute in Spain, where even now only one-third of the land is suitable for farming on a regular basis. The scarcity of arable land was one reason for the great importance of migratory herding in Spain. Since the Middle Ages, flocks of sheep totaling several million animals grazed on land unsuitable for agriculture, and shepherds moved them around seasonally, both to take advantage of optimal conditions for winter and summer forage and to lessen conflicts with farmers during the growing season.

Conflicts nonetheless arose and became particularly acute when population growth necessitated an expansion of cropland. At those times, notably in the sixteenth and eighteenth centuries, the organization of flock owners known as the Mesta faced pressure from farmers and from the government to yield some of their traditional rights to grazing lands. Like other modern bureaucrats, Carlos III's reform-minded ministers viewed agriculture as the basis for a prosperous economy and used government power to expand farming at the expense of herding. They viewed the traditional privileges of the Mesta, as well as the privileges of other corporate bodies, such as artisan guilds, as no more than obsolete impediments to economic growth. Government ministers were not alone in urging reforms and were joined by a wide swath of educated Spaniards well versed in the best new ideas. To encourage elite opinion in favor of the reform program, the government supported universities and philanthropic societies such as the Amigos del País (lit., friends of the country), a movement founded in the Basque country with enthusiastic groups of local reformers all over Spain. Like similar movements throughout enlightened Europe, the Amigos met to discuss the latest books about agriculture, commerce, science, and culture. With royal support, the Amigos also established schools for both boys and girls, with comprehensive curricula that included artisanal skills as well as standard academic subjects. A few of the societies also decided to admit women.

On balance, it is fair to say that the economic reforms had a salutary effect on the population as a whole, but they were not without cost. For example, whereas the government founded hospitals, schools, asylums, and almshouses all over the country, it also clamped down on vagrancy and begging, in effect restricting the movement and activities of thousands of impoverished citizens. In order to increase peasant landownership, the government attacked the Mesta and large landowners, and reforestation plans and irrigation schemes inevitably overruled traditional uses of Spain's natural resources at the local level. In some of the most visible initiatives, the government brought in foreign artisans and businessmen to found factories for the production of luxury goods that were formerly imported. These included factories for fine glass at the palace of La Granja, and for porcelains at the palace of the Buen Retiro in Madrid; cotton velvet in Ávila, leather goods in Seville and Córdoba; and a variety of fine machinery, watches, optical instruments, and other items. Some of these efforts were profitable, others were not, and they went hand in hand with government efforts to restrict the power of traditional artisan guilds.

Not surprisingly, the reform program faced opposition from everyone affected adversely by these initiatives, not only the large flock owners of the Mesta and officials of guilds, but also ordinary people who relied on custom and traditional privileges to earn a living. Also in the economic sphere, the government sponsored savings banks and benefit societies to update traditional forms of savings and insurance. In order to pay for the array of new initiatives and reduce government debt, Carlos and his ministers organized the Bank of San Carlos, which sold bonds that traded at face value.

In the cultural sphere, in addition to traditional activities such as sponsoring art and music, the crown reformed education and added to the university curriculum new scientific developments, such as the physics of Sir Isaac Newton. The king and his ministers also worked to raise the educational level of the clergy and to curb the remaining power of the inquisition, which was increasingly anachronistic by the eighteenth century.

Taken together, the changes in the first years of Carlos III's reign moved forward rapidly on a broad front and aimed to bring about a thorough restructuring of Spanish life. Not surprisingly, the changes generated considerable opposition on a broad front as well. The pace of reform approached a crisis after the government eliminated ceiling prices on grain in July 1765. In the traditional economy, ceiling prices shielded the poor from the rising cost of food in times of harvest shortages. As bad luck would have it, the harvest of 1765 came up short. With price ceilings removed and the population rising, the harvest shortfall led to exponential increases in the cost of food in the ensuing months, affecting poor city dwellers above all. Sermons against artificially inflated prices in Madrid and other cities added to the dangerous mood of the people in the spring of 1766, particularly among the working classes.

Matters came to a head over a seemingly minor incident. In an ill-timed move to discipline the rabble, the king's Minister of the Interior, the Italian marquis of Squillace (Sp. Esquilache), decided to ban the long capes and broad-brimmed hats favored by the street toughs of Madrid. These *majos* had long preoccupied the forces of law and order, who argued that their hats could mask their identities and that their capes could conceal weapons and stolen goods. Following the decree on March 10, 1766, Squillace ordered a table set up in the Puerta del Sol, the heart of Madrid, on Palm Sunday. Officials stationed at the table stopped men in the prohibited costume, cut off their capes, and pinned up their hats in the three-cornered style fashionable among the well-behaved classes. Not surprisingly, this set off a riot in Madrid, and disturbances soon spread to cities and towns throughout Castile. The twentieth-century Spanish composer Manuel de Falla immortalized the incident, known to Spanish history as the "Mutiny of Esquilache," in his ballet *The Three-Cornered Hat*, which neatly captures the complex nature of the uprising.

Another element in the unrest was the crown's religious policy. The king and his ministers were pushing beyond the Concordat of 1753 to assert royal authority, known as regalian rights, over the Roman Catholic Church in Spain, in opposition to the power of the pope. In Spain and elsewhere, the Society of Jesus led the defense of papal authority, which challenged royal authority. Carlos III and other contemporary monarchs viewed the Jesuit opposition as disobedient at best and potentially traitorous at worst. In the aftermath of the "Mutiny of Esquilache," royal officials blamed the Jesuits for inciting the riots, and Carlos III expelled the order from Spain and its empire in 1767. The Spanish action was part of a broader assertion of royal authority all over Europe that induced the pope to abolish the order in 1773. They would not be reinstated until 1814.

In the short term, government forces put down the riots and restored social peace. The king dismissed Squillace in April and appointed the count of Aranda to oversee the broad program of agrarian reform. The defenders of tradition in the countryside had opposed Squillace, and presumably cheered his dismissal. They fared even worse, however, under Aranda, a freemason steeped in the principles of physiocracy, which held that a country's prosperity depended on the well-being of small farmers. Aranda drafted a royal decree of May 2, 1766, that gave the government authority to sell municipally held lands in Extremadura that were not cultivated, in order to make them available to land-hungry farmers. The decree applied to other areas in Castile in the next few years. Although small farmers often lacked the resources to purchase the lands put on the market, and herding interests suffered, there is no question that the decree increased the supply of available farmland and set a precedent for other reversals of traditional patterns of landholding.

After the "Mutiny of Esquilache" the pace of internal reforms slowed in Spain, which some historians have attributed to royal wariness. Carlos III and his ministers had realized that too much change, too fast, could lead to dangerous social instability. Given the continued activism of Spanish foreign policy, internal peace was essential. Hostile diplomatic negotiations with Great Britain (1766–71) over the Falkland Islands (Sp. Malvinas) off the coast of Argentina brought the countries to the brink of war, and Spain did go to war with Portugal in 1776–7, winning back Uruguay. By then England was fighting to retain her colonies in North America in the face of a rebellion that began in 1776. Although Carlos III was pleased to see England in a difficult situation, he was reluctant to support the rebels openly, given the danger of inspiring rebellion in the Spanish colonies. France had less to fear from aiding American rebels, however, and poured considerable resources into that effort. Spain entered the war against England in 1779 as an ally of France, in what Spanish historians call the Second Maritime War (1779–83).

The man in charge of Spanish operations in Louisiana, Bernardo Gálvez, led three regiments of soldiers and militiamen against British forces on the Gulf coast, winning a victory critical to the success of the American rebellion. He also organized the Spanish naval victory at the battle of Pensacola Bay in Florida. Because of these successes, Spain was able to demand the return of Florida and the Mediterranean island of Menorca from the British when the war ended in 1783. King Carlos had also hoped to regain Gibraltar, but Britain would only trade that piece of territory for all of Spain's other gains, a trade that the Spanish government could not accept. Bernardo Gálvez became the count of Gálvez for his efforts in the war, and thereafter served as the Spanish governor of Florida and as viceroy of Mexico. Galveston Bay on the Texas Gulf coast was named after him.

The count of Aranda negotiated the Treaty of Versailles (September 3, 1783) that ended the successful American Revolution and the war that it engendered. Despite Spain's support for the revolution, Aranda had no illusions about the likely future of the former British colonies. As he wrote to Carlos III in 1783, "This Federal Republic was born a pygmy and needed the support of Spain and France to achieve independence. The day will come when it will grow into a giant and forget the benefits received from the two powers and will think only of its own enlargement... Then it will aspire to the conquest of New Spain."

Aranda was not far wrong. Nonetheless, the last years of Carlos III's reign saw the Spanish Empire in the Americas at its apex, with territorial claims running from Tierra del Fuego to the Bering Strait. In the far west of North America, Carlos's government continued to sponsor an active program of expansion and settlement to add substance to those claims. Moving north from New Spain, soldiers, citizens, clerics, and bureaucrats founded a series of fortified *presidios*, towns, and missions in the king's name. Every major city in California, and many cities and towns in Arizona, New Mexico, Colorado, and Texas, owe their origins to those foundations. The history of the United States has traditionally neglected the Spanish legacy of law and settlement across the southern tier of the country, although these so-called "Spanish borderlands" are increasingly finding a place in that history, as new generations of historians revisit and revise old views.

Back in Europe, Spain experienced an upsurge of piracy in the western Mediterranean at the end of Carlos III's reign, sponsored by the leaders of Algiers and Morocco. Although Spanish fishermen, merchants, ship owners, and even coastal farmers had suffered from such piratical attacks for centuries, the activity increased in the late eighteenth century, perhaps related to population pressures in North Africa. The Spanish crown had to spend large sums to combat it, and even sent expeditionary forces against Algiers in 1784 and 1785, to little effect. Nonetheless, by the end of Carlos III's reign, there is no question that Spain stood higher in prestige and economic clout than it had in the late seventeenth century. That is the legacy of the Bourbon reforms and of the active foreign policy pursued by Felipe V and Carlos III.

Like many other great rulers, Carlos III did not have an heir worthy to succeed him. By all accounts, Carlos IV of Spain was mediocre in every respect. Nonetheless, had he lived in calmer times, Spain might not have fared so badly under his rule. As it was, his reign coincided with perhaps the greatest political upheaval in European history – the French Revolution and its aftermath – and when the king abdicated under ignominious circumstances in 1808, Spain was dragged into a chaos of foreign invasion and economic collapse that shattered the country. Carlos IV bears at least part of the blame for that disastrous outcome.

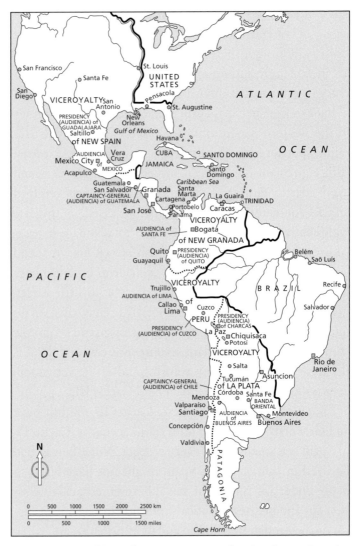

MAP 5.2 Map of Spanish America, *c.* 1790, showing the empire at its
greatest extent.

In domestic policies, the new king continued the reform program of his forebears, particularly with regard to the agrarian economy. Some of his principal advisers, most notably Gaspar Melchor de Jovellanos, were determined to wipe away traditional privileges that hindered the workings of the marketplace. Following upon the work of Campomanes, Jovellanos wrote a strongly worded "Report on the Agrarian Law" in 1795 that anticipated the arguments of nineteenth-century liberalism. To Jovellanos, the ownership of land and other private property was a "natural right," a basis for all other rights and privileges of citizenship. The state should not intervene to restrict that right in support of traditional ways of managing the economy through price ceilings, usage rights to un-owned land, or other restraints. Because of his firm convictions regarding private property, Jovellanos opposed the Mesta, the guilds, and other corporate groups that had in the past enjoyed royal protection from the harsh realities of the market economy.

Manuel Godoy, the most famous – or infamous – of Carlos IV's ministers, shared Jovellanos's views on the need for internal reform and had no compunction about alienating important sectors of Spain's economic and social elite after he came to power late in 1792. Godoy, born without any particular social distinction, rose to dizzying heights of prestige and authority through the patronage of the king and queen and was widely believed to be the queen's lover. That career trajectory did nothing to enhance his credibility as a bureaucrat or to make the internal reforms he promoted palatable to the traditional sectors of Spanish society. In any case, after the French

Revolution erupted in 1789, foreign affairs increasingly overshadowed internal affairs.

In Spain, as elsewhere in Europe, the early years of the revolution presented France's neighbors with a set of difficult choices, ranging from watchful waiting to outright hostility. For the English government, there was no choice: the revolution simply provided one more reason to oppose France. Nonetheless, many private citizens in England reacted with approval to the news of righteous reform at Versailles from May 1789 to May 1791. In Bourbon Spain, long allied with France, the official stance favored neutrality, at least as long as the king's cousin Louis XVI seemed to be sponsoring, or at least acquiescing to, the political and economic changes proposed in France. The count of Floridablanca, in charge of domestic policy since the previous reign, had no illusions about the revolution from the outset. While officially maintaining a neutral stance toward France, he hoped to keep the revolution from contaminating Spain. Until he left office in February 1792, he worked to restrict people, publications, and even news about the revolution from seeping over the Pyrenees and the Spanish coastal defenses. By then the French Legislative Assembly had declared war on some of its neighbors to combat threats to the revolution and to spread its message. Although Louis XVI publicly supported that policy, his fellow monarchs knew that the revolutionary leaders were effectively holding him and his family hostage.

The count of Aranda continued to support neutrality from February to November 1792, when Godoy replaced him, but by then neutrality had become untenable. French revolutionaries had arrested the king and his family as they tried to flee the country, and shortly thereafter declared a republic and tried the king for treason. After the National Convention of the revolutionary republic executed Louis XVI in January 1793, Spain had no choice. Putting aside past differences, Godoy's government joined Great Britain and other allies in a war against revolutionary France. The bloody horrors of the French "Reign of Terror" in 1793–4, dominated by show trials and huge public executions, confirmed the validity of that choice. After the Terror subsided and the more moderate Directory took over, Spain signed the Treaty of Basel that ended the war in July 1795.

From the point of view of traditional Spaniards, the situation remained deeply ambiguous. Despite the peace, France was still a regicide revolutionary republic and the purveyor of a range of ideas repugnant to traditional values, including violent hostility toward religion, private property, hierarchy, monarchy, and – many would argue – human decency. Yet England still posed the greatest objective danger to the Spanish Empire. Because neutrality was not possible, Manuel Godoy would try to steer Spain between these two unappealing allies for more than a decade, earning little more than hatred from all sides.

Making their choice based on the global interests of Spain, Godoy and Carlos IV first chose to collaborate with the French republic. The Treaty of San Ildefonso of July 1796 allied Spain with the French Directory and once again dragged her into a naval war against England for which she was ill prepared. The Spanish naval defeat in 1797 off Cape St. Vincent ended the conflict and helped to drive Godoy from power, at least temporarily. Quite apart from the damage to the navy, the nearly continuous wars on one side or the other took a tremendous toll on Spain's economic resources, both human and material, and not only at home but also in the colonies. With Godoy out of office, the government of Carlos IV pursued a more independent policy from 1798 to 1800, though the alliance with France remained in effect.

Napoleon Bonaparte, one of the three directors of the French republic, seized power in 1799, after a string of military victories in Europe and North Africa. As in 1793, French aggression forced the rest of Europe to take sides. Spain, with Godoy out of power but still influential, continued to stay with France, largely based on a hard-headed and cynical calculation of costs versus benefits. Had Spain bolted from the French alliance, the country would have been vulnerable to invasion by Napoleon's powerful armies, with no likely benefits or protection from Great Britain. Allied with Napoleonic France, Spain might hope for compensation for her support. With Godoy influencing Spanish foreign policy through his relative Pedro Cevallos, Spain ceded Louisiana to France in 1800, on the promise from Napoleon to enlarge Parma for the Bourbons in Italy. The following year, at Napoleon's bidding, Cevallos declared war on Portugal, an ally of Britain, and Godoy took the field as commander-in-chief of the Spanish forces. The so-called "War of the Oranges" lasted only a few weeks before Portugal capitulated, and was most notable for a brilliant portrait by Francisco Goya of Godoy on campaign. The artist portrays his subject in military uniform but hardly in a traditional military pose. Instead, lounging in a camp chair, Godoy displays the fleshy appeal of an indolent royal favorite, rather than the competence of a serious policymaker or commander of troops.

In that same epoch, Goya painted perhaps his greatest canvas – the devastating family portrait of Carlos IV, his queen, their progeny, and assorted relations. Historians often fault Goya for his tendency to drift with the prevailing political winds and to remain as an official court painter to an increasingly discredited court. Yet artists before and since took their commissions where they existed, in order to make a living. The notion of the artist as an independent social commentator, or even as a political rebel, is far too restrictive to contain genius. Goya painted Spain's social elite, to be sure, but he also painted the underclass of Spanish society, like other great artists before him, and imbued them with equal dignity, if he saw fit to do so. In his portrait of Carlos IV and his family, the trappings of majesty cannot hide his contempt for his subjects. Carlos IV, Queen María Luisa, and their eldest son Fernando stare vacantly into space, and most of the other members of the family display a similar lack of character. The king's former majesty has vanished, replaced by a look of confused stupidity. The queen, whom Goya once depicted as pretty and vivacious, appears coarse and vulgar; and the prince's lantern-jawed stolidity suggests a stubborn mediocrity. Only the young Prince Francisco de Paula, holding his mother's hand and gazing pleasantly at the viewer, has an appealing aspect – and he was widely believed to be Godoy's son. The royal family supposedly liked the portrait, which confirms the acuity of Goya's vision.

The war with Portugal ended quickly when England refused to aid Portugal, and the Treaty of Amiens in 1802 settled the conflict between France and England, if only for a year. Godoy was allowed to sign the treaty first for Spain, as France's ally, but otherwise Spain received little or nothing from the French alliance. Nonetheless, to honor Godoy's role at Amiens, Carlos IV gave him the title "Prince of the Peace," a rank that can only have further irritated Godoy's enemies among the Spanish nobility. Relations between France and Spain deteriorated thereafter, not because of increasing hostility, but because of Spain's increasing dependence on Napoleon's growing power. Violating his own earlier promise, Napoleon sold Louisiana to the United States in 1803, and signed a new treaty with Spain as he prepared to isolate England.

Because the French navy lacked the strength to confront England alone, Spanish vessels played an important role in the sea war against England. During his first stint in power, Godoy had revived the naval building program of his precursors, hoping to expand the roster of naval vessels from 200 to more than 300. To crew, supply, and maintain a fleet of that size would have required nearly twice as many men as the 65,000 listed on the marine registry. Although the building program fell short of its goals, the Spanish government nonetheless succeeded in strengthening the program of naval construction. Moreover, between 1800 and 1802, a set of new regulations placed the marine registry and the bureaucrats who ran it under centralized military control, replacing local civilian administrators. The gains in numbers and efficiency prepared Spain to confront the fleets of Britain and her allies after 1803, but they were not enough. In 1805, at the battle of Trafalgar off the Atlantic coast of southwestern Spain, Admiral Nelson's British fleet all but destroyed the

Spanish navy. In that battle, Spain lost not only her fleet and her pretensions to play a larger role in European politics, but also the means of expanding her internal economy through trade and defending her empire overseas.

In an eerie repetition of the situation a century earlier, Spanish hopes of avoiding even greater losses lay in the alliance with France. By the Treaty of Fontainebleau in October 1807, Spain acknowledged a humiliating dependence on Napoleon and his expanding empire and joined the "continental bloc" against England. Prince Fernando, the heir to the throne, publicly disapproved of the new treaty and led a poorly planned uprising to oust his father and Godoy from power. After loyal troops put down the rising, Carlos IV denounced his son. It was an embarrassing incident all around, adding to the discredit of the monarchy. Napoleon had nothing but contempt for the pathetic Spanish Bourbons and had already decided to remove them.

Preparations for another joint invasion of Britain's ally Portugal became the vehicle for their ouster. In late 1807 and early 1808, tens of thousands of French troops entered Spain, and Spaniards soon realized that they, too, were targets of French aggression. Even the feckless royal couple and their favorite Godoy had become preoccupied with the growing French presence in Spain. On March 18, 1808, they prepared to flee the royal palace at Aranjuez for Andalusia, and from there to South America, abandoning Spain to its fate.

Spaniards were not willing to let that happen. The result was the so-called "Mutiny of Aranjuez" on March 19, in which an organized mob from Madrid marched to Aranjuez and forcibly prevented the departure of the royal couple and their favorite. They roared their approval of Prince Fernando and demanded the ouster of Godoy. The king met their demands, dismissing Godoy and abdicating in favor of his son before departing for – of all places – France, to seek Napoleon's protection. The situation became even more confused thereafter. The mob had trapped Godoy, but the French General Murat, who arrested him, saved him from their vengeance. Fernando suspected that Godoy would join with the French to oust him, and he, too, departed for France.

Housed, fed, and cajoled by Napoleon, the Spanish royal family fell into his lap like rotten fruit. On May 6, Fernando abdicated and returned the throne to his father Carlos IV. Two days later, Carlos abdicated in favor of Napoleon. And less than a month later, Napoleon conferred the Spanish throne on his elder brother Joseph, sending him off to Spain with a new constitution in his pocket designed to bring enlightened rule to the Spaniards with the help of French troops. With that cynical and arbitrary transfer of power, the Spanish Bourbons forfeited all moral authority and legitimacy as sovereign rulers of Spain. In disillusion and disgust, many members of the elite willingly transferred their loyalty to Joseph Bonaparte. Most Spaniards, however, remained loyal to King Fernando, whom they considered a captive of Napoleon. For the next four years, Spaniards of all political stripes would fight the French occupation in the name of their absent king. That savage war on Spanish soil would shatter the political and economic structure of Spain's Old Regime, creating in its place a spectrum of competing visions for the future.

FIGURE 5.1 The Roman bridge over the Tormes River in Salamanca (Castile-León) evokes the city's importance in ancient times. The new cathedral in the background illustrates the city's continuing wealth and prestige. It took virtually the whole period covered by Chapter 5 to complete: 1509–1734. Over those centuries, the structure evolved, as a succession of architects, ecclesiastical officials, and builders incorporated changing architectural styles and decorative elements into the design.

FIGURE 5.2 Virtually every Spanish town has a main square (*plaza mayor*), which traditionally served as the center of its civic identity. Some are grand, such as the one in Salamanca (5.2a), others are modest, such as the one in Mérida (Extremadura) (5.2b), but they each contribute to the texture of urban life in Spain. Larger towns and cities have a variety of plazas, each one defining its neighborhood.

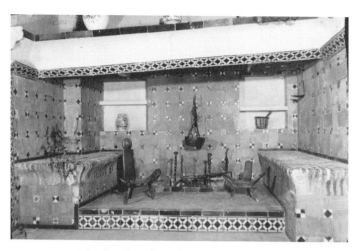

FIGURE 5.3 A kitchen hearth, such as this one in the house–museum of the painter El Greco in Toledo, was a standard feature in the early modern period. Similar hearths can be seen in Cervantes' house in Valladolid and in Lope de Vega's house in Madrid.

FIGURE 5.4 Seville's Casa Lonja (House of Trade), was built next to the cathedral in the late sixteenth century. Until then, the city's merchants had conducted their growing business on the steps (*gradas*) of the cathedral itself, and even inside that building during inclement weather, much to the annoyance of the archbishop. The Casa Lonja now houses the Archive of the Indies, with millions of documents and maps from Spain's 400 years of empire.

FIGURE 5.5 Located well inland on the Guadalquivir River, Seville was the official gateway to the Spanish Empire during the sixteenth and seventeenth centuries. This painting, attributed to Antonio Sánchez Coello, shows the city at the peak of its importance in the late sixteenth century, centering on the maritime activities along the river's sandy banks.

FIGURE 5.6 The royal palace in Madrid was begun in 1738 to replace the old fortress-palace (*alcázar*) that burned down in 1734. Substantially completed in 1764, the new palace represented the French and Italian tastes of the Bourbon dynasty.

6

Toward modernity: From the Napoleonic invasion to Alfonso XIII

~

Joseph Bonaparte was arguably the best of the Bonaparte clan, and Napoleon undoubtedly hoped that the Spanish people would accept him as a welcome replacement for the feckless Bourbons. He was wrong. By the time that Joseph arrived at the frontier, a spontaneous revolt against the French invasion had already begun. The rising began in Madrid on May 2, in reaction to news that the royal family had left for France. General Murat put down a riot in the Puerta del Sol quickly and brutally, using the Mameluke cavalry that Napoleon had recruited in Egypt. Given the long Spanish history of conflict with Muslim forces, the sight of turbaned horsemen charging a crowd of men and women in the heart of Madrid had a shocking effect. The next day, Murat's soldiers executed the supposed leaders of the riot on the hill of Príncipe Pío, at the western edge of Madrid near the royal palace. Various Spanish artists would paint their interpretations of those two actions, but the versions that history remembers are two arresting canvases by Goya, which capture the events in all their horror. In *The Charge of the Mamelukes on the 2nd of May*, the mad look on the face of the horseman in the center of the composition, and the tangle of bloodied bodies and enraged citizens in front of him, evoke the violent movement, confusion, and savagery of the confrontation. By contrast, the composition of *The Executions on the Hill of Príncipe Pío on the 3rd of May* is eerily still, as a terrified man in a white shirt raises his arms in surrender, while a contingent of faceless uniformed French soldiers aim their weapons at him in perfect formation. The viewer is left to complete the action, imagining the white shirt splattered in blood and the man collapsing in death to join the bodies of comrades who have fallen all around him.

In all, some 400 Spaniards were killed in those two days, and the stunning news spread to all corners of the country in record time. Although Murat thought he had ended the rebellion by his swift actions and exemplary punishments, in fact he had ensured fierce resistance to the French occupation would continue. Following Spanish traditions that dated back to the Middle Ages, committees (*juntas*) of citizens formed in cities and towns all over Spain to organize a war against the French. Considering that Spain had no national government at the time, the organization of Spanish resistance was astounding and demonstrated both the resolve of the citizenry and their strong sense that they were in charge of their own destiny. The first junta was organized in the northwestern city of Oviedo in late May, and other juntas and local militias joined the cause over the next few months. The officer corps of the Spanish army provided military discipline in some of the units, but for the most part the militias functioned simply because they included men who had known and worked with one another all their lives.

Despite his earlier conduct, Fernando's captivity in France rallied most Spaniards to his cause, and they organized their fight in his name. At the outset, they could not hope to challenge the well-trained French army on its own terms. Instead, the citizens' militias attacked isolated groups of soldiers wherever and whenever they had the opportunity, fighting a little war (*guerrilla*) with pitchforks and daggers against the guns and bayonets of the French. These unorthodox tactics had a demoralizing effect on the French as they moved farther into the countryside, and neither side gave any quarter to the enemy. Against all odds, a Spanish army organized by the juntas won a great victory against the French at Bailén in Andalusia on July 18–20, 1808. At the same time, Joseph Bonaparte was making his way toward Madrid from the north and becoming increasingly alarmed. As he wrote to Napoleon from Burgos on July 18, "It seems that nobody has wanted to tell the exact truth to Your Majesty . . . I am not frightened by my position, but it is a unique situation in history. I do not have one single partisan here."[1] Despite that gloomy assessment and the rebel victory at Bailén, the rebellion clearly needed outside help to oust the French.

A rag-tag Spanish army under General Palafox was the only major force between Barcelona and Madrid, and they managed to hold the city of Zaragoza through the summer and fall of 1808, aided by the heroic efforts of the citizenry. Meanwhile, the rebel leaders organized a supreme central committee of all the existing juntas, which in December declared itself the legitimate government of Spain, acting for the captive Fernando. The central committee signed a formal alliance with Great Britain in mid-January 1809, thus clearing the way for British troops to enter

---

[1] Quoted in John D. Bergamini, *The Spanish Bourbons: The History of a Tenacious Dynasty* (New York: Putnam, 1974), p. 136.

Spain and coordinate the war effort. They arrived too late to save Zaragoza, which fell to the French in February 1809. In all, the Spanish forces numbered some 35,000–50,000 men. The British would send 40,000–60,000 men to what they called the Peninsular War, and the French would eventually commit 200,000–300,000 men to the Spanish front, suffering enormous losses in numbers and prestige between 1808 and 1812, when Napoleon pulled them out to concentrate on the invasion of Russia. The French troops, confronting both conventional and guerrilla attacks, took their vengeance where they could, often at the expense of the Spanish population. Here again, the genius of Goya captured the moment, in his unblinking and deeply disturbing series of engravings called "The Disasters of War." Even viewers numbed by images of the savagery of modern warfare find it difficult to contemplate the horrors he depicted, to which he was an eyewitness.

The dramatic events of the French invasion of Spain and its aftermath have inspired modern film directors as well as historians and artists, though not necessarily with the same attention to historical accuracy. *The Naked Maja* casts the love story of Goya (Anthony Franciosa) and the duchess of Alba (Ava Gardner) against the background of the war. *The Pride and the Passion* features a romantic triangle involving a beautiful peasant girl (Sophia Loren), a heroic militiaman (Frank Sinatra), and a newly arrived British naval officer (Cary Grant), in the aftermath of the surrender of Zaragoza. And *The Mask of Goya* explores the complicated nature of the artist (Javier Bardem) in the treacherous political atmosphere of the times. The first two films are notable mainly for some nice scenes of the Spanish landscape, though the scenes in *The*

Pride and the Passion trace a hilariously confusing itinerary across northern Spain.

As the war continued across much of Spain, French troops managed to hold Madrid secure for Joseph Bonaparte, who reigned as José I, but whose kingship was contested from the start. He based his government on the first written constitution ever applied to Spain, written in Bayonne on July 6, 1808, by his brother Napoleon. Though both José and his constitution were foreign imports, imposed by force, they nonetheless attracted support from numerous members of the Spanish elite. These individuals included reform-minded bureaucrats who had given up on the Bourbons and sincerely believed that Spain should adopt the best legacies of the French Revolution. They also included opportunists who wanted to advance their careers under whoever held power.

Outside Madrid, while rebels continued the struggle to oust the French from Spain, rebel leaders created a Council of Regency to act in Fernando's name and organized elections for a new Cortes. The elected delegates convened in Cádiz in late September 1810. Although they were unified in their opposition to the French invasion, they represented a fairly wide spectrum of political opinion. About a third of the delegates were priests. The most radical delegates were known as the Frenchified faction (*afrancesados*) because of their admiration for the changes brought about by revolutionary France. Although they participated in the provisional government acting in Fernando's name, they made it clear that they did not trust the Bourbons to reform Spain. At the end of December, the Cortes appointed a commission of fourteen Spaniards and two representatives from the Indies to draft a constitution, supposedly based on medieval Spanish principles. The commission finished a draft by mid-August 1811, which the delegates debated for the better part of a year, before approving it on March 12, 1812. Reinforced by specific legislation such as the abolition of the inquisition, the new constitution was introduced into all of the areas outside French control, in the name of King Fernando VII. The areas controlled by the French already had a constitution, based on the French Revolution, and a king, imposed by the French. Moreover, the intellectual elite on both sides of the political divide claimed to be supporters of a modern, constitutional, parliamentary monarchy.

Meanwhile, the vast majority of the Spanish population, still loyal to the "captive Fernando," had little in common with the liberal reformers in Cádiz or the supporters of Joseph Bonaparte's government in Madrid. They remained conservative, traditional, religious, and fiercely independent. Rebel bands savagely attacked French troops whenever the occasion permitted, and they easily identified the havoc and disruption of their way of life with everything foreign, and especially French. They remained unwilling to accept Joseph Bonaparte as their king, but they also viewed the activities of the Cortes of Cádiz with suspicion. The constitutional changes espoused by various factions of the intellectual elite had little to do with their lives. Although they wanted social and economic justice, many of them seem to have trusted a traditional monarchy in the person of their "captive" King Fernando, rather than a revolutionary committee, to deliver them.

Spain's War of Independence formed part of the Europe-wide struggle against Napoleon. Though the brutal struggle affected Spaniards at all levels of society, British forces took the military lead. After several years of indecisive battles and continuing guerrilla attacks against the French, Sir Arthur Wellesley (later the duke of Wellington) led a combined army of British, Spanish, and Portuguese troops that defeated the French at Vitoria in July 1813. Joseph Bonaparte then decamped for France, but the war nonetheless dragged on until 1814.

With Napoleon's defeat, King Fernando VII, dubbed "The Desired One" ("el Deseado"), returned to Spain at the end of March, 1814. He soon proved to the liberal intellectuals of Spain that their doubts about him had been justified. Fernando immediately revoked the constitution of 1812, removed anyone who opposed him from the armed forces and the government, and set about trying to reinstall every aspect of traditional monarchical authority, as if the revolutionary upheavals of the previous quarter-century had meant nothing. Predictably, his actions angered the forces on the political left who had held the country together in his absence, as well as the leaders of the alliance against Napoleon. Yet Fernando also retained the services of many bureaucrats who had supported Joseph Bonaparte. Predictably, that angered his most loyal supporters on the political right. Fernando's blend of personal rigidity, political expediency, and outright stupidity thus marked his reign from the outset.

Many historians rank him as one of the worst monarchs in Spanish history, and his incompetent reign could not have come at a worse time. In the confused period during the Napoleonic invasion, political leaders in several areas in Spanish America had declared their independence from French-controlled Spain, either to support the provisional government represented by the Cortes of Cádiz, or to claim complete independence. In the years after Fernando established his benighted rule, most of the remaining areas of Spanish America decided that their interests would be better served as independent republics. Spanish America's independence movements stretched on for more than a decade, with each area in that vast region playing out its own political drama.

Without a navy, and with many of its most experienced military and administrative officials in America having joined the rebellions, Spain struggled to reassert authority. The upheaval in America had a direct effect on internal Spanish politics as well. Many army officers had come of age during the heady days of European revolution, and had fought the French under the authority of the Cortes of Cádiz. They disapproved of the reactionary policies of Fernando VII and had distinctly mixed feelings about fighting against their brother officers in the Americas. These liberal officers began to think of themselves as the most worthy defenders of the state, with a duty to intervene in politics and set the regime back on the path to good government. As one of the army units assembled in Cádiz late in 1819 to embark for America, their leader had other plans. On January 1, 1820, Captain Rafael Riego issued a proclamation (Sp. *pronunciamiento*) in defense of the constitution of 1812 and led his men to Madrid.

Riego's *golpe de estado* (coup d'état), the first in modern Spanish history, succeeded in the short term. King Fernando reinstated the constitution as the law of the land, and a new era of liberal legislation followed. It was spearheaded by the most radical of the "Men of 1812" (*doceañistas*), who had clearly lost faith in the Bourbon restoration.

Unfortunately, the attitudes and programs of these exalted politicians (*exaltados*) were out of touch not only with conservative Spaniards, but also with their fellow liberal constitutionalists and the army officers who had put them in power. The situation became so volatile by 1822 that many feared that Spain would disintegrate into civil war.

Similarly radical developments elsewhere in continental Europe had led to a conservative Holy Alliance of France, Austria, and Russia. With the blessing of the alliance, in April 1823 French forces invaded Spain once again, this time joining with Spanish troops loyal to Fernando to rescue him from supposed captivity. Styled "the 100,000 sons of St. Louis," they restored the king to power. Fernando made a deal with the French government in February 1824 to retain some 45,000 French troops in the country, based in Cádiz. The original term for this occupying force was only five months, but it was later made open-ended, a proof of the king's tenuous authority. In that same year, the rebellious American colonies won their independence and soon split into more than two dozen independent republics comprising nearly 20 million citizens. After more than 300 years, all that remained of the Spanish Empire in America were the islands of Cuba and Puerto Rico, although cultural and economic ties between the new republics and Spain continued.

When French troops finally left Spain in September 1828, the political landscape looked more placid. Although Fernando was hardly a model constitutional monarch, he had recognized the need to compromise with the liberal constitutionalists in order to stay in power and avoid further turmoil. He therefore supported fiscal and political reforms that served the interests of the conservative bourgeoisie – most notably the manufacturing elite in Catalonia and the banking elite in Madrid. In the process he offended the most conservative elements of Spain's church and state, including peasants defending traditional rights and privileges against the pressures of capitalist agriculture, and ultra-conservative clerics and aristocrats. Dubbed the *apostólicos* for their defense of ultra-conservative Catholicism, they rallied around the figure of the king's younger brother Carlos.

Because Fernando had no heir in the 1820s, despite three marriages, Carlos was the heir to the throne, and he and his supporters were willing to bide their time. But then Fernando was married a fourth time, to María Cristina, a Bourbon princess from Naples. When she gave birth to a daughter named Isabel in 1830, it provoked a succession crisis. Under the Habsburgs and their precursors, females had always had the right to ascend the Spanish throne if they had no brothers. The Bourbons had changed that, by bringing the succession rules of the Salian Franks to Spain. Under Salic law, Isabel had no right to succeed her father, even though she had no brothers. Instead, the king's brother Carlos still stood first in the line of succession, as long as the Salic law remained in effect.

Rather than let that happen, shortly before his death in 1833, Fernando revoked the Salic law to make Isabel his heir. Rather than accept the infant Isabel as legitimate queen, Carlos and the *apostólicos* launched a civil war – the first of the so-called "Carlist Wars" – determined to take power one way or another and to revoke the changes made by the constitutional monarchy. Although ostensibly defined by a dynastic struggle over which branch of the Bourbons should inherit the throne of Spain, the Carlist Wars in fact represented a much broader struggle over the very nature of the Spanish state. To the Carlists, the only legitimate bases for the state were the truths propounded by the Catholic Church. They favored autonomy for the Spanish church in religious matters, and a very close relationship between church and state overall.

The factions on the left of the political spectrum generally favored the liberal agenda that the Cortes of Cádiz defined during the Napoleonic war. The term "liberal" came to have various meanings in European politics during the nineteenth century. In Spain liberals defined themselves as free (*libre*) subjects of a constitutional monarchy, represented by an elected Cortes that shared power with the monarch. They believed the state should actively shape economy and society, guided by reason and the best new ideas regarding education and social legislation. Although most Spanish liberals in the early nineteenth century were not anti-religious, they favored a limited role for the church in education and society.

By contrast, many segments of Spanish society, emerging from the turmoil of the Napoleonic period and facing the unsettling social and economic changes of early industrialization, clung to religious traditions as their best hope in a hostile world. The factions on the right opposed the restraints that a constitution placed on the power of the monarch and on the role of the church. They favored traditional values, such as order, hierarchy, and morality, to guide the actions of the monarch and the state, with limited power for the individual in both the public and the private spheres. With regard to the role of the church in national affairs, they believed that religious values should inform every aspect of life, and that the economic basis of the church should be preserved, so that it could carry out the functions necessary for social stability.

During the First Carlist War, because the factions on the right supported Don Carlos, María Cristina, as regent for the three-year-old Isabel, had no choice but to embrace the agenda of the factions on the left. With both sides fairly evenly matched, the war lasted for six years (1833–9), and María Cristina had to accept radical measures to generate funds. These measures included closing down most monastic orders in 1835 and auctioning off their properties, as well as the secular property of the church in general. Viewed as an outrage by the factions on the right, these sales allowed the new moneyed classes to consolidate their economic power by becoming major landowners, and committed the monarchy irrevocably to the liberal political agenda. Further actions by the hard-pressed government included abolishing the tithe, which had supported the secular clergy since time out of mind, thus driving the wedge still deeper between traditional and liberal Spain. The government also wiped out various rights and privileges of the Spanish nobility, while leaving their landownership intact. Given that deeply held beliefs were at stake, the Carlist War was fought with exemplary brutality on both sides, to the extent that the international community became alarmed that it might spread.

To contain that threat, Isabeline Spain was included in the Quadruple Alliance formed in April 1834 by Britain, France, Spain, and Portugal. Defined as an alliance of constitutional monarchies against the reactionary states of

Austria and Russia, the alliance allowed foreign intervention in Spain to ensure that the Carlists did not win. England sanctioned the formation of a military expeditionary force of some 10,000 men to fight in Spain, and they would remain from 1835 until the end of the conflict in 1839. In August 1839, the so-called "Agreement of Eliot" laid out conditions for the proper treatment of prisoners of war, and the Peace of Vergara ended the conflict, negotiated by the liberal general Baldomero Espartero and the Carlist general Rafael Maroto. Although the constitutional monarchy remained in power, Carlist army officers were reincorporated into the national army, and Navarre, the Carlist stronghold, retained its traditional rights and privileges. In other words, though the war ended, the underlying conflicts that spawned it remained unresolved.

A new constitution written in 1837 defined the Isabeline state, broadly based on liberal political principles. Nonetheless, it was not clear which socioeconomic groups among the liberal factions would gain the greatest advantages from the state. The wealthy capitalists of agriculture, industry, and banking were determined to retain their position and consequently favored a legislative agenda that would not jeopardize their ownership of former church lands or intervene unduly in the economy. The middling capitalists who owned shops, along with landowning peasants, some of the wealthier artisans, and educated professionals, generally favored a more active legislative agenda that would extend political participation. The turbulent political history of Isabel II's reign would be defined by the alternation in power of these two broad groupings in the context of a liberal, constitutional monarchy. The Carlists would remain far to the right, and the landless farmers and urban wage-workers would remain far to the left, excluded from political participation.

In the immediate aftermath of the First Carlist War, the activist arm of the liberals, who became known as the Progressives, forced the government to shift toward the left, in order to broaden political participation and individual freedoms. They instituted this change by means of an army proclamation in 1840, reminiscent of Riego's proclamation two decades earlier. The "sword-arm" (*espadón*) who issued the proclamation was General Espartero, who replaced the queen mother as regent for the child queen, but acting as a civilian rather than as an army officer. Espartero would use his authority to promote a program of modernization that tried to foster the loyalty of the high and middling segments of the bourgeoisie at the same time, promoting free trade and civil liberties.

Instead of unity, however, Espartero's program alienated both right and left of the limited political spectrum. Large landowners, bankers, and industrialists opposed free trade, which favored British interests, and they conspired with María Cristina and King Louis-Philippe of France to oust Espartero. Segments of the army were appalled by the latter's execution of General Diego de León in 1841 for plotting to kidnap the "captive" young queen. Advocates of greater civil rights, and workers who wanted the right to organize labor unions, met with similar intransigence from Espartero. At the end of 1842, when industrialists and workers in Barcelona joined forces to protest against free trade, Espartero ordered the bombing of the city and even shut down the Cortes.

In May 1843, General Ramón María Narváez, an army leader who championed the more conservative or Moderate (Moderado) political factions, issued his own proclamation just outside Madrid. General Espartero left Spain for exile in England, and Narváez took his place as principal adviser to the young queen. That same year Isabel officially came of age, at thirteen, and ruled thereafter in her own name, but under the heavy influence of Narváez. From 1843 to 1854, he would develop mechanisms that made the constitutional monarchy function efficiently, the cost being what the modern world would term "corruption."

The constitution of 1845 set a more conservative tone than its 1837 precursor, enforced by a strong state bureaucracy at the national level and supported by a network of political bosses at the local level. The glue of state funds and patronage ensured the loyalty of the bosses, known cynically as *caciques*, the village headmen in parts of Spanish America in colonial times. With the management of these bosses, elections to the Cortes became a staged drama rather than an exercise in democracy. The paramilitary police force known as the Civil Guard (Guardia Civil), founded in 1843 as an arm of the government, swiftly put down any threats to civil order. The managed system of constitutional government in Isabeline Spain resembled similar systems elsewhere in nineteenth-century Europe, most notably in England. They worked for the most part, and they kept the lid on social protest for the most part, but at the cost of engendering cynicism and a growing anger among idealists and activists who wanted to promote a real and honest democracy.

As queen, Isabel II demonstrated an odd combination of traits and behaviors. Largely to meet the needs of international politics, she was married at the age of sixteen (in 1846) to her first cousin, Francisco de Asís, the duke of Cádiz, rather than to someone of royal rank from outside Spain. In a double wedding, her younger sister, María Luisa Fernandina, married the duke of Montpensier, a son of the king of France. If things had unfolded as England and France planned, Isabel, closely tied to Britain, would have had no children, because her husband was widely known to be homosexual. After Isabel's death, her sister, closely tied to France, would have ascended the throne. Events proved otherwise. Although Isabel greatly admired the English Queen Victoria, her direct contemporary, her personal life was anything but "Victorian." She would bear nine children, five of whom survived to adulthood, but her husband probably did not father any of them, though he acknowledged them as his own. Because Isabel was the reigning queen, there was nothing that her enemies, or the Montpensier faction, could do to challenge the legitimacy of the growing royal family.

Contrasting with this scandalous romantic history, the queen also demonstrated a fervent, sentimental, and even superstitious religiosity, surrounded by priests when she was not dallying with lovers. She displayed similar contrasts in her extravagant personal expenditures and her penny-pinching attitude as head of state. Perhaps the worst indictment of her rule is that she never seemed to understand the difference between her personal whims and wishes and her duties as a constitutional monarch to adopt the programs of Spain's elected officials. Vain, sensual, capricious, and foolish, she might have been a disaster for Spain in the days when monarchs held real power. As it was, in the modern world of the nineteenth century, she was a disaster mainly for the institution of monarchy itself.

With the stability created by Narváez's managed political system, the Spanish economy slowly modernized and industrialized. A relatively free press represented various political factions but posed no danger to the status quo. A Second Carlist War in 1847–9 affected little more than rural Catalonia, and the upheavals of 1848 elsewhere in Europe had no parallel in Spain, which already had some degree of political democracy, cynically managed though it was. With regard to church–state relations, Narváez's government negotiated a new Concordat with the Vatican in 1851, which gave the church more power, in exchange for the pope's all-important confirmation of the legal ownership of former church lands. In all, Narváez's system functioned well enough, although it solved none of the underlying tensions in Spanish society and bred cynicism because of its widespread corruption.

A new generation of progressive army officers grew increasingly restive under the system. In 1854 they issued a proclamation demanding better government, less corruption, more efficiency, and enhanced rights for citizens. When the government refused to resign, the plotters seized power violently, in a *golpe de estado* known as "La Vicalvarada." General Leopoldo O'Donnell then joined with older Progressives, including Espartero, who had returned from England, to prepare a new constitution. The new government acted to speed up industrialization by providing subsidies for large projects including railroad construction (1855). The funds came from the sale of lands of the noble military orders and municipal commons and wastelands, which harmed small farmers who relied on access to those lands to supplement their own small-holdings. A law to limit liability for corporate partners (the Madoz Law, 1855) had similarly mixed results. Industrial workers in Barcelona argued that it should protect their collective right to organize unions, and the resulting unrest destabilized the government. It was brought down in a proclamation by one of its own, General O'Donnell, in July 1856.

O'Donnell's government reinstated the more conservative constitution of 1845. In the interests of stability, it aimed for a coalition of the most moderate of the Progressives and the most progressive of the Moderates. With the rivalries among the most powerful elements of Spanish society muted, all of their energies could be focused on developing the economy. In addition, by presenting a united front, those in charge of the economy could keep a lid on social unrest and workers' demands for full economic and political justice. To a certain extent, O'Donnell and his administration succeeded, achieving greater efficiency with less corruption. On the other hand, it was clear that they made political decisions to favor those in power, and anyone who opposed the official agenda found the government increasingly repressive.

To raise funds, more municipal lands were sold, further privatizing what had previously been communal property. Like the earlier sales of ecclesiastical and other entailed lands, these new sales benefited the propertied classes and deprived poor farmers of access to land. Even with this new infusion of public funds, however, the government lacked sufficient capital to carry out major improvements to the infrastructure, and dared not risk alienating the propertied classes by increasing taxes. Given this dilemma, and to go forward with projects such as completing a national network of railways, the government borrowed foreign funds on the international market and encouraged foreign capital to flow into Spain.

Some historians have argued that these policies did little to develop the economy while widening the gap between rich and poor and allowing foreign goods to enter the Spanish market to the detriment of local production. Others argue that the policies were necessary for the industrial development of Spain, despite their negative aspects. There is no question, however, that the Spanish economy grew substantially in the mid nineteenth century. Even though Spain clearly lagged behind the major industrialized countries in Europe, such as Great Britain, the government's push to modernize the economy enjoyed limited success.

To modernize society as well, a Law of Public Instruction (1857) established government control of all schools, private as well as public. Thereafter, the state would set the curriculum, oversee examinations, and award degrees. Nonetheless, to mollify traditionalists, the law still privileged Catholic doctrine as the basis for Spanish education. These changes did not go nearly far enough for the most progressive voices among the intellectual elite. Increasingly, many of them favored a clear division between church and state, and secular values in place of the religious values of the past. Ironically, the most distinguished university professors also objected to the state's control of education. In the 1860s, professors who held senior positions demanded the right to control the curriculum and examinations, and above all to be free to express their opinions, regardless of what the government thought. This ferment of intellectual opposition occurred largely outside government circles, and a segment of the press took up their call for more thoroughgoing change.

The government also used the press to rally support and launched a series of overseas expeditions and minor wars, designed in part to foster national unity. In 1858–60, Spanish expeditions were sent to Cochin China (today, Vietnam) and Morocco, the latter resulting in the conquest of Tetuán, long a base for pirate raids against the Spanish coasts. In the period of the American Civil War (1861–5), Spain occupied Santo Domingo, lest it fall into other hands, and participated with France's Napoleon III in an expedition to Mexico (1861–2). Spain also fought with Peru and allied republics on the Pacific coast over access to the nitrate-rich deposits of bird guano on islands off the Peruvian coast, a valuable commodity. This so-called "Guano War" (1864–6) did little to enhance the country's prestige. Nonetheless, in the European scramble for colonies and colonial products that marked the mid nineteenth century, Spain was determined to maintain a presence.

The growing economy made these overseas adventures possible, and they were useful for the government as it faced increasing opposition at home. Unfortunately, the European economy as a whole entered a recession in 1866, related to disruptions in the supplies of raw cotton during the American Civil War. The situation was made worse by crop failures in the Spanish countryside. With the population exceeding 16 million, even a small shortfall in the harvest led to higher prices for food and bread riots in the cities. Despite increasingly repressive policies, the government of Isabel II could not withstand the crisis that unfolded in 1868. The queen was ill equipped to serve as a stabilizing force, given her scandalous romantic life and her failure to play the role of a constitutional monarch.

On September 19, 1868, another military proclamation in Cádiz demanded a change in government and "a Spain with honor." General Juan Prim and General Francisco Serrano (duke of La Torre) acted for a diverse group of conspirators, many of whom were civilians. After a brief skirmish between the military rebels and the forces that remained loyal to the queen, Isabel II went into exile on September 30, though she did not abdicate. The conspirators then formed a provisional government and began shopping for a replacement monarch.

The search would not be easy. By then, a new generation of idealistic reformers, politicians, and intellectuals had become so alienated from the policies of the constitutional monarchy that some of them began plotting to create a republic. Disillusioned also with the notion that a strong central state could effect change, they shifted their goals toward decentralization, believing that the common people could best be schooled in representative government at the local and regional levels. And some of them, at least, angered by the power and intransigence of the religious establishment, moved toward the goal of a secular state, separate from, if not actively hostile to, the Catholic Church.

In the short term, the republicans could not take power, but the provisional government set up by the leaders of the coup nonetheless instituted several radical changes in the constitutional monarchy. First, they organized elections to a new Cortes, based on universal adult male suffrage. All males of twenty-five years and older could vote, which was the most inclusive electorate in the world at the time. The Cortes wrote a new constitution dated June 6, 1869, that placed all legislative power in its own hands. It retained the monarchy but defined it in advisory and ceremonial terms. As advanced as the new constitution was, it was bound to disappoint those who favored abolishing the monarchy and instituting a republic. Marginalized by the new constitution, republicans moved outside official political discourse to plot a seizure of power, an ominous sign for the future.

In the meantime, the provisional government headed by General Juan Prim, with General Francisco Serrano serving as provisional head of state, or regent, searched for a new monarch willing to reign under the terms of the new constitution. In Paris, Isabel II finally abdicated the throne in 1870, in favor of her son Alfonso. Any alternative candidate who agreed to become Spain's monarch would have to contend with challenges not only from the Carlists but also from Alfonso's partisans.

The political situation in Europe further complicated the search, which lasted for a year and a half. When the Cortes offered Leopold of Hohenzollern the throne, his acceptance provoked the Franco-Prussian War of 1870, in which France suffered a humiliating defeat and Paris, besieged by Prussian troops, collapsed into chaos and revolution with the Paris Commune (March–May, 1871). This "first workers' revolution," in the designation of Karl Marx, encouraged the socialist theoreticians of the International Workingmen's Association (1864–76, also known as the First International) to believe that a widespread socialist revolution was at hand. Spain's search for a new monarch took place in this highly volatile political and social atmosphere.

After Leopold of Hohenzollern withdrew his candidacy, the Cortes extended an offer to a son of King Victor Emmanuel II of the House of Savoy in Italy on November 16, 1870. To the relief of Spain's constitutional monarchists, he accepted. Designated Amadeo I, the new king arrived in Spain on December 30, only to find that his principal supporter, General Prim, had died at the hands of assassins that same day. Amadeo arrived in Madrid at the start of the New Year, and it is fair to say that his reign was doomed from the start. Although he accepted his role as a constitutional monarch and filled it with intelligence and care, Spain's political classes seemed to have no talent for fulfilling their responsibility to legislate and govern in the best interests of the country.

Amadeo's supporters, ostensibly the most powerful group in the Cortes, split into factions and failed to agree on a legislative program. Individuals out of power at a given moment spent their time conspiring to overthrow their rivals, rather than serving as a "loyal opposition." Moreover, the constitutional monarchy as a whole faced continual challenges from republicans on the left and supporters of Alfonso XII on the right. As if that were not bad enough, rebellion in Cuba continued (1868–78), and the Carlists launched their third war in favor of the Carlist pretender in 1872. In addition to the financial strains that the wars caused to Amadeo's struggling government, ordinary Spaniards greatly resented the system of military conscription that took young men from their homes, and they did not support either war wholeheartedly.

Internally, and despite universal adult male suffrage, the political classes failed to resolve the issue of political rights for Spanish workers and peasants who owned little or no property. Factory workers provided the muscle for Spain's push to expand industrialization; rural wage-workers fed the country and enriched capitalist landowners, but they had no right to bargain collectively, and the state did little to protect them from unsafe and unfair working conditions. In Spain as elsewhere in the first century of industrialization, the propertied classes were also the political classes and they showed little inclination to sacrifice their interests in order to benefit the workers. Moreover, although radical republican intellectuals were prominent among Spain's political classes, they were as unresponsive to the problem of worker unrest as their colleagues.

Faced with this array of intractable problems, Amadeo I abdicated on February 11, 1873, after just two years on the throne. It is hard to fault him on this or any other aspect of his brief reign. The day after the abdication, the Cortes proclaimed Spain a republic, using heady and overblown rhetoric that compared their rebellion to England's Glorious Revolution of 1688. But "La Gloriosa," far from transforming the Spanish political and economic landscape, lasted just eleven months and displayed the same dreary combination of uncompromising factional politics and governmental incompetence. One after another, four presidents scrabbled to the top of the political heap, dragging the executive power back and forth from left to center-right, focused on the question of how much power the central government should delegate to regional authorities. Estanislao Figueras, a moderate Catalan federalist, took power on February 11, 1873, but the more radical federalists replaced him the following June with Francisco Pi y Margall, a Catalan writer and public intellectual. Pi y Margall's tenure, which lasted only from June 11 to July 18, coincided with two major uprisings. The affiliates of the First International launched a brief attempt at socialist revolution in Alcoy (Valencia) on July 9; and the Cantonalist revolt that began on July 12 represented the extreme of federalist beliefs, aiming to reduce government to its most local level. Pi y Margall took the blame and Nicolás Salmerón replaced him, aiming to restore order. He failed, lasting in the presidency only from July 18 to September 7. Pulling the radical republic back toward the center, Emilio Castelar took power on September 7. With an immediate need to restore order, he collaborated with the army, which cost him the support of his colleagues in the Cortes. In short, the intellectuals who held power during "La Gloriosa" proved themselves incapable of fulfilling the minimal requirement of a government. They could not govern.

Given the failure of civilian politicians to address the needs of Spain or its citizens, army leaders once again concluded that they were the only force capable of putting the state back on track. On January 3, 1874, General Manuel Pavía marched into the fractious Cortes and essentially told the delegates to go home, as they were no longer in charge. For the rest of the year, General Francisco Serrano governed without a legislature, appointing a group of conservative but competent civilian ministers to run the country. The government immediately outlawed the labor movement, driving it underground. Although the radical revolts of 1873 did not recur, the Cuban rebellion and the Third Carlist War continued, draining funds and political confidence. Despite Serrano's contempt for the civilian leaders of what would become known as the First Republic, he agreed with them in rejecting the notion of a Bourbon restoration.

Behind the scenes, however, many of General Serrano's colleagues in the army had concluded that a constitutional monarchy, with a Bourbon restoration, offered the best chance to bring peace and stability to Spain, after nearly a decade of political chaos. Many civilian politicians, frozen out of power by General Serrano, agreed, among them Antonio Cánovas del Castillo (1828–97). A distinguished historian of Spain, Cánovas worked to gather support for a Bourbon restoration, hoping to effect this change without another military intervention. He succeeded and failed at the same time. On December 29, General Arsenio Martínez Campos issued a proclamation in Valencia demanding the restoration of the Bourbons, with Alfonso XII as Spain's constitutional monarch. The young king was in England at the Royal Military Academy at Sandhurst, but he returned to Spain in early January 1875 to take up the role that his mother had failed to perform.

After the years of turmoil and uncertainty, most of the Spanish people accepted the Bourbon restoration with something resembling joy and gratitude. Republicans remained committed to the abolition of the monarchy, however, and the Carlist pretender continued the third war against the state. Alfonso's army defeated the Carlists in 1876, however, ending another phase in that ongoing struggle.

The second Bourbon restoration settled in quickly and smoothly, guided by the carefully crafted policies of Cánovas, who worked to create a consensus among Spain's fractious political classes. A new constitution in 1876 restated the highest ideals of the constitutional monarchy, enshrining the rule of law, civilian control of the government, and secular authority over education and culture, though respectful of Catholic believers – a program designed to appeal to the broadest cross-section of the population. Under the new constitution, the legislative parliament (Cortes) held most of the power in its two chambers: a Senate with 360 elected delegates, and a Congress with 409 delegates. In this parliamentary structure, the head of government held the office of president of the Council of Ministers and sat in the lower chamber (Congress). The king was head of state and had to countersign all legislation to enact it into law.

Early in 1878 the young king married his cousin María de las Mercedes, and the handsome royal couple basked in their popularity among the Spanish people. Tragically, María de las Mercedes died just six months after the wedding. Before the end of the year, a Spanish anarchist fired a shot at the king, a shocking reminder of the growing contingent of extremists in Europe and the United States, who justified extreme violence to achieve their ends. Those ends rarely included a practical program of reform, but merely aimed at assassinating leaders to destabilize the power structure and bring it down. The last half of the nineteenth century and the first decade of the twentieth would see a rash of such assassinations.

Anxious to produce an heir, Alfonso XII married again late in 1879, this time to a distant cousin, the Archduchess María Cristina of Habsburg-Lorraine. As if to underscore the dangerous times in which they lived, the newly married couple survived an assassination attempt as they rode in their carriage in Madrid. Despite the unease that these violent episodes created, general economic prosperity served as a counterweight favoring stability. The European economy enjoyed an extraordinary surge of growth until around 1886, and Spanish prosperity continued until almost the end of the century.

Bolstered by the growing economy, the parliamentary structure functioned smoothly, with elections managed at the local level to make sure that the Liberals and Conservatives alternated in power and enjoyed a majority in the lower house when they controlled the government. Like his counterparts in the mid nineteenth century, Cánovas modeled his system on Great Britain's parliamentary monarchy; in fact, many dubbed the system "the English style" (*el estilo inglés*). Cynical though it was, Spain's system of alternation in power (*el turno*) aimed to keep all political factions under the umbrella of the official governing structure. As a measure of its success, Liberals and Conservatives as well as moderate republicans and even moderate Carlists saw more advantages in staying within the structure than moving outside.

Alfonso XII won the affection of Spaniards not only by his appealing personality, but also by his willingness to face danger; for example, he visited areas affected by a cholera outbreak in 1881 and traveled to comfort the victims of a devastating earthquake in 1885. He won the loyalty of the political classes by adhering strictly to his role as a constitutional monarch. Under the system, the king had little independent power, except to designate the president of the Council of Ministers – the head of government. Cánovas del Castillo tried to limit royal power further by a law in 1881 that would have set a term in office of eighteen months for the head of government, whether or not that official enjoyed the confidence of the king. Alfonso refused to sign it. In consequence, Cánovas resigned, and the king then called Práxedes Mateo Sagasta, the leader of the Liberals, to form a new cabinet. In other words, the king followed the principle of *el turno* even in the exercise of his independent power, giving control to those who favored more rapid change.

Sagasta instituted many changes in the government's approach, including allowing the labor movement to organize openly and to bargain collectively with employers. And, as of 1887, the Law of Associations established those rights in law. In 1888, socialist politicians under the leadership of Pablo Iglesias (1850–1925) formed both a political party, the Socialist Workers' Party of Spain (Partido Socialista Obrero Español, or PSOE), and a labor union, the General Union of Workers (Unión General de Trabajadores, or UGT). Both the party and the union drew most of their strength from the mining and industrialized areas of northern Spain. The PSOE participated in national elections to the Cortes after the Law of Universal Suffrage took effect in 1890, but for several decades they lacked sufficient votes for anyone to be elected. Nonetheless, the party remained within the legal framework of the Spanish state and formed an integral part of the international socialist movement as well.

Alfonso XII and his second wife had two daughters, and Queen María Cristina was pregnant again in 1885 when Alfonso XII died of tuberculosis on November 25, three days before his twenty-eighth birthday. The widowed queen gave birth to a son on May 17, 1886, and the infant immediately became king as Alfonso XIII, displacing his two older sisters. María Cristina would act as regent for her son until he attained his majority at the age of seventeen in 1902. During the regency, the widowed queen and her adored son formed a sympathetic pair in the public image. By all accounts, María Cristina presided over the parliamentary system with skill and tact, without entering into the fray of electoral politics. This helped to insulate the monarchy from the contentious issues of the day and from the consequences of unpopular government policies.

One of the most divisive social issues concerned education. At the end of the nineteenth century, some 63 percent of the Spanish population remained unschooled. Only the state had the resources to expand and extend education, but debate centered on whether that education would be state-run and secular or run by the Catholic educational establishment, with subsidies and supervision by the state. In either case, a further issue concerned the curriculum and the values that formed its basis. Throughout the Western world at the time, similar questions arose, centered on the best way to educate individuals as law-abiding and productive citizens. The issues were particularly acute in Spain, however, because of the continued power and influence of the Catholic Church.

The education of Spain's future leaders held special importance as it continued its push to industrialize and modernize. Several important and rival movements to reform secondary schools and universities coincided with the Bourbon restoration. Within the Catholic fold, the Society of Jesus led the way in educational reform, after decades of difficult relations with the Spanish government since their reconstitution as an order in 1814. The

Jesuits' counterpart in the secular sphere was the private school movement known as the Free Institution of Teaching (Institución Libre de Enseñanza), founded in 1876. The guiding intellects behind the Institución Libre were Francisco Giner de los Ríos (1840–1915) and Manuel B. Cossió (1857–1935). In the public sphere, elite educational reform began in earnest in the first years of the twentieth century, with the Committee for the Expansion of Historical Studies and Scientific Research (Junta para Ampliación de los Estudios Históricos e Investigaciones Científicas). The Center for Historical Studies (Centro de Estudios Históricos), under the direction of Ramón Menéndez Pidal, was an early result of the reform movement, along with the Students' Residence (Residencia de Estudiantes) for males and the Young Ladies' Residence (Residencia de Señoritas). Each in its own way, the various avenues of elite educational reform produced generations of political and economic leaders, but their values and approaches to public policy were often at odds with one another.

The Spanish military establishment, so active politically through most of the nineteenth century, remained strangely quiet during the Bourbon restoration. In part, this was the product of an increased professionalization of military careers through the foundation of military academies. With economic prosperity, career officers could aspire to comfortable middle-class lives if they rose in rank. Ironically, however, Spain's economy benefited from continued peace, and there were few opportunities for military officers to advance their careers in peacetime. Intermittent rebellions in Cuba in 1866–79, 1883–4, and from 1895 on provided limited scope for battlefield glory, and the Spanish army failed to distinguish itself in that ongoing conflict.

The Cuban rebellion that began in 1895 coincided with a burst of belligerent nationalism in the United States, and irresponsible journalism on both sides of the Atlantic pandered to the taste for sensationalism in popular culture. The United States presented itself as the protector of an oppressed Cuba and accused Spain of brutality beyond measure. The strong anti-Catholic sentiment in the United States added to the mixture of mutual contempt. Spain and the United States went to war in April 1898, a war welcomed on both sides as an opportunity to win military glory.

Resigning his post as assistant secretary of the United States navy, Theodore Roosevelt joined a large voluntary expeditionary force, soon dubbed "the Rough Riders," that went to Cuba to wrest control of the island from Spain. At the same time, the United States sent naval forces both to Cuba and to the Philippines, which, along with Puerto Rico, were among the last remnants of the Spanish Empire. The war was a disaster for Spain, with humiliating defeats in naval battles at both Santiago Bay in Cuba and Manila Bay in the Philippines. Due to Roosevelt's talent for self-promotion, he would emerge as the public face of the American victory, second only to Admiral George Dewey, the victor at Manila Bay. When the war ended on December 10, 1898, Spain lost what remained of its historic empire, and suffered a tremendous blow to its national self-image. The echoes of that defeat would reverberate well into the twentieth century.

In confronting the reality of the 1898 disaster, the Spanish elite of all political stripes felt an urgent need to reform

Spain and bring the country up to date within the European context. Their definitions of the crisis, and their proposed remedies, differed greatly, however. In some ways the so-called "Generation of '98" recalled the soul-searching of the *arbitristas* exactly three centuries earlier. Did Spain's problem lie in a lack of leadership at the highest levels of the government? Was the political system itself responsible for the crisis? Or was all of society to blame, with each group pushing its own agenda instead of working for the benefit of Spain as a whole? For the first three decades of the new century, Spain's intellectual elite threw itself into an anguished examination of the nation, defining its ills and arguing for profound changes in both public policy and private behavior.

The Generation of '98 included a brilliant array of cultured individuals, unquestionably the largest and most energetic display of creativity since the Golden Century. That earlier movement had included not only reformers such as the *arbitristas*, but the poets, playwrights, novelists, and composers whose work still defines the cultural brilliance of the Habsburg centuries. The Generation of '98 included writers such as the philosopher and novelist Miguel de Unamuno (1864–1936); the poet Antonio Machado (1875–1939); and essayists such as Ramiro de Maeztu (1875–1936), Pio Baroja (1872–1967), and José Martínez Ruiz, known as Azorín (1873–1967). Together, and separately, they analyzed the failings of Spain, drawing the intellectual elite into an emotional debate about the very essence of the nation. Many countries, in the contemporary world as in the past, do not have the stomach for such critical introspection, viewing it as a kind of treason, but self-criticism has always been part of the Spanish character. In many ways, Spanish intellectuals from the sixteenth century on bear as much responsibility for the "Black Legend" of Spanish history as do her enemies.

The anguished critics did not represent all of the intellectual elite, however. Many educated Spaniards reacted to the dark view of their compatriots with a spirited defense of Spanish values, and with pride in the overall legacy of four centuries of Spanish imperial rule. On the surface, the critics generally favored more radical reform, and the defenders favored more gradual reform. It is fair to say, however, that they all knew that things could not remain the same, especially in the face of increasing demands from Spanish workers and peasants.

In the waning years of the nineteenth century and the first years of the twentieth, militant labor movements gained strength all over the Western industrialized world. Governments had easily suppressed protests, strikes, and riots during the mid nineteenth century, and the general prosperity of the 1870s and 1880s had blunted the calls for radical change. At the end of the century, however, the economic downturn reminded workers that they were still not receiving their fair share of industrial profits, while factory owners and investors grew richer by the year.

In countries such as Spain that lagged behind the industrial leaders of Western Europe, the militancy could take extreme forms, not only in cities but also in rural areas among landless laborers and poor peasants. Anarchism had arrived in Spain in 1868 and gathered adherents among the most alienated peasants and workers. Anarchists favored direct action to bring about a total revolution, over better wages and working conditions. They planned the failed Alcoy uprising in 1873 as the start of that revolution. In subsequent decades, anarchism gained adherents, both during the period when labor movements were illegal (1874–81) and thereafter.

Anarchism was inherently hostile to central organization, and the movement suffered continually from factional disputes based on how far, how fast, and how violently to push for change. Nonetheless, anarchism flourished as Spain's slow pace of industrialization failed to absorb displaced peasants, landless laborers, and artisans, and successive governments moved cautiously to avoid threats to order and private property. Using the slow pace of change as a justification for violence, individual anarchists committed terrorist acts such as throwing bombs in public places in the 1880s and 1890s, which resulted in police repression and an identification of the whole anarchist movement with indiscriminate and uncontrolled violence.

A shocking example of that violence occurred in 1906, when an anarchist assassin attacked the wedding procession of Alfonso XIII and his bride Victoria Eugenia of Battenberg. Wedding preparations had been going on for at least a year, and the king's marriage to a granddaughter of Britain's Queen Victoria promised to make the occasion a celebration of the constitutional monarchy. The Palace Hotel, newly built near the Prado Museum, housed official wedding guests, who included many members of the European aristocracy. On May 31, with the streets filled with festive crowds hoping to catch a glimpse of the newly married couple on their way to the wedding reception, the Catalan anarchist Mateu Morral threw a bomb at the royal carriage. Although the newlyweds escaped harm, many members of the public died or sustained wounds in the attack, along with the horses pulling the carriage. The public outrage that followed the attack generated considerable sympathy for the monarchy, faced with growing challenges both inside and outside official circles.

At the start of the twentieth century, Spanish anarchism had grown and matured enough to attempt to form a national movement. The Federation of Workers' Societies of the Spanish Region came into being between 1900 and 1905, bringing together groups that identified with anarchism as well as with traditional labor union movements, or syndicalism. In Barcelona, a parallel movement called Workers' Solidarity, which shared anarcho-syndicalist values, began in 1907. These movements came together in 1910 as the National Federation of Work (Confederación Nacional del Trabajo, or CNT) and held their first conference in 1911. The anarcho-syndicalists alarmed the government even more than the socialist labor movement, and the CNT was outlawed from 1912 to 1918.

Republicans remained committed to the abolition of the monarchy in the long term but worked within the constitutional framework in the short term, gaining support from both workers and segments of the middle class. Nonetheless, the various factions among the republicans continually squabbled among themselves, over both political issues and personal loyalties. The enigmatic Alejandro Lerroux led the older faction most identified with uncompromising republicanism. Melquíades Álvarez led the faction most identified with a more flexible approach to working within the constitutional monarchy. Sharing the leadership, but stymied by internal strife, the republicans did little to bring about the changes they espoused.

Outside the political system, Joaquín Costa articulated the disaffection with the government felt by segments of the middle class. The focus of his copious writings and mass rallies was on widespread opposition to government taxation – always a popular platform – but also on forward-looking proposals such as a nationwide irrigation system to aid agriculture. Despite his provocative stances, he stayed within the legal norms of political activity open to the citizenry and garnered much support for his positions. Nonetheless, because that support depended so much on Costa's own vision and energy, it inevitably faded as his health declined and never presented a serious challenge to the government.

Within the system, elected politicians from the Liberals and Conservatives made a concerted effort at reform. In part, they acted to blunt pressures from republicans within the system and from labor militancy outside it, but they also worked to make both government and the economy function more equitably and efficiently for the population as a whole. There is no reason to doubt their sincerity, even while recognizing the fear that motivated it. The driving force behind the reform movement was Antonio Maura y Montaner, a Mallorcan and former Liberal who shifted to the Conservatives and became that party's leader in 1903. Chosen as president of the Council of Ministers in 1907, he aimed to end the power of local bosses to control the political process (*caciquismo*) and thereby to increase confidence in the government on the part of the country's economic leaders in every party. With confidence restored and the constitutional monarchy strengthened, Maura's government hoped to address the demands for autonomy from Catalonia, the most dynamic region in Spain, where dreams of regional autonomy frustrated in the First Republic had grown along with the local economy.

Worker unrest in Catalonia erupted in rebellion in July 1909, aimed first at the military adventurism in Morocco and the power of industrial bosses, and then shifting to a violent outburst of anti-clericalism. Mobs in Barcelona attacked churches and monasteries and their inhabitants, burning buildings, desecrating cemeteries, and in the process outraging those who continued to value the role of the church in Spanish society, whatever their political beliefs. Although military units soon quashed the rebellion, the events of the "Tragic Week" had serious repercussions. The government arrested a firebrand orator, Francisco Ferrer y Guardia, as the instigator of the rebellion, hoping to thwart any thoughts of similar uprisings. Though Ferrer's trial could not tie him to any capital offenses, the court convicted him, and his execution provoked international outrage against Spain. In short, the government executed Ferrer for his ideas, not for his acts, and the fallout brought down Maura's government and his ambitous program of reform.

King Alfonso XIII made clear his dislike for Maura and did not reappoint him. Instead, he chose José Canalejas as the new president of the Council of Ministers in 1910. A scholar and academic, as well as the leader of the Liberal Party, Canalejas had no desire to push for changes that would further destabilize the country. Instead, through a series of compromises and agreements, he aimed to keep the lid on the explosive tensions in Spanish society. Responding to the violent anti-clericalism that had surfaced during the Tragic Week, he sponsored a law in 1910

that forbade the foundation of any new religious establishments until the government could negotiate a new
Concordat with the Vatican. The church saw a sinister
impulse behind this "padlock law," in part because Canalejas was anti-clerical, but it is fair to say that he was not
anti-religious; he was simply trying to defuse tensions by
preventing provocative actions from either side of the religious divide.

In the international sphere, Canalejas negotiated
an agreement with France over control of Morocco
(Hispano-French Treaty, 1912), preserving a well-defined
role for Spain. Domestically, he initiated talks to bring
Maura back into the parliamentary system, despite the
king's disapproval of the former head of the government. Canalejas continued Maura's firm stance regarding
worker unrest, which meant that no compromise was possible. In 1911, his government suppressed a general strike,
as well as a naval mutiny. In 1912, Canalejas responded to
another general strike by drafting railroad workers into
the army. From the point of view of the violent elements
outside the parliamentary system, the government's stance
justified direct and violent action against the state. In
November 1912, Manuel Pardiñas, a twenty-six-year-old
anarchist well known to the police on both sides of the
Atlantic, shot Canalejas to death in the Puerta del Sol, as
he paused outside a favorite bookshop.

For the next five years, the reform program came
to a standstill, as successive governments merely kept
the machinery going in support of the economic and
social elite. The Cortes drifted into inaction, meeting
for only a few months of each year and then only to
pass legislation such as budget bills needed to keep the

administration functioning. Both inside and outside government, Liberals and Conservatives continued to bicker amongst themselves and with one another, postponing any serious attempt to address the fractures in Spanish society. Remarkably, the Spanish governments and the country as a whole continued to function fairly well, buoyed by the economic prosperity that accompanied Spain's neutrality in the First World War. Spain, and influential Spaniards, earned large profits from selling agricultural and industrial production, and the government was able to reduce part of Spain's foreign debt.

King Alfonso and his English queen Victoria Eugenia, nicknamed Queen Ena, produced seven children in the first eight years of their marriage. Pictures of the royal family filled the popular press, providing a welcome distraction from the grim news emanating from the battle zones of the First World War. Queen Ena had brought a tragic genetic legacy into the marriage, however. Hemophilia afflicted two of her sons, including the first-born, Alfonso, just as it afflicted other royal descendants of Queen Victoria and her consort Albert, including the son of Czar Nicholas II of Russia. The second son of Alfonso XIII and Queen Ena, Jaime, also experienced a tragedy in childhood, becoming deaf because of a botched surgical operation. These very human tragedies no doubt gained sympathy for the royal family, even among critics of the monarchy. The king and queen had relatives on both sides of the First World War, making Spain's neutral stance an understandable choice during the conflict. The king used his international connections and the services of Spanish diplomats to intercede for the humane treatment of war captives on both sides of the carnage.

Despite prosperity and social stability, however, Spanish writers and intellectuals decried the self-serving hypocrisy of their elected leaders and the government's failure to enact true reform. Like diehard republicans, labor leaders, anarchists, religious leaders, and some military officers, Spain's intellectual elite saw a deep breach between the attitude of the government and the needs of the country as a whole. The essayist José Ortega y Gasset (1883–1955), one of the country's leading intellectuals, defined the breach as a split between "official Spain" and "vital Spain" and saw little hope for its resolution. The various interest groups in "vital Spain" had lost faith in the constitutional monarchy and the parliamentary system that administered it. Increasingly they treated the government as irrelevant and pursued their goals by direct action, outside the system. In Ortega's analysis, the country lacked a central core of values and programs that could unite all Spaniards in a common cause. Spain had become a body without a spine – "invertebrate" – with the vital forces outside the system tearing the body apart.

Although the anarchists were the most marginalized of the pressure groups alienated from the system, other groups were central to the country's future. In Catalonia, industrial leaders, middle-class lawyers, and workers had all suffered from the loss of Spain's last colonies in 1898. Their disaffection with the government coincided with a rising tide of regional pride that led to demands for more power to run their own affairs, and more respect for the rich history and literate culture of Catalonia.

Even the army, the bulwark of the restored Bourbon monarchy, began to move outside the system. Despite the greater sense of professionalism fostered by the service academies, the Spanish army had not performed well in the Cuban rebellions or the 1898 war with the United States. Humiliated and widely blamed for that defeat, army leaders at first relied on the protection of the Liberal Party and gained the right to bring charges of sedition against the press in 1907. In the absence of strong civilian leadership after 1912, army officers once again began to think of themselves as the best guarantors of the integrity of the state.

From about 1916 on, army leaders reverted to the traditions of the early nineteenth century, favoring direct action to put an errant state back on track. They found an ally in the king himself, who had lost faith in the constitutional monarchy as well, though he was supposed to be its best guarantor. Alfonso XIII cultivated friendships with army officers and took a personal interest in the army's activities in Morocco – the last major foreign outpost in which Spain had an official position. For that interest, the king acquired the nickname "the Africanist."

The rebellion in Morocco quietened down during the First World War, but other problems continued to fester, despite the wartime prosperity of neutral Spain. Although the leaders of industry and banking profited handsomely during the war, along with some skilled workers, ordinary workers did not. Their wages stagnated, except in war-related industries such as coalmines and railroads, even as inflation eroded their standard of living. The middling ranks of army officers, as well as enlisted men, also saw their wages eroded by inflation. The government's decision to use wartime profits to pay off foreign debt, while laudable, lost the opportunity to modernize the economic infrastructure, and the country's economic leaders tended to spend their profits rather than investing in the future. Together, these characteristics meant that the Spanish economy was not well positioned to grow after the war.

The war also affected neutral Spain politically. The massive destruction elsewhere in Europe shattered whole populations, and traditional political structures and politicians had to bear the blame for the catastrophe. In that atmosphere of disillusion, the entry of the United States into the war in 1917, and President Woodrow Wilson's "Fourteen Points" for the reconstruction of Europe, opened a new range of possibilities for forces on the political left. In Spain, Wilson's support for "self-determination" encouraged Catalan separatists to renew their demands for autonomy. And the Russian Revolution of March 1917, which toppled Czar Nicholas II and put the republican Mensheviks in power, encouraged Spanish republicans to renew their push to oust Alfonso XIII.

Matters came to a head in the summer of 1917 as the war wound down and radical movements on the political left pushed for change all over Europe. In Spain, army officers in clandestine military unions (*juntas de defensa*) demanded government recognition to negotiate for better wages and rights, claiming to represent the nation much better than the traditional political parties did. The Liberal government could not mollify or quell the army's demands, and resigned. A large faction of the Conservatives, under Eduardo Dato, formed a new government more willing to compromise in order to retain army support, but unable to stop the erosion of central authority. With the Cortes out of session, republican politicians and business leaders in Catalonia organized support for an alternative legislative body, which met in Barcelona in mid-July, composed mostly of republicans and socialists, and denounced by Maura's Conservatives. Although the government declared the meeting illegal and disbanded the group, they vowed to meet again. In short, even duly elected political leaders had moved outside the official system, an ominous development for the future.

Labor leaders of both the UGT and the CNT chose the summer of 1917 to launch a "general strike," less for wages and working conditions than for political purposes, as a prelude to revolution. Radical republicans and socialists began making plans for a provisional government that would take power after a successful strike, following the examples of Russia in March and ongoing strikes all over Europe during the summer. In the event, the Spanish plan failed. Railroad workers went on strike on August 10, before national leaders had fully prepared. During the subsequent general strike on August 13–17, the republicans and even the CNT failed to support the action, no doubt sensing disaster. The army put down the strike with little opposition, but the government itself was in such disarray that it is hard to speak of a government victory.

The system of alternating power between elected representatives of one political party or another, under a constitutional monarchy, had clearly broken down. Even worse, none of the governments formed under Alfonso XIII had been able to solve the corrosive problems that divided Spaniards or to find a new sense of national purpose that would unite them. In the six years after the revolutionary summer of 1917, the king would attempt to find a new combination of government officials and policies that would make the system work again. Dissolving the traditional parties, he appointed political leaders willing to work together in non-partisan coalitions, focused on addressing the two most pressing problems facing Spain: continuing labor unrest; and the renewal of the rebellion in Morocco. Although able men such as Antonio Maura would form a series of such governments, the problems continued to fester. Moreover, a series of well-organized interest groups continued to grow on the fringes of the official political system. Socialists, communists loyal to the Russian Bolshevik Revolution of November 1917, anarchists, regional separatists, and various republican groupings on the left, and Carlists and traditional Catholic groupings on the right, all distrusted the government.

The labor problem was worst in Barcelona, descending periodically into something resembling open warfare, as the various factions hired thugs and gunmen (*pistoleros*) to carry their grievances into the street. The strife involved not only management versus labor, but also a range of mutually hostile labor organizations. Company unions (*sindicatos libres*) and unions organized by the Catholic Church were the most conservative, working for better wages and working conditions but not for radical political change. Industrial unions (*sindicatos únicos*) organized by the CNT represented all the workers in a factory, rather than separating the workers by occupational specialty. They were the most radical of the groups, committed to anarchist goals.

The socialist union, the UGT, had much less presence in Catalonia, and was split – like its political wing, the PSOE – by the international blow-up between socialists and communists. With the Bolsheviks firmly in control in Russia, the Third or Communist International

(Comintern) held its first gathering in March 1919. To join the Comintern, socialist parties had to accept a list of "Twenty-One Conditions" regarding their organization and goals, most notably to accept the leadership of Russia and to expel so-called "Social Democrats" who did not support the goal of communist revolution. In Spain, this would have meant the expulsion of iconic figures such as Pablo Iglesias, in many ways the father of Spanish socialism. When the PSOE majority rejected the "Twenty-One Conditions" in 1921, the minority split off and formed the Communist Party of Spain (PCE). In other countries – France, for example – the majority voted to accept the conditions, and the minority split off to form socialist parties. The net result of the debates centering on the Comintern led to a "red scare" that alarmed the middle classes everywhere and made them fear all labor agitation as revolutionary. Such an atmosphere heightened tensions surrounding negotiations for wages and working conditions. The Liberal politician Eduardo Dato fell to an assassin's bullet in March 1921 – a reminder of the persistence of violent direct action in the political sphere.

The renewal of rebellion in Morocco became a similarly intractable problem in the aftermath of the First World War. In 1919, the dynamic rebel leader Abd-el-Krim and his followers attacked Spanish *presidios* in Melilla and Ceuta, demanding independence from Spain and the formation of a republic. Even the new generation of Spanish officers found it difficult to overcome this new threat from the rebels, given the demoralization and anger among their own soldiers. Poorly paid conscripts complained about inferior rations and equipment, knowing that dishonest suppliers were getting rich at their expense. Young officers such as Francisco Franco y Bahamonde worked to remedy the defects and to recruit units of loyal Moroccans to Spanish service, at the same time imposing army discipline on the disgruntled conscripts. They had some success, but not enough.

Anxious to solve the Moroccan problem, General Manuel Fernández Silvestre led a huge Spanish force against Abd-el-Krim on July 21, 1921, at the battle of Anual. It was a complete disaster, with the deaths of 15,000 men. General Silvestre, closely linked to the king, died in the battle, which saved him from taking the blame. That honor fell to the military high commissioner, General Dámaso Berenguer, but the whole Spanish army felt the shame and humiliation of the catastrophic defeat.

For the next two years, politicians in the Cortes began to demand a full investigation of the disaster and to assess the responsibilities of everyone in charge, from army officers and government officials to the Prime Minister, even as the war in Morocco continued. The stain of defeat threatened to spread to the king himself, because of his close connections to the army high command and the Moroccan campaign. After acrimonious debate, the government finally appointed a "commission of responsibilities," set to meet in the fall of 1923. Despite growing national revulsion at the continuing cost of the war, the Liberal coalition government at the time also announced a new Moroccan initiative and a new round of conscriptions into the army. In response, the socialists began to organize another general strike, also set for the fall of 1923. The upcoming confrontation over the Moroccan war lurched toward a crisis during the summer of 1923, even as violent labor confrontations continued in Barcelona.

With the king and the government still in the unofficial summer capital of San Sebastián in the north, General Miguel Primo de Rivera issued a proclamation in Barcelona on September 13, calling for a change of government. As the captain-general in Catalonia, General Primo had won the support of the Catalan business elite. After years of labor upheaval, they were in no mood for a fresh round of political turmoil. Moreover, a new tariff agreement in 1922 promised a return to the prosperity of the war years, as long as the government could keep the lid on unrest. General Primo seemed to offer a hope for stability, which the governments since 1917 had failed to deliver.

General Primo traveled from Barcelona to Madrid by train, and Alfonso XIII joined him there from San Sebastián. At their meeting, the king asked General Primo to form a government in the time-honored tradition of earlier nineteenth-century military proclamations. Instead of forming a new civilian government under the existing constitutional structure, however, General Primo suspended the Cortes and the constitution of 1876 and announced the formation of a military government to restore order. He announced that this would mean only a "brief parenthesis" in the history of the constitutional monarchy, but it was nonetheless Spain's first military dictatorship, and it had come to power under the auspices of the king. General Primo's takeover followed the precedent of Benito Mussolini's "march on Rome" in October 1922, which had left King Victor Emmanuel II on the throne of Italy. Alfonso XIII's acquiescence in Primo's dictatorship served a useful short-term goal from the point of view of the king and the army: it derailed the campaign to determine "responsibilities" that would surely have damaged both the army high command and the king. In the long term, however, the king's actions fatally undermined his position as a constitutional monarch.

None of that mattered in 1923, however. Weary of strikes, street warfare, bad news from Morocco, and sterile political haggling, most Spaniards greeted General Primo's takeover with overwhelming support. A military dictatorship governed Spain from September 1923 until December 1925, and, because Primo barred both the Liberals and the Conservatives from power, both parties collapsed. In their place, he organized a single party, the Patriotic Union (Unión Patriótica) in April 1924 and had his military governors recruit civilian politicians to join it. Many of them did so, including supporters of Antonio Maura, some socialists, most Carlists, and bureaucrats of various political loyalties. They were more interested in helping to find a workable political system for Spain than in a principled rejection of the military takeover. Like the king, however, their acquiescence tied them inextricably to the regime.

Consciously following the example of Mussolini's Italy, Primo tackled the labor problem by separating demands for higher wages, better working conditions, and a voice in industrial organization from the more radical political demands favored by the extreme left of the labor movement. To address the non-political demands of the working classes, Primo worked with the socialist leaders of the PSOE and the UGT to form twenty-seven corporations that included representatives of workers, employers, and the government. Like Mussolini's corporate state, Primo's initiatives enjoyed moderate success among the more pragmatic of the working-class leaders. To isolate the radical labor leaders, he outlawed the CNT. It did not disappear, however, but instead went underground and moved toward even more extreme positions. In July 1927, a group called the FAI (Federación Anarquista Ibérica) emerged as an offshoot of the CNT, dedicated to violent direct action in the tradition of the bomb-throwing anarchists of several decades earlier. Primo's support among Catalan businessmen eroded slightly when he made clear that he would not support demands for regional autonomy. Nonetheless, as long as he could maintain stability, they had little reason to abandon the regime.

Primo's greatest achievement was the victorious end of the war in Morocco. Beginning in the summer of 1925, he worked with General Henri-Philippe Pétain of France to mount a joint Hispano-French expedition against Abd-el-Krim. Francisco Franco, rapidly rising through the army ranks, helped to organize it. The joint force landed in North Africa in early September 1925, and Abd-el-Krim surrendered to French forces in mid-June of the following year. Support for Primo and his government rose to its greatest height. On the strength of that support, Primo backed away from his promise of providing only a "brief parenthesis" in the history of the constitutional monarchy and moved to make his regime permanent.

The Patriotic Union and the industrial corporations were already in place as bases for a new political system. In addition, in December 1925, even before the victory in Morocco, Primo had appointed civilians to replace army officers in governing the state. The king authorized the change publicly, thus tying himself even closer to the regime. On the strength of the victory in Morocco,

Primo held a plebiscite to ask citizens to approve a Civilian Directory to govern Spain, plus the formation of a national assembly to write a new constitution. The vote in September 1926 included the total adult population, both male and female, and gained the approval of nearly two-thirds of them. An appointed National Advisory Assembly then proceeded to write the new constitution, which the king and another plebiscite approved.

In the heady economic atmosphere of the late 1920s, the government invested heavily in public works such as railroads, irrigation schemes, and roads, finally paying attention to the modernization of the infrastructure that previous governments had neglected. Foreign investments helped to finance these ambitious programs, as did monopoly corporations such as CAMPSA, which controlled gasoline. Overall, the regime could boast that it had restored social and economic order and had drawn the middle ranks of labor into willing cooperation with the government. Politicians of various political stripes, but mostly from the center and right of the political spectrum, also participated willingly in Primo's regime, in part because it provided the only avenue of open participation in public life. That was both its strength and its weakness.

Despite the outward appearance of success, however, the regime had merely papered over some of the widest cracks in Spanish life. The various political groups outside official circles continued to meet quietly and organize support. Although the PSOE cooperated with the regime until 1929, various other socialist and republican groups remained in quiet opposition. More than a few disillusioned monarchists joined their ranks. Catalan nationalists, thwarted in their hopes for regional autonomy, also moved into opposition. Moreover, many Spaniards who had welcomed Primo's intervention as a "brief parenthesis," would not accept a permanent corporate state. The hierarchy of the Roman Catholic Church, initially in favor of the regime, resented its lack of support for Catholic trade unions. Many intellectual leaders, including members of university faculties and their students, disapproved of the regime on principle, inspired by the philosopher and novelist Miguel de Unamuno. The Scholarly University Federation (Federación Universitaria Escolar, or FUE), formed in 1927, provided a focus for their discontent.

Opposition to the regime also came from quarters closely allied to the dictatorship. In 1926, a remnant of the old Liberal Party staged an unsuccessful uprising (the "Sanjuanada"), and, in January 1929, José Sánchez Guerra led a rising of disgruntled Conservatives. The army put down both disturbances with little trouble, but the mere fact that they occurred put the regime on notice that it had failed to achieve a national consensus. Even the army, which had spawned Primo's regime, contained officers opposed to Primo, who were just biding their time, among them some who had lost confidence in the monarchy as well as in the dictatorship.

A student strike in January 1930 marked the beginning of the end, suggesting the breadth of opposition to the regime. When both the king and the army leaders signaled their withdrawal of support from Primo's government, he resigned, leaving behind a complicated legacy. Despite the pacification of Morocco and the restoration of social and economic order, Primo had deliberately destroyed the parliamentary basis of the constitutional monarchy.

By shattering the Liberal and Conservative parties, and by drawing many of their leading figures into his government, he destroyed the center of the Spanish political spectrum. In opposition to his regime, radical groupings both to the left and to the right grew stronger and more resolute during the dictatorship. The attempt to create a national consensus, which Primo had worked so hard to achieve, had not only failed: it had left Spanish political life more polarized than ever.

FIGURE 6.1 Paper factory in Prat de Llobregat (Barcelona), in the early twentieth century, illustrating the industrial power of Catalonia.

FIGURE 6.2 *Comida de bodas en Bergantiños*, by Fernando Álvarez de Sotomayor (1875–1960). Despite the changes in Spanish society with industrialization, local traditions remained strong, especially in rural areas. This wedding meal in the coastal town of Bergantiños (Galicia), dates from about 1900, but the scene and the people would have looked very much the same 300 years earlier.

FIGURE 6.3 The building in Barcelona known as "La Pedrera" (the stone quarry) by the architect Antoni Gaudí, is a classic example of Catalan modernism. Built in 1906–10 for the industrialist Pere Milà, its undulating lines continue to astonish visitors and residents alike.

7

The struggle for the Spanish soul: Republic, civil war, and dictatorship

∼

After Primo's dictatorship ended in January 1930, the king asked General Dámaso Berenguer to form a new government, based on the constitution of 1876, in an attempt to reestablish the constitutional monarchy. Berenguer had served as the military high commissioner at the time of the disastrous battle of Anual in 1921. His appointment to head the government signaled the king's continuing support for the army, but it can hardly have inspired confidence in the country as a whole. In a play on words that is typical of Spanish political humor, Berenguer's government was dubbed the "dictablanda" or "soft dictatorship," as opposed to the hard dictatorship (*dictadura/dicta-dura*) under Primo. Berenguer lasted just over a year in office, during which the republican opposition organized support. In the Pact of San Sebastián in August 1930, republican leaders joined with Catalan nationalists and the Socialist Party (PSOE) to plan a provisional government after the ouster of the monarchy. Military leaders sympathetic to the republican cause staged an uprising in Jaca (Aragon) in December 1930. After forces loyal to King Alfonso put down the rising, the king ordered its leaders executed, creating martyrs – military martyrs – for the republican opposition.

The king dismissed General Berenguer in February 1931 and replaced him with Admiral Juan Bautista Aznar, no doubt hoping that the navy leadership would prove more steadfast than the army had been. Aznar called elections for municipal officials on April 12, 1931 – the first elections under the 1876 constitution since 1923. In Spain's largest cities, republican candidates won a majority of the votes, although their victory was not a landslide. Nonetheless, the king knew all too well what the vote portended. Joyous republicans took to the streets to celebrate the victory, and their leaders proclaimed Spain a republic on April 14, announcing a provisional government under the leadership of Niceto Alcalá Zamora. When army leaders made clear that they would no longer support King Alfonso, on the night of April 14 he simply left Spain without abdicating, as his grandmother Isabel II had done in 1868. Queen Victoria Eugenia also went into exile – separately from her husband. Their marriage had become increasingly strained over the years, not least because of the king's numerous extramarital affairs.

The Second Republic – dubbed "the Pretty Girl" ("la niña bonita") by its supporters – faced distrust and charges of illegitimacy by its detractors from the outset. The provisional government had not been elected by a national mandate, but had simply decreed a republic as a result of municipal elections. It would be months before its leaders put in place the machinery to legitimize its authority. In the interim, Alcalá Zamora's provisional government nonetheless moved swiftly to establish the tenor of the new regime. From April 14 to June 28, 1931, the government issued decrees touching on a wide range of issues, including land reform and the relationship of the government to the army and the Roman Catholic Church. On June 28, 1931, Spaniards went to the polls to elect representatives to a Cortes that would prepare a new constitution. The task was finished on December 10 of that year but the Cortes continued to sit as a legislature for the next two years – in other words, far exceeding their electoral mandate. To their enemies, that provided additional evidence of the illegality of the republic.

Alcalá Zamora had resigned as Prime Minister in October 1931, when the Cortes enacted legislation to place church financing and religious orders under state control. Although the majority in the Cortes justified this action as necessary for good management, the church hierarchy and its supporters viewed it as an attack and a gratuitous insult. Manuel Azaña took on the role of Prime Minister and therefore of the head of government. Under the new constitution, Alcalá Zamora became the President, technically the head of state, but with a largely ceremonial role.

Azaña, a lawyer and intellectual with a long résumé in politics but never an office-holder, had a coherent and ambitious vision for the new republican Spain. In addition to separating church and state, he aimed at no less than the resolution of conflicts that had bedeviled Spanish politicians for a century. The solutions he favored fell generally on the left of the republican political spectrum. One problem was that the army had grown too large and costly for a country at peace and with almost no overseas responsibilities. To reduce the top-heavy command structure, Azaña's government provided incentives for early retirement. Many – perhaps most – of those who accepted the offer were confirmed republicans. Many of the officers who remained in their posts, it is fair to say, were willing to support the republic only so long as it appeared able to govern.

The Azaña government also addressed the problem of land reform, moving toward expropriating unproductive private holdings and redistributing them to land-hungry peasants. The government also implemented an ambitious program of investment in irrigation and fertilizing schemes, aiming to make Spanish agriculture both more equitable and more productive. The programs got off to a slow start but huge numbers of peasants nonetheless welcomed the initiatives, finally seeing a chance to realize their dreams of landholding. Azaña's government also gained the loyalty of Catalonia and the Basque provinces by ceding power over many functions of government to local authorities. These included finance, education, social policy, and the maintenance of public order, satisfying long-standing demands by regional political leaders.

From the outset, the Second Republic worked toward the ambitious goal of transforming Spanish society. Two key elements in the government's program were the provision of subsidies for the construction of schools and the extension of literate culture into the remotest corners of rural Spain. By the end of 1932, the Education Minister could boast that nearly 10,000 new schools had been built, and more than 15,000 teachers had applied for government-sponsored courses to improve their knowledge and teaching skills. Idealistic university students and others, as well as theatre troupes such as the poet Federico García Lorca's "La Barraca," brought examples of high culture to small, isolated towns. They also brought examples of popular modern entertainment such as silent films. Overall, the government's goal was not simply to raise the cultural level of the masses, but to make them more politically aware and less resistant to change.

The maintenance of public order proved to be the thorniest problem faced by the Second Republic, as disgruntled factions of both right and left decided to test the government's authority. In December 1931, an anarchist uprising at Castilblanco (Badajoz) challenged the republic from the left. In August 1932 army officers under General Sanjurjo issued a proclamation against the republic. The army as a whole, however, remained loyal to the republic and put down Sanjurjo's challenge on the right just as it had put down the anarchist uprising on the left. The army also crushed another leftist rising at Casas Viejas in January 1933. Although Azaña's government, with the army's support, withstood these challenges, his administration was clearly losing the confidence of the public by the end of summer 1933. Azaña and his government resigned on September 12 of that year. When no alternative leader was able to form a government, Diego Martínez Barrio agreed to form a caretaker government to prepare for new elections.

Spanish voters went to the polls again on November 19, and this time they voted for a government to the right of center in the republican spectrum. As the new Prime Minister, Alejandro Lerroux formed a coalition government aiming to reverse much of the legislation passed under Azaña's leadership. By doing so, he hoped to keep conservative forces from moving outside the political process, but without fatally alienating forces on the left. If he succeeded, he could bolster the image of the Spanish Republic as an effective parliamentary system, in which both left and right had a place, but he faced a very difficult task. Adolf Hitler had come to power in Germany in the first months of 1933 and was rapidly undermining German democracy. Elsewhere in Europe as well, extralegal movements on both right and left were destabilizing parliamentary governments, their support fueled by the spreading effects of the global collapse of financial markets and the resultant economic depression.

Even before the 1933 election in Spain, forces on the right had gathered strength. Monarchists, of course, were opposed to the republic on principle. Antonio Goicoechea organized one monarchist group – Spanish Renewal (Renovación Española) – early in 1933. Lerroux's government lifted the ban on another monarchist group in April 1934: José Calvo Sotelo's Spanish Action (Acción Española), which was the remnant of Primo de Rivera's Patriotic Union. Primo's eldest son, named José Antonio, organized the Spanish Falange (Falange Española) in October 1933 in conscious imitation of fascist movements elsewhere. The Falange merged early in 1934 with a right-wing labor organization known as the Committees of the National Syndicalist Offensive (Juntas de Ofensiva Nacional Sindicalista, or JONS). Their strong advocacy of labor justice, coupled with José Antonio's effective rhetoric, gained the growing movement widespread support on the right, outside government circles. In the army, leaders skeptical of the republic found a voice in the Spanish Military Union (Unión Militar Española), founded late in 1933, one of whose leaders was General Emilio Mola.

Christian Democrats had helped to put Lerroux in power, but they did not form part of his coalition until October 1, 1934, when three members of CEDA (Confederación Española de Derechas Autónomas) joined the government. To republicans on the left, this was an intolerable sign that Lerroux had caved in to conservative pressure. In response, the socialists called a general strike on October 5, hoping to bring down the government. Miners in Asturias launched their strike on October 4, and an armed coalition of socialists, communists, and anarchists briefly captured the city of Oviedo, posing the most serious challenge yet to Lerroux's government. In Catalonia, Lluis Companys proclaimed the "Republic of Catalonia within the Federal Republic of Spain" on October 6, using the occasion of the general strike to push for regional autonomy. The government called upon army leaders to put down all of these rebellious actions, which they did. The chief military commander in Barcelona, General Domingo Batet, remained cool-headed and restored order with a minimum of fuss. Elsewhere, the army dealt harshly with the rebels, particularly in Asturias, where Francisco Franco, the youngest general in the Spanish army, led a force of soldiers from Spanish Morocco and foreign legionnaires from North Africa. The leaders of the diverse uprisings ended up in prison.

Leftist politicians of all stripes saw the repression as a reason to join forces against Lerroux's government, even though the republican left, and especially the socialists, could hardly deny their role in provoking that repression. In the summer of 1935, a coalition of Spanish socialists and communists formed a Popular Front movement, coinciding with, and reinforced by, the program of the seventh Congress of the Comintern. They pledged to work together at the next election to shift the government back to the left. As Lerroux's ability to govern steadily weakened, his Minister of Agriculture, Manuel Giménez Fernández, nonetheless carried out more land redistribution than in the previous three and a half years of the republic combined, an ironic development. A financial scandal involving members of Lerroux's inner circle in late October accomplished what the leftist uprisings had failed to do. The government fell, and a caretaker replacement organized new elections for February 16, 1936.

Given the constitutional structure of the republic, a small shift in the popular vote could mean a substantial change in the composition of the Cortes. Individuals ran as part of a slate of candidates; the winning slate in any given locality then sent 80 percent of that locality's delegates to the Cortes, regardless of the margin of victory in the elections. That assured the new government of a workable majority in the legislature, but it did not necessarily reflect the popular vote. On February 16, 1936, the Popular Front coalition of republicans, socialists, and communists won control of the government, even though they garnered less than 50 percent of the vote nationwide. As the coalition leaders had agreed before the election, Manuel Azaña then formed a government solely of republicans, in part to counter fears of a radical change in policy.

The early actions of Azaña's new government did little to counter such fears. Less than a week after the election, the government granted amnesty to everyone involved in the uprisings of 1934. The government also supported regional movements toward autonomy by sponsoring plebiscites on the issue in Galicia and the Basque provinces. The suspicion that the government might willingly dismantle the country alarmed leaders on the right, particularly those outside the political process and in the army.

Meanwhile, maneuvers within the Cortes aimed to put more authority into fewer hands, to ensure that the coalition would be able to govern. The socialist leader, Indalecio Prieto, organized a vote to oust Niceto Alcalá Zamora as President of the Republic, the post he had held since 1931. Azaña replaced him as President, and a friend of Azaña's, the Galician Santiago Casares Quiroga, took over as Prime Minister. The net result of this cynical maneuver was to restrict the ruling coalition to a small group of republicans and socialists, which weakened support for the government within the Cortes as a whole.

Even worse, despite its legal authority, the new government could not keep order. Wildcat strikes, open clashes between leftist and rightist gangs in Spain's large cities, and sporadic attacks on churches and members of the clergy continued through the spring and early summer of 1936. In an attempt to disable the Falange, the government had arrested José Antonio Primo de Rivera in March, and moved him from Madrid to Alicante in June, where he would pose less of a threat.

The republic's security forces, the Assault Guards, could do little to quell the violence, and the government did not trust the traditional forces of order, the army and the Civil Guard, to move against rightist disturbances. Street violence in the cities continued unabated, and the government seemed powerless to stop it. In the countryside, legally sanctioned confiscations of unused land gave way to extralegal takeovers by bands of armed peasants, and landowners suspected that the republican government had no interest in stopping them.

In the army, a small group of determined plotters organized support for a military coup, claiming the necessity to defend the nation from the possibility of disintegration and the effects of incompetent civilian rule. General Mola led the plotters and planned very carefully, to avoid repeating the failure of similar plots in the 1920s and early 1930s. Several key commanders joined the plot, but Francisco Franco, then posted in the Canary Islands, cautiously held back as planning continued and rumors circulated that a military coup was imminent. The chaos in Madrid reached a critical point in the second week of July. On the evening of July 12, right-wing assassins killed José Castillo, a lieutenant in the Republican Assault Guards. After midnight, the left had its revenge. During a sweep of possible suspects for Castillo's murder, a contingent of the Assault Guards arrested José Calvo Sotelo, the leader of Acción Española. By morning, his bullet-riddled body had been dumped at the entrance to a local cemetery. With Calvo Sotelo dead, and José Antonio jailed in Alicante, there were no civilian right-wing leaders of sufficient stature to replace them. The army plotters decided that their moment had arrived.

With Franco at last committed to the plot, the rebellion began in Morocco at 5 p.m. on Friday, July 17. Mola proclaimed the overthrow of the Popular Front in Spain the next day. Similar proclamations in the past, dating back to 1820, had succeeded almost immediately, when the governments had caved in. Casares Quiroga was not willing to do that. Instead, he resigned on the evening of July 18. Diego Martínez Barrio took over as Prime

Minister and tried unsuccessfully to negotiate with the rebels. He could not trust the armed forces to defend the government, but he was not willing to arm the citizenry to fight the rebellion. He resigned as well. José Giral, a university professor of chemistry, became Prime Minister on July 19 and ordered state arsenals to hand out arms to the various militias associated with workers' unions and political parties. What began as a military rebellion thus became a civil war, and all over Spain militants and ordinary citizens alike took sides.

It is not an exaggeration to say that all of the anger, frustration, class antagonism, and other corrosive forces that had eaten away at Spanish society for at least a century spilled over into the conflict, making the Spanish Civil War one of the worst internal confrontations in European history. Individuals defined their true loyalties based on religious adherence or rejection, political ideology, economic class, occupation, family history, or a combination of factors. Many citizens, however, had little choice but to adapt to the side that held control of the town or region where they lived. Others fled the control of one side in order to fight for the other, risking their lives in the process. Like civil wars everywhere, the Spanish Civil War shattered families and communities. Neighbors turned on each other through sincere conviction, fear, personal animosity, ambition, cowardice, or any number of other motives. Alongside the suppressed resentments and hatreds of the past, the civil war created a new set of horrors to remember.

The war continued for nearly three years, exacting an enormous toll on the people of Spain. The rebels were a well-organized military force, with most of the army on their side. Nonetheless, the republican government controlled the resources of the state and most of the navy, and could claim moral superiority in the international community. It was not clear at the outset which side had the better chance to succeed. The rebels immediately captured about one-third of the country, with strongholds in Seville in the south, Old Castile and Galicia in the north and northwest, and Navarre and Zaragoza in the northeast. The republican government held Madrid and nearly all of central Spain, from Extremadura to the Mediterranean coast. In the first four months of the war, the rebels, dubbed the nationalists, launched assaults in every direction, gaining much ground. They were not able to capture Madrid, however, despite a fierce offensive in early November 1936. The fiery speeches of Dolores Ibárruri, dubbed "La Pasionaria" (the passion flower), inspired the defenders of the capital. In addition, volunteers from elsewhere in Europe and from America came to Spain to aid the republican cause, contributing to the successful defense of Madrid. These International Brigades, named for heroes in their own national histories, also bolstered the image of the republic as a bastion of democratic freedom against the fascist threat exemplified by the nationalists.

The democratic governments in Europe and the United States also recognized that threat but hoped to avoid having the Spanish conflict spill over into a wider confrontation. Great Britain and France sponsored a non-intervention movement in the summer of 1936, monitored by a committee in London, and twenty-seven states eventually signed up, pledging not to aid either side. The signatories included fascist Italy and Nazi Germany, though it is clear that their adherence was nothing more than a smokescreen to mask more or less open support for the nationalists. German and Italian planes had already carried troops from Morocco to Spain at the start of the rebellion. The United States passed its own Act of Neutrality on May 1, 1937, but private companies such as the Texas Company (later Texaco) continued to sell petroleum products to the nationalists. Similarly, private companies elsewhere followed their economic interests, supplying one side or the other with munitions and other war material, as long as the buyers had the cash to pay for them.

Alone among the democracies, Mexico under President Lázaro Cárdenas openly sent aid to the republic. The other international ally of the republic was the USSR under Josef Stalin, and his support aimed less to aid the Spanish republic than to protect the Soviet Union and the Communist International. Russian aid began to arrive in the form of arms and advisers in early October 1936, and they helped to arrange the recruitment and organization of the International Brigades. Eventually, Russia would send about 2,000 men to Spain in the first two years of the war, about half of them as combatants and the rest as political operatives. In return, the republic sent all the gold in the Bank of Spain to Moscow in November 1936, both for safekeeping and to pay for the Russian aid.

After the rebels failed to capture Madrid in the fall of 1936, they turned their attention elsewhere. Nationalist forces pushed across the south from Seville to Málaga by February 1937, and launched a major offensive in the north in the spring and summer of 1937. General Franco, by then head of the nationalist forces, had received major reinforcements in the spring of 1937, when Mussolini sent thousands of Italian soldiers to his aid, after their successful conquest of Ethiopia. Called "volunteers" to avoid violating the non-intervention pact, the Italian forces suffered heavy casualties at the battle of Guadalajara in March 1937, where, ironically, some of their opponents were true volunteers on the republican side. During the civil war as a whole, Mussolini would eventually send some 120,000 troops to Spain, and their dead and wounded would number at least 50,000. Germany sent 20,000–30,000 troops in all, but rotated them in and out through the Condor Legion of the German air force. By so doing, Hitler could provide combat experience for as many men as possible without committing them all at the same time.

A crucial turning point in the northern offensive came in April 1937, with the bombing of the small Basque town of Guernica by the Condor Legion. Several planes from the Italian air force also participated in the raid. The town of around 5,000 inhabitants held a munitions factory and a strategic bridge on the way to Bilbao; it also held enormous historical significance for the Basque population. The great oak tree of Guernica was a powerful symbol of Basque identity and aspirations to autonomous rule. The incendiary bombs launched against Guernica on the afternoon of April 26 destroyed 70 percent of the town and killed some 250 people – about 5 percent of the population. The bridge, the munitions factory, and the oak tree remained standing, as the nationalists had requested. In the face of international outrage at the bombing, as well as among his own Carlist and Basque supporters, General Franco long denied publicly that he had known about it in advance, much less requested it. Nonetheless, historians eventually turned up overwhelming evidence proving his responsibility for the raid.

Franco's nationalist troops captured Bilbao in June 1937, Santander in August, and Gijón in October. The bombing of Guernica, designed to weaken resistance to the nationalist offensive in the north, succeeded in that aim. Bilbao surrendered without a fight, and historians have discovered persuasive evidence that the Basque Nationalist Party (PNV) secretly cooperated with the nationalists and with Italian forces in the north to expedite the nationalist victory and thus prevent further damage to their region. The PNV betrayal of the republic that had granted the Basques autonomous rule illustrates the complicated nature of the Spanish Civil War. Outsiders could define the conflict in simple terms of nationalist versus republican or fascism versus democratic freedom. Insiders experienced the surreal complexity of hatreds and multi-layered loyalties and animosities. True believers on both sides might set aside their doubts in favor of a united front against the enemy. Honest men and women had to face the unvarnished anguish of their situation, as their country tore itself apart.

Republican forces continually lost ground to the nationalists in 1938, despite several determined campaigns. The nationalists pushed eastward across central Spain, reaching the Mediterranean in mid-April south of Barcelona, isolating Catalonia from the corridor linking Madrid with Valencia. Republican forces launched a major counter-offensive from July to November, known as the battle of the Ebro. In the middle of this crucial juncture for the republic, Soviet aid ceased. Great

Britain under Neville Chamberlain had sanctioned the Nazi takeover of the Sudetenland in Czechoslovakia in September 1938. Stalin knew that it was only a matter of time before he would have to face German aggression as well. By withdrawing his support for the Spanish republic, he hoped to postpone that eventuality by adhering to the non-intervention pact and removing a source of irritation to Hitler.

After breaking the republican resistance along the Ebro, the nationalists were able to conquer Catalonia between late December 1938 and late February 1939, at which point Great Britain and France recognized General Franco as the leader of Spain. The civil war was all but over. Despite a desperate resistance in Madrid by the remnants of the republican government, nationalist troops entered the capital at the end of March. The United States recognized the Franco government on April 1, 1939, a month after Britain and France had done so.

The timetable of military actions in the Spanish Civil War tells only part of the story, however. While Spanish and foreign troops fought on the battlefields, another set of struggles took place in the country at large. At the beginning of the military revolt, civilians ended up willy-nilly on one side or the other, few of them having the luxury of making a conscious choice. Thereafter, both sides worked to mobilize civilian support in the areas under their control. For the nationalists, this meant organizing a stable, effective government that would end the turmoil associated with the republic. General Franco's background as an astute military leader stood him in good stead as he established control, first over territory, and then over the citizenry in that territory. A few days after the rising on July 18, 1936, a Committee of National Defense met in Burgos and transferred power to Franco, both over the military forces and as head of the government that the nationalists had proclaimed. By October, he had gone beyond that mandate to sign himself the head of state. He organized a military government and consciously drew the various strands of anti-republican sentiment into his hands.

Most of the hierarchy of the Roman Catholic Church supported the uprising from the beginning, after the hostile treatment they had faced under the republic. All but two of the Spanish bishops signed a letter in July 1937 that defined the uprising as a modern crusade against godlessness. Nonetheless, a sizeable number of priests in the Basque areas aligned themselves with the movement for autonomy, and therefore with the republic. For Franco, the autonomy movements in the Basque areas and Catalonia were anathema. He defined the state as an indivisible unit and called upon the patriotism of the citizenry to support it and to resist outside influence, especially from the communist government of the Soviet Union.

Instead of the divisive and chaotic squabbles typical of parliamentary politics, Franco promised an orderly and effective government under a single party representing all legitimate interest groups. José Antonio Primo de Rivera had been killed by republican forces in Alicante on November 20, 1936. That gave Franco the opportunity to make José Antonio's movement the centerpiece of his government. Under its aegis, supporters could hope for the revolution promised by José Antonio – social justice, fair wages, and, above all, an orderly state in which to live one's life. In a brilliant stroke, Franco put José Antonio's sister,

Pilar Primo de Rivera, in charge of the Feminine Section of the Falange. Under her direction, women dedicated to Franco and his goals became a formidable force in Spanish society, distributing food, caring for the wounded, and organizing women all over Spain in support of the nationalist cause. When the most radical of the Falangists – the so-called "Old Shirts" – rebelled against the takeover of their movement, Franco crushed them and executed their leader, Manuel Hedilla.

Next, Franco solidified his support among the Carlists, incorporating them and turning the Spanish Falange and Labor Movement (FE y de las JONS) into the Traditionalist Spanish Falange and Labor Movement (FET y de las JONS). By April 1937, most of the elements of the new government were in place, defined by the promulgation of the Twenty-Seven Points of the Falange. Although the government's program of social justice aimed to appeal to the masses, Franco made clear that it would be centrally organized and implemented. The army, both old and new recruits, would fight the war, and the Falange would administer the country and organize support behind the lines. That formula proved to be remarkably effective for the nationalist cause as a whole.

The republican side also espoused social reform; indeed, many of the republic's most notable achievements aimed to give power to the powerless, land to the landless, and social justice to all. During the civil war, however, the aspirations unleashed by the republic proved to be divisive rather than unifying. Movements for regional autonomy clashed with the need for coordinated resistance to the rebellion. Workers' demands for freedom and higher wages clashed with the exigencies of wartime production.

Even worse, the most radical elements in the labor movement were opposed to the bourgeois republic on principle. These and other internal struggles on the republican side helped to ensure the nationalist victory.

The republican governments during the civil war lurched from crisis to crisis, trying to reconcile a set of irreconcilable objectives. The regional autonomy granted to Basques and Catalans worked against republican unity; to rescind it would lose their support altogether. The promise of social revolution had won the loyalty of many factions on the left. Nonetheless, to win the war required a postponement of those promises, at the risk of alienating many of the republic's most fervent supporters. Had the republican side promoted a true social revolution, however, the bourgeois democracies would surely have given up on non-intervention. With every new crisis, and the accumulation of bad news from the battlefield, the leadership of the republic shifted toward individuals who seemed to have the willpower necessary to fight the war.

The government of José Giral, composed only of republicans, lasted only until September 4, 1936, gutted by its inability to overcome the military rebellion. Francisco Largo Caballero, a labor leader from the UGT, then formed a predominantly socialist government, which supported social revolution as a means to ensure the loyalty of Spanish workers. Although republicans continued to participate in Largo's government, some of them were uneasy with the shift to the left. Anarchists from the CNT entered the government on November 4, 1936, and two days later the government left Madrid for the relative security of Valencia, as the nationalist offensive pounded the western defenses of the city. Although

General José Miaja and the Madrid Defense Committee, supported by the International Brigades, held off the
nationalists, the government of the republic remained in
Valencia, and communists joined a government for the
first time in Western Europe.

The following spring, the city of Barcelona erupted
in an attempted social revolution, which lasted most of
the first week in May 1937. The CNT, which virtually
controlled Aragon, and the revolutionary Marxist militia known as the POUM, led the rebellion, which turned
the streets of Barcelona into an internal war zone, far
from the battle lines between nationalists and republicans.
The English radical writer George Orwell had come to
Spain to fight for the POUM, exhilarated by the purity of
their cause. He lived through the rebellion in Barcelona
and later chronicled his bitter downward spiral into dis-
illusionment, fear, and despair in *Homage to Catalonia*.
Nonetheless, it is doubtful that he ever really understood
what was going on.

Largo Caballero had little choice but to crush the rebellion in Barcelona, alienating most of the republic's most
loyal supporters. Socialists, communists, and republicans
then united to vote Largo out of power on May 15, with
the communists taking the lead. Ironically, the Communist Party of Spain, which had more than 1 million members by then, was far less radical than some other leftist
factions. Its leaders were against collectivizing agriculture
and other revolutionary actions, arguing that it was more
important in the short term to mount an efficient war
effort.

On May 17, Juan Negrín, a socialist who enjoyed communist support, formed a new government, dedicated

above all to winning the war. He moved quickly against the leftist groups responsible for the rebellion in Barcelona, arresting the leaders of the POUM in mid-June. One of those leaders, Andrés Nin, died in government custody, undercutting the moral authority that justified the purge. On August 11, Negrín disbanded the CNT-controlled Council of Aragon and its revolutionary communes. Four days later, the government created a new intelligence agency called the SIM (Servicio de Investigación Militar), dedicated to identifying traitors to the republic, on both the left and the right.

In the peculiar context of the times, Negrín's government looked more moderate than many alternatives, because it favored central control and a postponement of revolution in aid of the war effort. Unquestionably, however, Negrín was pro-USSR and pro-communist. Moreover, to retain Soviet support, he often acceded to Russian pressure, either direct or channeled through the PCE. In the Soviet Union, Stalin was in the process of purging his own supporters at the same time, and news of those purges eroded support for Negrín's government among many sectors of the Spanish left.

As his support declined, Negrín dug in his heels. In October 1937 he crushed the revolutionary faction of the UGT and sent Largo Caballero to prison, after ousting him as the head of the union. Shortly thereafter, the anarchists left the government. Negrín moved the headquarters of the republic from Valencia to Barcelona at the end of October, as his support continued to erode. In April 1938, Indalecio Prieto, the last moderate socialist in the government, resigned, in opposition to the growing Russian influence over Negrín. In August 1938, the

last remaining republicans also resigned – the Basque
Manuel Irujo and the Catalan Artemio Aiguade. Thereafter, Negrín presided over a cabinet that was predominantly communist, with a minority of left-wing socialists.
When the Soviet Union ended its support for the republic
in September 1938, the Negrín government stood alone
as nationalist forces closed in.

The government fled across the Pyrenees to France
on February 6, 1939, a week before Franco closed the
frontier. The day after Britain and France recognized the
Franco government on February 27, Manuel Azaña, still
President of the Republic, resigned. Negrín went back
to Valencia, determined to continue the fight, appointing communists to most positions of command. Desperate to separate the republican cause from Negrín and
the communists, in Madrid Colonel Segismundo Casado
launched an uprising against the government on March
5, supported by factions of the republican army and civilian leaders such as Julián Besteiro of the PSOE. At the
same time, they tried to negotiate terms with the nationalists. Franco, by then approaching Madrid from the west,
had every reason to applaud the internal war among the
republicans, but he had no reason to accept anything less
than their unconditional surrender.

The war took a terrible toll. In 1930, Spain had a population of 23.7 million; in 1940, the number stood at 25.9
million, but those figures hide the horrors of the war
and its aftermath. At least half a million Spaniards died
between 1936 and 1943. According to one careful esti-
mate, about 100,000 of those deaths occurred in battle. The rest were due to air raids (10,000), disease and
malnutrition (50,000), and executions and reprisals on

both sides. In the republican zones, militants killed some 20,000 people for political reasons, among them about 6,800 priests, 1,000 Civil Guards, and 2,000 members of the Falange. The rest were ordinary citizens of various political stripes, left as well as right.

In the nationalist zones, the toll was far higher, but, with rare exceptions, the nationalists targeted only enemies on the other side of the struggle. In addition to summary executions during the war, a Tribunal of Political Responsibilities had already begun to identify more "enemies of Spain" as Franco's troops entered Madrid in late March 1939. From 1939 to 1943, an estimated 200,000 republican prisoners died, some by execution, others from disease. It is not clear if a republican victory would have been any more merciful to its enemies. The great tragedy on the republican side was that they sometimes killed their own as well, leaving a legacy of bitterness and recrimination that continues into the present.

For three decades after the end of the Spanish Civil War, a sense of helplessness fueled the internal divisions on the left. That is how long the victor in that war, General Francisco Franco, held power in Spain. Although the Western democracies recognized him as a dictator, none would move against him. Inside Spain, substantial portions of the citizenry agreed with the aims of his regime. Even those who hated him and nearly everything he represented – at least in retrospect – did not want another civil war. It is necessary to understand how the regime functioned to appreciate its extraordinary longevity.

Franco himself, born in 1892, was not a prepossessing individual, though he distinguished himself early in his army career for personal bravery in the Moroccan wars and for an innate ability to command. By the time the military rebellion broke out in July 1936, Franco had become the youngest general in any of the European armed forces – in fact, the youngest general since Napoleon. After he took control of the uprising, he developed a set of positions that would define his regime. National unity served as the keystone of the structure, in which divisive politics had no place. In fact, Franco saw democracy, socialism, anarchism, communism, and even freemasonry as foreign movements alien to the authentic character of Spain. Instead of political parties, his dictatorship fostered citizen identity through families and local communities, the Roman Catholic Church, and the workplace. The regime respected the rights of private property and favored capitalism, although, as we shall see, it dabbled in state management of the economy as a matter of necessity.

For most of Franco's long dictatorship, the secretary-general of the Falange supervised the administration of the country. Syndicates, encompassing both workers and employers, replaced labor unions of all stripes, governed by the Work Charter (Fuero del trabajo) of 1938. In January 1940, Franco gave the Falange control of the syndicates as well, by the Law of Syndical Unity. By the Law of the Cortes in 1942, he reestablished the Cortes as an advisory body, clearly subservient to the interests of the regime. Franco served as both head of state and head of government, advised by a Council of Ministers, and the Cortes reverted to the passive role it had held under the Bourbon monarchy of the eighteenth century.

Although some historians argue that Franco was as much a fascist as Mussolini or Hitler, he clearly lacked the charisma to build a cult of personality around himself, even had he wished to do so. Above all, he was a military officer, an anti-communist, and – he would later claim – a monarchist. He often described his regime as an "organic democracy," adopting a traditional term but stripping it of its traditional meaning. Political scientists, while recognizing the regime as a dictatorship, struggled to fit it into the standard mold of totalitarian dictatorships such as those of Nazi Germany and Soviet Russia. In 1964, the political scientist Juan Linz defined a new category, the authoritarian regime, to characterize Spain. Scholars since then have adopted the phrase to describe other modern regimes as well.

Several characteristics define the authoritarian regime. Unlike totalitarian states, Franco's regime did not try to foster active citizen participation in controlled political activities. There were few mass rallies, and, once the regime was established, it aimed at passive acquiescence on the part of the citizenry, rather than active participation. Moreover, the regime devoted few resources toward policing thought. Instead, the leadership relied on the power of traditional institutions to maintain social stability and to shape succeeding generations.

The Roman Catholic Church formed the cornerstone of the regime's traditional structure. After the hammering that the established church had suffered, arguably since the nineteenth century, the hierarchy was happy to accept the role of a staunch ally of General Franco. The regime also supported other traditional forces such as the military establishment; the nobility; the Carlists; and the economic elites in agriculture, industry, and banking. Individuals in these institutions were generally free to pursue their own interests, as long as they did not oppose the regime. Together with the family, the church, and the labor syndicates, these traditional institutions provided social and economic stability, and thus passive acquiescence toward the regime, even on the part of its enemies.

Within the regime, Franco tolerated and even encouraged various interest groups to compete for attention and support. Unlike a totalitarian state, in which such internal conflict tends to be rare or spasmodic, the competing voices in the Franco regime allowed it to change in response to changing conditions, but never so abruptly as to destabilize the structure as a whole. Moreover, the internal competition ensured that no one cadre of leaders could ever become a threat to Franco's control. That, of course, is the same principle that effective monarchs had used in the past, from Fernando and Isabel in the fifteenth century to Carlos III in the eighteenth.

The entry paths into the elite of the Franco regime were fairly open, varied, and unpredictable. In other words, aspiring leaders did not have to belong to the Falange or enter the army in order to succeed. Most of the men who rose to the top had law degrees. Others were educators, or had trained in economics or other technical fields. If Franco decided that he needed their expertise, he appointed them to positions of authority and supported them as long as they were successful.

Overall, unlike totalitarian states, the regime did not worry about the travels of ordinary citizens, as long as they did not oppose the regime openly. They could move from place to place, or emigrate, if they saw fit, without meeting government opposition. In fact, as the population grew, the regime actively encouraged temporary or permanent emigration as a way to relieve pressure on the economy and to provide a source of outside income. This was one of the most striking differences between totalitarian regimes and the authoritarian regime defined by Juan Linz.

Overall, Linz proposed that the plurality and tolerated opposition of an authoritarian regime made it more flexible than a democracy or a totalitarian regime, neither of which can change much without losing their essential character. An authoritarian regime, according to Linz, could shift either toward democracy or toward totalitarianism without seriously disrupting the structure of the state. As we shall see, his analysis predicted and helped to explain how Spain could shift almost seamlessly to democracy after Franco's death.

The regime went through several phases over its four decades in power, decades marked outside Spain by the Second World War and the subsequent Cold War. The Second World War began just five months after the end of the Spanish Civil War. Whereas Franco owed his victory in part to the aid from Germany and Italy, he was appalled by Hitler's non-aggression pact with the Soviet Union in August 1939, and Spain was in no shape to join the larger conflict. Instead, at the start of the war, Franco adopted an official policy of neutrality, though his actions betrayed a pro-Axis stance. The only part of Hitler's aims that really interested him, however, was the offensive against the Soviet Union, which he enthusiastically supported, sending the so-called "Blue Division" of Spanish soldiers to fight alongside the German army on the eastern front. Although Hitler kept pressing Franco for access through Spain to attack Gibraltar, Franco held him off. At a meeting of the two dictators in a railroad car on the French border in 1940, Franco famously kept Hitler waiting while he took a nap after lunch. He did agree, however, to sell the rights to Spanish tungsten – a crucial war material – to Germany.

Sometime in 1942, Franco realized that Germany might not win the war and began to shift his support away from the Axis. He started permitting Allied fliers shot down in France and elsewhere to travel through Spain to Portugal. Franco also gave orders to issue Spanish passports to Jews in Salonika, arguing that they were descendants of the Jews expelled from Spain in the fifteenth century. He pressured Hitler to let them leave with their wealth and evidently saw no value in the Nazi push to exterminate them. In Eastern Europe, Spanish consulates also issued passports to Jews trying to escape the Nazis, and Franco allowed those who arrived in Spain to travel on freely to Portugal, where they could find transport to the western hemisphere. Although these actions displeased Hitler, he did nothing to stop them, as he still hoped that Franco would openly join his cause. The Allies also hoped to win Spain to their side.

As for Franco, though neutrality seemed the only practical course for Spain during the war, he knew that policy risked alienating both sides. Suspecting that Spain would be isolated once the war ended, he implemented a policy of autarky – total economic self-sufficiency. Despite his slide toward the Allies from 1942 on, Franco had guessed right. The founding members of the United Nations barred Spain from membership in 1945, even as it admitted a long list of states with similarly dubious credentials. Many politicians in Europe and the United States despised Franco as one of the last dictators to survive the war. They favored measures that might cause the regime to fall; some even argued for an invasion of Spain in 1945–6, spurred on by the pleas of republicans in exile. However, Europe was exhausted, and the United States had no stomach for a continuation of the combat. Efforts by guerrilla fighters to go back into Spain failed as well. Franco stayed in power, and Spaniards of all political beliefs suffered for it. Ironically, the international quarantine of Spain by the Western democracies may actually have bolstered support for the regime among Spaniards, especially as Franco moved to redefine his government.

In an attempt to align Spain with the Christian Democratic governments of postwar Western Europe, Franco abandoned the remnants of fascist rhetoric and leadership and allied more closely with a lay organization, Acción Católica. He also issued a constitution in 1945, known as the "Charter of the Spanish People" (Fuero de los Españoles), which emphasized the human rights of the citizenry, though not political rights. None of this had much effect on the international community, though it may have persuaded some Spaniards that the regime was loosening up. The harsh repression after the civil war eased off in 1943, as any remaining opposition had been eliminated or co-opted. Nonetheless, any overt resistance to the regime ran up against a rigid legal structure that punished seemingly minor acts with imprisonment.

Franco redefined his regime as a monarchy without a monarch in 1947, promising that the monarchy would return after his death. Spaniards validated the change with a plebiscite, but that did not end the regime's isolation. That same year, the United States barred Spain from aid under the Marshall Plan, designed to rebuild the shattered economies of Europe, including the former Axis powers. Spaniards had hoped to share in that aid, and their exclusion was another humiliating reminder of their isolation. They felt abandoned by the rest of the world. Only Argentina, under the populist dictator Juan Perón, offered aid, in the tangible form of shiploads of Argentine beef and wheat. Autarky probably intensified Spain's economic problems in the 1940s, especially for agriculture, as skeptical farmers reduced production in response to price ceilings. The National Institute for Industry (INI) had greater success, developing national industries to replace foreign imports.

By the end of the 1940s, the international community began to realize that the Franco regime was likely to remain in power. Spain was peaceful and stable politically, with a population that had grown to over 28 million. Although several hundred thousand republican Spaniards lived in exile, they were scattered throughout the rest of Europe and the western hemisphere. Moreover, like the Second Republic in its day, they represented diverse and mutually hostile factions. They did not offer a viable alternative to Franco.

During the 1950s, the Cold War that pitted the United States and its allies against the Soviet Union and its allies provided an opening for Francoist Spain to reenter the international political system. As a staunch anticommunist, Franco began to look more appealing to the anti-Soviet bloc, and Franco used this appeal to his advantage. The regime negotiated a new Concordat with the Vatican in 1953, which gave Franco a good deal of control over the Roman Catholic Church in Spain. That same year, the United States, under the leadership of President Dwight D. Eisenhower, signed a bilateral treaty with Spain, the Pact of Madrid, which provided for a series of three United States air bases on Spanish soil, in exchange for promises of American financial and military aid. One base was located at Torrejón de Ardoz near Madrid; another at Zaragoza (Aragon) in the northeast; and the third at Morón de la Frontera near Seville in the southwest. A purpose-built petroleum pipeline guaranteed a fuel supply for the aircraft. Under the terms of the pact, the United States was also able to establish a small naval base at Rota on the Atlantic coast near Cádiz. For the remainder of the Cold War, these facilities provided an extremely important link in anti-Soviet defense planning for the United States. Spain, after more than a decade of isolation, gained a grudging acceptance by the Western democracies, illustrated by the startling image of President Eisenhower embracing Franco on an official visit to Spain.

In material terms, the bilateral treaty provided funds needed to rebuild the Spanish economy, but the regime had to spend most of those funds in the United States, mainly on military equipment. Critics of the Franco regime, both inside and outside Spain, viewed the treaty as a humiliation. In their judgment, the country gained little more than the ability to purchase outmoded military equipment in return for ceding control of part of its national territory. Mindful of the criticism, Franco tried to limit the visibility and the influence of the American presence in Spain. In general, the regime preferred that only married Catholics serve tours of duty in Spain, and they could not wear their uniforms outside the bases. In

357

subsequent renewals of the pact, Spain negotiated better terms, but both sides saw advantages in continuing the arrangement.

The implementation of the bases pact was followed by other marks of acceptance. By the late 1950s, Spain was part of a growing list of international organizations, including the World Bank, the International Monetary Fund, and the United Nations. During the 1950s as well, a dialogue on the pace and nature of change began within the regime, with some bureaucrats arguing for thoroughgoing reforms. Dionisio Ridruejo emerged as the main spokesman for a range of critics who had supported Franco during the civil war but subsequently turned against the regime. Little came of these internal debates at first, and those who criticized official policy openly found themselves excluded from power. Nonetheless, the discussions began.

The most serious challenge to the regime came from the economy. Although autarky had been relaxed, the regime still aimed to foster economic independence rather than collaboration with other countries. To bolster both economic and social stability, the regime also continued to laud traditional rural life and social values, and to enhance the agrarian economy with ambitious irrigation schemes and a modest attempt to reclaim and redistribute unused property. Even so, the rural population continued to drift toward the larger towns and cities of Spain. By 1960, some 56 percent of the population lived in municipalities with 10,000 or more inhabitants, an increase of 7 percent since 1940.

In the industrial sphere, the regime supported full employment and job security, as well as encouraging excess workers to seek employment outside Spain. By the late 1950s, despite some success, the Spanish economy still lagged far behind many of its European neighbors while nonetheless experiencing growing inflation, despite a shortage of money. Spain's exclusion from the European Common Market in 1957 dampened any hopes for an immediate improvement in the situation.

To confront the economic challenge, the Franco regime carried out a major socioeconomic transformation, beginning with the Stabilization Plan of 1959 to stop inflation. With a population of 30.4 million people in 1960, Spain had to modernize the way it did business, and that required infusions of capital. However, a report by the World Bank in 1962 said that Spain would not be creditworthy unless it took fundamental steps to change the economy and provide greater opportunities for foreign investment.

The World Bank report goaded the regime into further action. In a major cabinet shake-up, Franco appointed a large group of trained economists and other technocrats to institute the necessary changes in a national development plan. Some of the most prominent of these new men, such as Laureano López Rodó, belonged to a lay Catholic organization called Opus Dei ("Work of God"). Founded by the Spanish priest Josemaría Escrivá de Balaguer in 1928, Opus Dei defines itself as a lay prelature that promotes economic progress for the benefit of individuals and society as a whole. Its most visible members tend to be highly educated, especially in fields related to the law, business, and government. Although the organization claims to be largely apolitical, it is fair to say that its members are conservative, and critics on the left of the political spectrum have long viewed Opus Dei as a conspiratorial, sinister force. There is general agreement, however, that the experts appointed by Franco opened the Spanish economy to foreign investment, and that this helped to spur rapid economic growth in the 1960s.

Laureano López Rodó, the architect of several successive economic plans, emphasized industry rather than agriculture, recognizing that industrial growth would generate more jobs. The government defined a number of cities as industrial "growth poles," including some that already had substantial industry but needed encouragement to grow, and others where the government planned to establish new industries. Valladolid and Salamanca in north-central Castile, and Huelva in Andalusia were among the cities designated as growth poles. The government's efforts to reduce traditional regional disparities had measurable success, even as economic leaders such as Madrid, Catalonia, and the Basque region continued to dominate industrial production.

With government investment in industry, the outmigration of excess rural workers, and the increased mechanization of agriculture, Spain experienced a sharp drop in the rural population, a marker of advanced economies. Half the population in 1940 was rural; less than one-quarter was rural by 1975, and most of that change occurred in the period after 1960. This signaled the growth of industry and solved the age-old problem of land-hunger in rural Spain. In other words, as agriculture was mechanized and became productive enough to require less labor, and as workers found jobs outside agriculture, the issue of land redistribution became irrelevant. As Spain moved to establish a free-market system, the regime applied for admission into the Common Market, filing its first application in 1962. Although Spain would not be allowed to join that body for more than two decades, the government had made a long-term commitment to modernize the economy and join the rest of Europe.

During the 1960s, tourism emerged as a major source of foreign exchange for the Spanish economy, and the government worked hard to promote Spain as an attractive destination, particularly in the sun-starved countries of Northern Europe. Year by year, increasing numbers of tourists flocked to Spanish beach resorts, bringing their customs and attitudes with them. To Spaniards used to the moralistic constraints of the Franco regime, those customs were shocking and titillating at the same time. Despite the best efforts of the government to limit the social impact of tourism, many segments of Spanish society used the example set by foreign tourists to press for change. Foreign scholars also flowed into Spain in considerable numbers from the 1960s onward. Some of them had to face the disapproval of their colleagues at home for seeming to provide further legitimacy for the regime. On the other hand, the flow of scholars into Francoist Spain probably strengthened the growing pressure for change within Spanish society.

Social change often brings demands for political change in its wake, and the Franco regime worked hard to keep any such demands within acceptable limits, in part by making minor changes in the structure and functioning of the government. In 1962, Franco approved the creation of the post of vice-president of the Council of Ministers, an assistant head of government. More importantly, in 1966 the regime abolished prior censorship of the press. Before, government censors had to approve virtually all publications, as well as films, plays, and other cultural productions. After the 1966 law, if the government did not approve of something that was published, it simply confiscated the publication. Because publishers suffered a substantial loss of revenue when that happened, they tried to avoid openly provoking the regime, even as they tested the limits of government tolerance. Overall, the tentative political changes of the early 1960s marked a step forward in opening up the regime, but they hardly satisfied the growing chorus of demands for greater changes.

The Spanish economy enjoyed enormous growth during the 1960s as it opened to the world. In the period 1960–73, Spain had the fastest rate of growth in the Western world, far higher than its European neighbors. Critics argue that this "economic miracle" only reflected the prior backwardness of the economy, but the growth was nonetheless impressive. Through it all, the government kept a wary finger on the pulse of Spanish society, attentive to the potential for unrest that might accompany economic changes, either good or bad. The Institute of Public Opinion carried out numerous polls about diverse aspects of Spanish life, while sociologists, historians, and other academics carried out independent research on a wide range of topics that had political implications, such as rural-to-urban migration. The government both sponsored and facilitated such research, whether or not its authors were associated with the regime. In that way, those in power could gauge the effects of their policies, including potential political demands.

Adding to the pressure for change in the 1960s, underground opposition to the Franco regime's unchanging political structure grew as society and the economy rapidly evolved. The Communist Party of Spain (PCE) played a key role in that opposition, under the leadership of Santiago Carrillo, who became the party's secretary-general in 1960. The PCE faced problems, however. Not only did it remain illegal in Spain, along with all other traditional political parties, but it faced opposition from within. On the right of the PCE, a pro-Soviet faction led by Enrique Líster emerged in 1968 and, on the left, Trotskyites and Maoists opposed the relatively moderate stance of Carrillo's leadership. Other leftist parties emerged as well, all of them clandestine but well known to the government. In the peculiar political atmosphere of Spain in the late 1960s, the leadership of a wide range of opposition parties met openly in social settings such as the bar of the Hotel Suecia behind the Cortes building. As long as they observed the letter of the law regarding associations, the government left them alone.

In the late 1960s as well, students and faculty at Spain's major universities, in particular the Universidad Complutense in Madrid, followed the lead of their counterparts in France and the United States in demanding major educational reforms. Although they succeeded in changing the university, they were unable to use that success as a template for social revolution in general, as many of them wished to do.

The government removed labor syndicates from the control of the Falange, and passed a law in 1958 that allowed limited collective bargaining. As a result, Laborers' Commissions (Comisiones Obreras), or CCOO, bargained for affiliated workers and organized a series of de facto strikes, acting as unions in all but name. Nonetheless, the regime refused to make the commissions autonomous, despite demands from international labor organizations and the European Common Market. Led by Marcelino Camacho, the CCOO workers also grew increasingly restive during the 1960s, and, in the interests of social peace, the regime often accommodated the workers' demands, as long as they remained outside the political sphere. Although Camacho was a communist and a member of the Comintern, he denied it until the late 1970s. One of the remaining leftist heroines of the civil war, Dolores Ibárruri, in exile in Moscow, was also a member of the Comintern, though she too denied it. By remaining circumspect, leaders of the Spanish left, both inside and outside Spain, could work for the improvement of workers' lives with the tacit compliance of the regime.

Although Spanish industrial production rose rapidly in the 1960s, the economy had a limited capacity to absorb new workers from the countryside. Consequently, the Franco regime encouraged and facilitated worker emigration to the more developed parts of Western Europe and abroad. The government even arranged subsidized trains to bring Spanish workers home for vacations, well aware that the temporary out-migration provided a safety valve against unrest at home. The workers sent money back to their families in Spain and thus directly contributed to the growth of the home economy.

By the late 1960s, Franco and his regime had confounded critics by their longevity, but Franco at least could not last forever. Age and infirmity, particularly

Parkinson's disease, had rendered him a seemingly frail and stiff shadow of the man who had taken power in 1936. His regime therefore attempted to prepare for a perpetuation of Francoism without Franco, instituting minor changes to the legal and governmental system aimed at deflecting demands for more thoroughgoing changes. A new set of fundamental laws – in effect, a new constitution – passed through the Cortes in 1966, ratified by a referendum in January 1967. The government then passed three important laws to implement key provisions in the new constitution. One law allowed non-Catholic groups to operate in the open, rather than in private. Another law provided for the election of one-fifth of the deputies to the Cortes, rather than having the whole body appointed. And a third law reduced the role of the Falange in government and renamed its remnant as an amorphous "Movement." Although these changes, together with the 1966 removal of prior restraint on the press, fell far short of the democratic freedoms demanded by the clandestine opposition, the regime hoped that they would be sufficient to defuse open unrest.

To a certain extent, they succeeded, but, ironically, the continuing economic progress sponsored by the regime also continued to spawn demands for social and political change. Industrial production in Spain rose 7.9 percent a year between 1959 and 1972, a phenomenal record surpassed only by Japan. One stunning success story involved the workers' cooperative enterprise founded in 1956 at Mondragón in the Basque region. Starting with twenty-three workers, the Mondragón project grew and prospered to become a model of worker-controlled industry and social services. With both conventional and

unconventional enterprises, Spanish exports of manufactured goods rose to 78 percent of total output by
1975. Foreign investment flowed into Spain through huge
banking consortia that held enormous economic power.
Tourism also brought in vast sums of foreign capital.
Although scholars debate about the role that government
planning played in the growth of the Spanish economy,
that growth itself is well documented and undoubtedly
increased the pressure for reform.

During the late 1960s, various opposition forces escalated their demands, coinciding with widespread protest
movements in the democratic West, and terrorism by
Palestinians in the Middle East and the Irish Republican Army in the United Kingdom. In Spain, the terrorist
group known as ETA began a campaign of assassinations
and bombings to press for the independence of the Basque
provinces in the north of the country. ETA's audacious
challenge to the government served as a catalyst for other
opposition, even as the vast majority of Spaniards decried
the violence. Even the hierarchy of the Roman Catholic
Church, long allied with the most conservative forces in
Spanish society, moved deliberately away from the Franco
regime, following the progressive social decrees of the
Second Vatican Council (1962–5). Both directly and indi-
rectly, priests and some members of the church hierarchy
in Spain supported the opposition.

In a further attempt to preserve the regime into the
future, on July 21, 1969, Franco named Prince Juan Carlos
de Borbón y Borbón to succeed him, finally fulfilling his
1947 promise to restore the monarchy. Laureano López
Rodó, the Opus Dei government leader, and Admiral
Luis Carrero Blanco, a trusted confidant of Franco, had

worked together to persuade Franco that the decision was necessary. Opposition leaders scarcely knew what to make of this move, though Franco had been grooming the prince as his presumed successor for more than two decades. To strict monarchists, Juan Carlos's father Don Juan was the only legitimate monarch. Diehard Carlists favored their pretender. Nonetheless, it is fair to say that the majority of conservative Spaniards welcomed the nomination of Juan Carlos as their future king.

The leftist opposition did not. They viewed Juan Carlos as a puppet of Franco and a passive figurehead for the continuation of the regime. Although the official press had reported myriad details about his military training during his teenage years, his marriage to Princess Sofía of Greece in 1962, and their growing family, the Spanish public knew very little about him as a person. In the aftermath of his nomination by Franco, jokes circulated that his nickname as king would be "Juan Carlos the Brief," assuming that the military would overthrow him at the first opportunity. In monarchist circles, many favored his father Don Juan instead of the untested prince. During the final years of the Franco regime, these and other stories and rumors flew around opposition circles.

During those final years, the regime confronted crisis after crisis, trying to keep a lid on opposition movements. By 1970, the Spanish population had grown to some 34 million, and it is fair to say that at least half of them opposed the regime. In December 1970, the trial of a group of ETA members accused of terrorist acts brought the opposition into the public eye. Despite warnings from the international community, a military court in Burgos condemned six of the sixteen accused to death, although they were not executed, pending judicial appeals. Franco later commuted their sentences. Regardless of the actual guilt or innocence of the accused, the trial galvanized a tactical coalition of Catholic clergy, students, workers, communists, socialists, and "left" Christian Democrats to press for civil and political rights denied by the Franco regime.

Faced with this widespread opposition, in the early 1970s the regime did not resort to the repressive measures employed in earlier decades, though scholars argue about the reason for that restraint. Some point to external pressure and Spain's perennial application for admission to the European Common Market, which required democracy, civil liberties, and an autonomous labor movement. Others, notably the distinguished historian Juan Pablo Fusi, called this reluctance to use force "the bad conscience of the regime," giving the crisis an internal rather than an external cause. According to Fusi, those in charge of the government in 1970 either lacked the will to employ repressive tactics or judged them counterproductive, given the changed conditions both inside and outside Spain. Moreover, the oil crisis in Europe and the United States in 1973 led to a reduction in the number of Spanish workers employed abroad and in the ability of the Spanish economy to employ the returnees. Thus, fears of economic instability may have added to the government's decision to respond to protests with restraint.

Several events in 1973 marked a critical juncture in the leadership and direction of the Franco regime. In June, Franco appointed Admiral Carrero Blanco as president of the Council of Ministers, and therefore as the effective head of the government. In other words, for the first time since 1936, the aging dictator no longer simultaneously held the positions of head of state and head of government. The change was necessary, given that Prince Juan Carlos would become head of state after Franco's death. Nonetheless, opposition forces drew the unmistakable conclusion that Carrero Blanco's appointment meant a perpetuation of the regime. That same year, a financial scandal involving members of Opus Dei in the government forced Laureano López Rodó out of power. As the architect of Spain's economic resurgence, he had enjoyed enormous prestige; the economic downturn of 1973, his dismissal, and the discrediting of his Opus Dei associates, cast the competence of the leadership into doubt.

The most stunning blow to Franco's hopes for the future occurred on December 20, 1973, when ETA terrorists assassinated Admiral Carrero Blanco. They accomplished this by relying on the admiral's regular habits and digging a tunnel underneath the street where his official vehicle always passed after he attended mass. The explosion blew the admiral, his car, and his chauffeur so high that pieces of the car lodged several stories up in the walls of an adjacent apartment building. As appalling as the act was, it gave hope to the various opposition groups that it was possible to act against the regime, despite the vigilance of the security forces.

Franco appointed Carlos Arias Navarro to succeed Carrero as president of the Council of Ministers. Arias dismissed the last of the Opus Dei technocrats from the Council and otherwise tried to run the country in a situation that was increasingly fraught. When Franco fell seriously ill in 1974, the government functioned well, which encouraged many Spaniards to hope that the transition after Franco's death would be smooth. Nonetheless, Spanish newspapers and magazines carried numerous articles about "Who's Who in the Military," as if preparing for another military coup once Franco finally disappeared from the scene. Coincidentally, Portugal went through a chaotic transition to democracy in 1973–4, following its largely bloodless ouster of the successor to Antonio Salazar, the long-term Portuguese dictator. By implication, Portugal's experience served as an example of how not to shift toward an open, democratic society. In Spain, the government was well aware of the breadth and depth of the forces pushing for change. An extraordinary series of public opinion polls and sociological studies made that quite clear to the regime.

Matters reached a critical point in the fall of 1975, as the Council of Ministers reviewed eleven death sentences earlier handed down to Basque terrorists in military trials. The council commuted six sentences and confirmed the other five, carrying out the executions on September 27, 1975. Whether or not those executed were guilty as charged, in the international community the executions confirmed long-standing hatred of the Franco regime and produced an explosion of horror and outrage. With Spain cast as an international pariah once again, Franco entered his final agony. Doctors kept his failing body alive on machines for more than a month, providing material for tasteless humor on television in the United States. When his family faced the inevitable, doctors disconnected the machines, and Franco died on November 20, 1975, after nearly four decades in power. Two days later, his designated successor took the oath of office as Juan Carlos I, promising to uphold the constitution. No one knew what would happen next, but it is fair to say that most Spaniards were apprehensive about what the future might bring.

FIGURE 7.1 This poster, produced by the Communist Party of Spain, urges voters to choose the affiliated parties of the Popular Front in the elections of 1936. It portrays class struggle with the image of a working-class mother, held back by the forces of religion, the privileged classes, and capitalism.

las niñas
de hoy
y las mujeres
de
mañana

UNIDAS SIN DISTINCION DE CLASES
EN ORGANIZACIONES JUVENILES DE F.E.T. Y DE LAS J.O.N.S.

FIGURE 7.2 The Falange Party also appealed to class and gender to consolidate public support in the aftermath of military victory. Denying the class struggle propounded by the left, this poster portrays young women from the upper and lower classes united in the youth organizations of the Falange.

FIGURE 7.3 The Franco regime strove to contain separatist sympathies by restricting the use of languages other than Castilian. Nonetheless, this street sign in Oñate (Guipúzcoa), photographed in August 1975, used both Castilian and Euskera.

8

New Spain, new Spaniards: European, democratic, and multicultural

~

Few things changed in the immediate aftermath of the Bourbon restoration of 1975. Most of the political figures who had served in the last years of the Franco regime continued to serve under King Juan Carlos, including Carlos Arias Navarro, the Prime Minister. The continuity dismayed Spaniards and outsiders hoping for dramatic change, but it provided stability and reassurance for Spaniards who feared change and the disruption it might bring. Newspapers and magazines debated the future of Spain in serious articles and political cartoons alike. The new daily newspaper *El País* began as a voice for change, strongly allied to the still clandestine Socialist Party but aiming to provide analysis rather than polemic. Farther to the left, the weekly magazine *Cambio16* emerged as a harsher critic of the government and its continuity with the Franco regime.

Beneath the surface, however, the king and his close advisers prepared to transform Spanish political life. Inadvertently, the assassins of Admiral Carrero Blanco in 1973 had made a transition toward democracy easier, removing a powerful opponent of change. One of the first indications of that transformation occurred seven months after Juan Carlos came to the throne. Carlos Arias met with the king on July 1, 1976, at the latter's request, and resigned as Prime Minister after the meeting. Arias had taken on a difficult and thankless task two and a half years earlier and had presided over the administration during a crucial period. Pressured from all sides and visibly exhausted, he once reputedly commented that he felt as if he were walking a tightrope, while someone kept oiling the rope.

Two days after Arias resigned, the king chose Adolfo Suárez to form a new government, stunning political observers both inside and outside Spain. Relatively young, handsome, and politically astute, Suárez had risen through the ranks of the Francoist political machine to head the national radio and television network, RTVE. The public knew his face and his background, and conservative forces in Spanish society thought they knew his political stance. They were mistaken. The king had come to know Suárez through official and social contact and recognized in him an ideal partner for his political agenda.

Like the king, Suárez took his oath of office promising to uphold the Francoist constitution, but both of them knew that Spain had to change. With the king's full support, Suárez used his trusted position in the old power structure to persuade his colleagues to abolish the old regime and its constitution and prepare for a transition to democracy. In less than a year, the Cortes in effect voted itself out of existence, and Suárez prepared the country for democratic elections. The king, in public and in private, supported the process and worked to bring the military in line with their new role in a democratic Spain. It is impossible to overestimate his importance in the transition or the intense political pressures he faced from all sides.

Political observers inside and outside the country watched in amazement as the clandestine political parties of Spain emerged from the shadows, applied for legalization, and campaigned for election to a new Cortes. Two important dates in that process were April 9, 1977, when the Communist Party won legalization, and May 27, 1977, when the king issued an amnesty to political prisoners. That same month, Don Juan de Borbón, Juan Carlos's father, formally abdicated his claim to be the legitimate Bourbon king of Spain, clearing the ambiguity that had surrounded Juan Carlos's position. Suddenly, even the most skeptical observers knew that change had arrived. In the elections held on June 15 – the first full, free elections in Spain in forty-one years – Adolfo Suárez's party, the Union of the Democratic Center (UCD) won 165 of the 350 seats in the new Cortes. The Socialist Party (PSOE), in alliance with the Socialist Party of Catalonia (PSC) won 118 seats; a collection of smaller parties of the left and right made up the balance. The international community of Western democracies welcomed Spain back into the fold, and at least one Spanish journalist wrote a full column apologizing for his anti-Suárez writings the year before.

In the next several years, with Suárez as Prime Minister (technically Presidente del Gobierno, President of the Government), his administration oversaw the writing of a new constitution (1978) and enacted legislation to implement it. One of the most difficult issues to resolve was the push for more autonomy from Madrid by the Basque provinces and Catalonia. The Cortes approved autonomy statutes for both regions in December 1979, giving local leaders considerable authority over education, cultural matters, and policing powers, among other things. Despite the increased local autonomy, those two regions still have strong minority support for complete independence, well into the twenty-first century. The government resisted pressure for similar statutes in other regions, however, and Suárez's party increasingly lost support. He resigned as Prime Minister in January 1981 but continued to hold his seat in the Cortes.

Spanish democracy faced its greatest challenge a month later. On February 23, 1981, a renegade officer in the Civil Guard, Lieutenant Colonel Antonio Tejero, burst into the Cortes with an armed group of followers and announced a coup to take over the government. Most of the deputies in the Cortes chamber dove for cover as the invaders fired shots into the ceiling. Suárez remained in his front-row seat defiantly; the communist deputy Santiago Carrillo stayed in his seat and lit a cigarette. The most dramatic defiance came from General Manuel Gutiérrez Mellado, the Vice-President for Defense. Gutiérrez Mellado was seventy years old, and after serving the Franco regime loyally for decades had transformed the Spanish army into a modern democratic force during the transition. He ordered the invaders to desist, claiming superior military rank, but they tried to shove him aside. Television cameras that were present in the Cortes that day to film ordinary business instead captured the whole event and broadcast it to a horrified public, until the invaders shut them down. In the tense hours that followed, the invaders held the Cortes – and Spanish democracy – hostage.

When the king learned of the attack, he telephoned leaders of the armed forces to enlist their support to resist the coup. He knew them all, having gone through officer training programs in all the branches of the armed forces. After assuring himself of military support, the king went on television shortly after midnight to assure the citizenry that he stood solidly behind Spanish democracy and to order the plotters to release the deputies and surrender. They did so, to the immense relief of Spaniards. In the aftermath of the attempted coup, the king met with the leaders of all Spain's political parties. He told them what they must already have known. Any future plotters would kill him first. Spain's political leaders realized that they shared responsibility to nurture and protect Spanish democracy, regardless of their political rivalries.

Throughout the first five years of the democratic transition, four political parties dominated the electoral spectrum: the centrist Union of the Democratic Center (UCD), the Socialist Workers' Party (PSOE), the Communist Party of Spain (PCE), and the rightist Popular Alliance (AP). By tacit and explicit agreement, they all worked to solidify and stabilize Spanish democracy, rather than arguing for positions that would have polarized Spain's political life. The shock of the attempted coup in February 1981 reinforced the value of that approach. The major parties, along with Spanish society as a whole, showed little interest in dredging up the past or reopening the wounds left by the civil war and the long Franco regime. Smaller parties, especially those linked with local militants in Catalonia and the Basque region, often disagreed with the strategy and tactics of the larger parties, pushing for more local autonomy from Madrid. In the Basque region, especially, the most militant parties often condoned street violence in order to gain complete independence for what they called Euskadi – the Basque homeland. The most extreme of the groups – the terrorist organization ETA, which had assassinated Admiral

Carrero Blanco in 1973 – continued to enjoy considerable popular support in the Basque region, although it remained outlawed for its continued criminal activity. In 1978, Basque nationalist politicians sympathetic to ETA's aims founded Herri Batasuna, a Marxist-Leninist party that was widely perceived as the political arm of the terrorist organization.

Between April 1981 and August 1982, the Cortes passed autonomy statutes for most of the remaining Spanish regions, giving them the same control over local affairs earlier granted to the Basque region and Catalonia in 1979. In 1982, Spain also joined the North Atlantic Treaty Organization (NATO), a bulwark of the Western democracies against the USSR during the Cold War. The soccer World Cup, held in Spain in the summer of 1982, took place in an atmosphere of renewed confidence among Spaniards in their future, despite the continuing problems of terrorist violence in the north.

As proof of that confidence, when voters went to the polls in late October 1982, they entrusted the Socialist Party with the responsibility for leading them, giving the PSOE the greatest electoral victory in its hundred-year history. The socialist victory came at the expense of both the Union of the Democratic Center and the Communist Party. Like the leftist socialists, the rightist Popular Alliance gained greatly from the 1982 election, emerging as the second-largest party in the Cortes. Political scientists attribute the great electoral shift of 1982 to the internal dynamics of the various parties and the ways that the electorate perceived them. In short, the socialists and the Popular Alliance both appeared to be stable and responsible parties, having resolved their internal disagreements in favor of a unified agenda and self-definition. In both cases, the unity was hard won after considerable internal strife, but definitive nonetheless. By contrast, the Union of the Democratic Center and the communists appeared to be faction-ridden and therefore unstable. Spanish voters in 1982 above all wanted stable and responsible government and voted accordingly. With the peaceful handover of power to the socialists in 1982, political scientists defined the Spanish transition to democracy as a stunning success and a potential role model for other transitions worldwide. This was all the more noteworthy, given the widespread skepticism that had greeted the first steps toward changing the regime in the mid 1970s after Franco's death.

The socialists would hold power for fourteen years after the 1982 elections, under the dynamic leadership of Felipe González, enacting an ambitious legislative program. In addition to completing autonomy statutes for the rest of Spain, the socialists aggressively pursued corruption in the business world and de-criminalized abortion in 1983, despite strong opposition from the Catholic Church and its supporters. Although the church declined greatly in political power from the 1960s onward, it retained considerable authority in social and cultural matters.

The socialist government pursued an active economic agenda, determined to raise Spanish living standards and economic performance, but at the same time holding wages down to control inflation. They aimed at an economy that would grow steadily and employ more workers to lessen the persistently high unemployment rates. Over the period from 1973 to 1992, the productivity of Spanish labor nearly doubled, as did the educational level

MAP 8.1 Map of current administrative divisions. Adapted from Peter J. Donaghy and Michael T. Newton, *Spain: A Guide to Political and Economic Institutions* (Cambridge: Cambridge University Press, 1987), p. 99.

of the population. By the 1980s, Spain had a population of 39 million, with a high proportion of its young people enrolled in institutions of higher learning. The Spanish economy nonetheless continued to lag behind the leading European countries, making Spanish agricultural and manufacturing production cheaper than in most of its European neighbors. That is one of the reasons why the European Economic Community (EEC, or the Common Market) did not admit Spain as a member until 1985.

By the mid 1980s, Spaniards had reason to question their country's continued membership in NATO. A new generation of leadership in the Soviet Union, led by Mikhail Gorbachev, led many to view the alliance as counterproductive to stability in Europe. The anti-Soviet stance of the United States, and especially the belligerent rhetoric of President Ronald Reagan, seemed outmoded and counterproductive to many Spaniards, who also resented the continued American military presence in Spain. Felipe González seemed to share those misgivings, and promised to hold a referendum on whether Spain should leave NATO. Before the referendum in March 1986, however, González shifted course, urging voters to confirm Spain's role. They did, by a narrow margin, but pollsters predicted that they would take out their irritation by voting against the socialists in June. Instead, despite voters' frustration with González's about-face on NATO, Spain's high unemployment rate, and the government's economic austerity measures, they returned the socialists to power.

In persuading Spaniards to ratify Spain's membership of NATO, González promised to take a hard look at the United States' military presence in Spain. For many Spaniards, the original treaty with the United States in 1953 remained a sore point – the moment that the Franco regime won legitimacy in the eyes of the international community. Rightly or wrongly, they thought that the regime would have collapsed without the boost that Franco received as an anti-communist during the Cold War. In the new Spain, with the socialists in a second term in power, the bases pact stood as a continuing reminder of the mistakes and humiliations of the past. The United States failed to understand the symbolic and historical significance of that past, and its negotiators for the treaty's renewal in 1988 had to climb a steep learning curve to produce a revised agreement that Spain could accept. They eventually arrived at terms acceptable to both sides. The result greatly reduced the American military presence in Spain, while retaining elements of mutual security that both sides considered essential.

On the economic front, the socialist government's austerity measures aimed to curb inflation in a period of rapid economic growth. Between 1985 and 1986, Spain's gross domestic product increased by one percentage point. In the following year, it grew by about 2.5 percentage points, the highest in Europe, and far higher than Canada or the United States. Although Spain's per capita gross domestic product still lagged far behind the European and North American leaders, it was clearly on the rise and had the potential for continued growth. Living standards were also increasing; by 1992, life expectancy in Spain was among the highest in Europe. Economic growth and the government's supportive stance toward the business world helped to keep the socialists in power.

In addition to profound political change, Spain underwent profound social change in the first decades after Franco's death. Many of these changes had been building for some time, but they came into the open in the 1980s. Perhaps most notable was the emergence of a robust feminist movement, belying the image of Spanish women as passive and submissive in the face of masculine authority. Despite opposition from conservative sectors of society, including the Catholic Church, in the 1980s the government legalized divorce, family planning, and abortion in certain cases, implementing women's equality under the new constitution. Women also entered the workforce in record numbers, including professions once exclusively male. In universities, women accounted for 50 percent of the student body by the late 1980s, many of them preparing for careers that their mothers could only imagine. The Socialist Party prepared the way for women to rise in politics as well, ruling that 25 percent of appointments in their party had to go to women. The more conservative political parties also recognized the electoral power of women and began to nurture talented women in their ranks.

Not surprisingly, these changes affected the sexual lives of Spaniards, both inside and outside marriage. Although a large percentage of Spanish men said they supported women's equality, many remained ambiguous about the implications of that equality in their private lives. Women working outside the home found that they still had to bear most of the responsibility for housework and childrearing. The changes also had a demographic impact. Spanish couples were tending to marry later, or not at all, and the birthrate fell steadily, as couples delayed having children, or opted to remain childless. This change had been developing for at least several decades, however, and did not begin with the death of Franco. Statistical studies by Spanish sociologists in the mid 1960s estimated that around 50 percent of the Spanish population used some form of contraception. Despite laws granting four months of paid maternity leave and one month of paid paternity leave in the early 1990s, by the year 2000 Spain had the lowest birthrate in the world, below the level that would guarantee the replacement of generations. Similar changes had occurred elsewhere in the developed world in the transition from premodern to modern population behavior, but they were notable in Spain because they came so fast and accompanied so many other social and cultural changes.

By the beginning of the 1990s, Spanish banking and business interests were consolidating their enterprises within Spain and expanding outward to invest in Europe and Latin America. Media conglomerates figured prominently in that expansion, even though many of the major Spanish newspapers and magazines did not come into being until after Franco's death. Alongside daily publications focusing on serious national and international news, raucous weeklies cover sensational topics in political and cultural life and feature an open sexuality that can shock even other Europeans. Moreover, some of the major newspapers accept advertisements for prostitutes of various gender identities, with pictures and salacious text that would be unthinkable in major newspapers elsewhere in Europe or in the United States. The Spanish government gave up its monopoly of television stations in 1990, opening the door to the private ownership of stations and international competition. All of these developments integrated Spanish society and culture into the European community more fully, and prepared Spaniards to take their place in the European economic unification that began in 1992.

In 1992 as well, Spain hosted two major international events, the world's fair "Expo 92," which opened in Seville in April, and the Summer Olympics and Paralympics in Barcelona in August. Both events tied in with the five-hundredth anniversary of Columbus's first voyage west in search of a new route to Asia, which marked the beginning of the global network of trade. Despite the ambiguous legacy of those developments, modern Spain was proud of its role in the development of empire and global trade and saw itself as the ideal representative of Europe in relations with the nations of the former Spanish Empire in the Americas.

Tourism continued to grow apace during the first mandate of the socialist government, along with the international convention business that the government actively encouraged. With the Spanish population at just over 39 million in the 1990 census, the number of tourists visiting Spain in a given year could equal or surpass that figure. International concerns came along with international integration and tourism. Drug use and drug trafficking, often associated with travelers and immigrants from Colombia, became a major worry for Spaniards by the late 1980s. Although the full range of illegal substances gradually penetrated Spanish society, as they did elsewhere in the developed world, cocaine has proven to be particularly prevalent. Because of Spain's extended coastline, beach resorts attract not only a growing flood of tourists, but also a growing flood of smugglers. The Civil Guard often takes the lead in the interception of drug traffickers, because of its authority over transportation, and Spanish law-enforcement agencies in general work with their counterparts elsewhere in the international fight against crime. The Civil Guard also takes the lead in enforcing wildlife and hunting laws, along with a wide range of other law-enforcement issues in the countryside. Although these activities are a natural outgrowth of the Civil Guard's historical role in policing rural areas, it marks a notable redefinition of a force that has often inspired as much fear as respect.

By the early 1990s, the Socialist Party showed the inevitable strains of nearly a decade in power, accompanied by ongoing scandals both political and financial. In January 1991, the courts found several law-enforcement officials guilty of extralegal actions against ETA targets. Though Felipe González and other socialist leaders denied complicity in the so-called GAL case, the political opposition argued that responsibility ran far higher in the socialist chain of command than the guilty parties. In May 1991, evidence became public that major banks and businesses had paid huge sums of money to two small companies in Barcelona owned by top officials in the Socialist Party. This financial scandal, known by the name of one of the companies involved – Filesa – along with the fallout from the GAL case, caused major internal ruptures in the socialist ranks, which cost Felipe González considerable effort to repair. Despite these problems, plus overspending for the 1992 celebrations and a slowing of Spain's economic growth, Spanish voters returned the socialists to power in the June 1993 elections.

Immigration to Spain grew exponentially in the 1990s and continued to be among the highest in the European Community. One reason was that Spain's historic ties with Latin America encouraged increasing numbers of immigrants, and Spain assiduously maintains those ties. From the early 1980s, the government pumped money into the preservation and restoration of historic archives and colonial buildings throughout the former Spanish Empire in the Americas. Spain's location on the Mediterranean also makes it the destination for clandestine immigration from North Africa and sub-Saharan Africa. Many of these would-be immigrants arrive after risking their lives in small boats and perilous conditions, only to be intercepted by the Civil Guard and returned to their points of origin. Those who escape often find jobs in agriculture and industry that many Spaniards are unwilling to take, but others settle into a marginalized existence, in constant threat of exploitation and arrest. As their numbers grow, and Spaniards perceive a connection between immigration and growing criminality and social disruption, immigrants face increasing resistance to their presence in Spain.

The creation of the European Union (EU, successor to the EEC) in 1993 made it easier for citizens in all the member states to shift their residence, which has led to migration flows both into and out of Spain. The expansion of the European Union in 2004 to include countries in Eastern Europe added to the flow. Attracted by economic opportunities lacking at home, Eastern Europeans – notably from Poland and Romania inside the EU, and Russia, from outside – moved to Spain in large numbers. Economic opportunities and the declining birthrate in Spain created a niche for these new workers, even as they strained educational and social services in some areas.

The labor market in Spain has long posed analytical problems for government agencies and scholars alike. In the midst of the economic boom of the 1990s, Spain nonetheless had the highest official unemployment rate in the EU, hovering around 23 percent in late 1993. Yet house-to-house polls indicated that the true rate was only about 8 percent. Many of those officially unemployed and collecting benefits were instead working at one or more jobs, treating unemployment payments as a kind of insurance against hard times. The gap between official statistics and reality still defies analysts of the Spanish labor market, but immigration figures suggest that the economy continued to have the capacity to absorb new workers throughout the 1990s.

The mid 1990s saw several important milestones that served as reminders of the extraordinary nature of the new democratic Spain. Cardinal Vicente Enrique y Tarancón, a key figure in the Catholic hierarchy in support of democracy, died in November 1994. The following year, Adolfo Suárez received a series of public awards for his crucial role in leading that transition. At the end of 1995, General Manuel Gutiérrez Mellado, who helped to redefine the role of the military in a modern democracy, died in a highway accident. All three men – representing the Roman Catholic Church, the political classes, and the military establishment – served as models of intelligent and courageous leadership in a very difficult time. All of them enjoyed the confidence and support of King Juan Carlos I, arguably the most extraordinary figure of all.

The king regularly topped public opinion polls as the most admired man in Spain in the 1990s and into the early years of the twenty-first century. He and the other members of the royal family filled diverse public roles, representing Spain and its government in a wide range of activities, from sporting and cultural events to official conferences. Each member of the family tended to favour a particular set of activities, and they all seemed to take their responsibilities seriously. Queen Sofía regularly presided over cultural and scholarly events, as well as attending official functions, and her devotion to her family served as a model for Spaniards at all levels of society. As Prince Felipe, the heir to the throne, grew to manhood, he received careful tutelage from his parents in the duties and comportment of a modern constitutional monarch, and he learned his lessons well. As he reached his late twenties, after stints in all the armed forces, he took on an increasing list of official appearances on his own, charming the press by his good looks and obvious dedication to his duties. His two older sisters, Princess Elena and Princess Cristina, also took on increasing public responsibilities as they finished their education. During those years the popular press in Spain covered their activities, both public and private, with great interest, and all three of the royal children grew to maturity as responsible citizens, nurtured and supported by their parents.

In March 1995, Princess Elena married Jaime de Marichalar, a younger son of a noble family from Navarre. Their wedding in Seville, the first royal wedding on Spanish soil in nearly a century, brought together the full range of the Spanish political classes, along with royalty and aristocrats from many parts of the world. Two years later, Princess Cristina married Iñaki Urdangarín, a Basque commoner and member of the Spanish Olympic handball team, whom she had met at the 1996 Olympic Games in Atlanta. After their wedding in Barcelona, they continued to live and work in that city.

When Spanish voters went to the polls in 1996, the conservative Popular Party (Partido Popular) won the election, turning the socialists out of power. Since 1989, José María Aznar had led the PP, restructured from the Alianza Popular, which had not been able to overcome its association with figures from the Franco regime. Aznar survived an attempted assassination by an ETA bomb in April 1995, and under his leadership the PP became the logical choice for centrist voters disillusioned with the PSOE. At the end of 1996, the Spanish Cortes honored the foreign volunteers, known as the International Brigades, who had fought against Franco's nationalists during the Spanish Civil War. The election of a conservative government and the homage to the International Brigades, coming in the same year, demonstrated that Spaniards felt secure enough about their democracy to start dealing with the wounds left by the civil war and its aftermath.

The Aznar government held power for eight years, from 1996 to 2004. During that time, Spain reinforced its presence in the European Union and cultivated its position as the logical link between Europe and the Islamic world, as well as the traditional connection between Europe and Latin America. Spanish businesses poured money into Latin American banking, communications networks, and transportation and tourism, among other ventures. The Spanish government encouraged those

investments and sponsored regular Ibero-American sum-
mit meetings to ensure ongoing, if not always smooth,
relationships with Latin American leaders. In all of these
initiatives, King Juan Carlos and Queen Sofía continued
to play important roles as hardworking representatives of
the New Spain. This was particularly important in the
country's relationships with the conservative monarchies
of the Islamic world.

In Spain, in addition to fostering a broad political
consensus against ETA terrorism, the Aznar government
focused on bolstering economic performance. Spain modeled its capital markets and competitive atmosphere on
the United States, while retaining Europe's committed
approach to social welfare. Spain was among the original
twelve countries to qualify for and adopt the new European common currency – the euro – which came into
existence on January 1, 1999. The actual euro bills and
coins did not circulate until January 1, 2002, allowing the
twelve countries to prepare their economic infrastructure
and their citizens for the momentous changeover.

In addition to other foreign policy initiatives, Aznar's
government cultivated more cordial relations with the
United States than his precursor had done. In the aftermath of the terrorist attack on the United States on
September 11, 2001, the Aznar government openly supported the United States in the wars in Afghanistan
and Iraq. In 2003, Aznar's Foreign Minister Ana Palacio worked with the US Secretary of State Colin Powell
in consultations with the Islamic world regarding those
conflicts. Although a large majority of Spaniards opposed
the wars in Iraq and Afghanistan and Spain's participation in them, they were willing to acquiesce in the

government's actions, as long as the wars remained far away.

Socially and culturally, Spain gained in stature, maturity, and international reputation during the late 1990s. Culturally, the 1997 opening of the Guggenheim Museum in Bilbao, designed by Frank Gehry, caused a sensation. Architects and cultural tourists from all over the world made the new Guggenheim into a must-see destination and infused new life into the old industrial city of Bilbao and its surroundings in the Basque region.

According to a variety of objective measures of economic and social welfare, in 1998 Spain ranked as the eleventh-best country to live in in the world, ahead of many of its European neighbors. As the millennial year approached, the Spanish economy continued growing rapidly, and Spanish voters returned the Popular Party to power for another four years in 2000. In 2001, more than half of Spanish families invested at least part of their savings in the stock market, the highest percentage in Europe. This "popular capitalism," as the newspapers dubbed it, provided evidence of their confidence in the future.

Many Spaniards also invested in second homes and rental properties, a pattern that was common even during the late Franco regime. One of the most interesting recent developments among urban dwellers has been investment in refurbishing or building second homes in their families' ancestral villages. For many middle-class urbanites, the weekend pilgrimage to the old "pueblo" has become a standard feature of family life. Small, quiet towns and villages all over Spain, after decades or even centuries of isolation, now come back to life on weekends and during the summer. Local festivals rooted in ancient traditions attract huge crowds of Spaniards as well as tourists. In addition to making rural Spain a more interesting place to live in, this regular interchange between city and country-side provides urbanites with a needed break from the pressures of city life. Those pressures include social problems such as crime and drug use, as well as a huge gap between the life experiences of younger Spaniards and their parents and grandparents.

In the new millennium, a boom in construction, information sciences, and a host of other technological careers shape the professional aspirations of young Spaniards, many of whom had not been born during Spain's extraordinary transition to democracy. For them, their country is a "mismocracia" – a democracy the same (*mismo*) as all the others – and they think of themselves as citizens of Europe and the world, not just as Spaniards. A European poll in December 2000 found that Spaniards were more tolerant of other religions than any other country in the European Union: 92.9 percent of Spanish respondents to the poll said they had no problem accepting the presence of other religions, compared to a European average of 80 percent. At the same time, Spanish Catholicism retains much of its historic fervor, and church leaders have no qualms about speaking out against many aspects of modern life that they consider immoral and anti-religious. Tainted by its long association with the Franco regime, the church, like other conservative elements in Spanish society, continues to redefine itself in the New Spain.

During the transition and for several decades thereafter, there was a tacit agreement, widely shared by Spaniards of all political stripes, that Spanish democracy would take hold more easily without reopening the wounds of the past. Although historians and others had published serious analyses of the Franco regime, and various films such as *Los años bárbaros* ("The Barbaric Years") had dealt with police repression during the 1940s, public debate remained muted, by tacit agreement. As 1999 marked the sixtieth anniversary of the end of the Spanish Civil War, various communications media in Spain seized the opportunity to run stories and analyses about the war and the Franco regime. With the new millennium, Spaniards increasingly seemed ready to face their ghosts.

Perhaps the most stunning proof of that readiness was the popularity of a television series that began in 2001. Called *Cuéntame como pasó* ("Tell me how it happened"), the weekly drama told the story of several generations of the fictional Alcántara family, following them from 1968, through the last years of the Franco regime, and onward toward the present. When the series began, every Thursday night after 10 p.m. – the Spanish dinner hour – millions of Spaniards sat transfixed in front of their television sets as the story of their lives and their country's recent history played out in front of them. The skilled team of writers, producers, and actors presented those intertwined histories with balance and humanity, and the series became an overwhelming success and a social and cultural phenomenon in its own right. As the series moves toward the present, *Cuéntame* provides a window on their common past to its fascinated audience, which includes a broad cross-section of Spaniards, including members of the royal family.

With his older sisters both married by 1997 and starting families, Prince Felipe faced increasing pressure to find a suitable wife and secure the next generation. The popular press covered each real and rumored romance of the prince with keen interest, and he had to face the uncomfortable reality that Spaniards would always treat his private life as a public matter. In fact, Spanish public opinion played a major role in ending one serious romance with a Norwegian fashion model. Most Spaniards, including his parents, simply did not think she was the right sort of potential queen for Spain. The prince reluctantly ended the relationship late in 2001 and went on with his duties, putting the interests of the country ahead of his own. He took on an even more active schedule of official responsibilities and built his own residence on the same property as his parents' Zarzuela Palace on the outskirts of Madrid. Hurt and disappointed by the public discourse regarding his previous courtship, the prince and his close circle of family and friends took care to protect his privacy.

In the fall of 2003, Prince Felipe surprised nearly everyone outside that circle by his choice for a wife: Letizia Ortiz Rocasolana, an award-winning television journalist from a middle-class family. Highly intelligent, well educated, articulate, and beautiful, she was successful and respected in her profession. The Spanish public knew her face and voice well, from her regular appearances as a news anchor on TV-1, the premier Spanish television channel. Admiring her work, the prince had arranged to meet her through a mutual acquaintance in media circles. She was divorced and romantically involved with someone else when she met the prince. When she was again unattached, he began courting her, and eventually won over her reluctance to take on the formidable responsibilities of Spain's future queen. His parents approved, and so did most Spaniards. She resigned from her job the night before the announcement of her engagement to the prince on November 1, 2003. In the seven months before the wedding, Letizia Ortiz lived in an apartment in the Zarzuela Palace, nurtured by the royal family and learning all of the ancillary skills necessary to be a modern queen. She already knew what it meant to be a public figure; she soon learned what it meant to have her every move scrutinized – a hard lesson, but a necessary one.

The holiday season of 2003–4 saw Spain preparing for an election in mid-March, which the Popular Party expected to win, based on opinion polls, and looking forward to the royal wedding in May. No one could guess that in the spring of 2004 Spain would undergo an unprecedented catastrophe. On Thursday, March 11, during the morning rush hour in Madrid, terrorists detonated bombs on several crowded commuter trains. They had designed the location and timing of the explosions to produce the maximum casualties. In all, nearly 200 people died from the attacks, and many more sustained injuries. In the initial reports of the outrage, the government of José María Aznar suspected that ETA bore responsibility, in part because the police had thwarted an ETA attempt to blow up trains just a month before. From forensic evidence, however, it soon became clear that Islamic extremists lay behind the attack, presumably in retaliation for the government's support of the United States' war in Iraq. With elections scheduled for March 14, the bombing seriously eroded support for Aznar's party.

The day after the attack, 11 million Spaniards – nearly a quarter of the total population – participated in peaceful demonstrations all over Spain to protest the train bombing. In Madrid, Prince Felipe, Princess Elena, and Princess Cristina led the procession. Two days later, when voters went to the polls, they turned the PP out of office. The police very quickly identified the likely perpetrators of the bombing by supplementing their own investigation with intelligence reports from other countries. They were able to trace the movements of dozens of suspects for the months before the attack and identify potential sources for the explosives they used. Judicial proceedings against more than two dozen men – most of them from Morocco – continued for several years, serving as a continual reminder that Spain was as vulnerable as any other country to the ravages of international terrorism, as well as attacks from ETA. The courts handed down a final verdict in October 2007, finding twenty-one of the twenty-eight men accused guilty of various levels of involvement in the attacks. Nonetheless, controversy continues about the full context of that involvement.

After the March elections of 2004, José Luis Rodríguez Zapatero, the leader of the Socialist Party, took over as President of the Government. Fulfilling a campaign promise, he immediately removed Spanish soldiers from combat roles in Iraq and made clear that in other ways as well he would follow a different agenda from that of Aznar and the Popular Party.

One of the thorniest issues faced by the government of Zapatero (as the press called him) was the continuing violence by ETA terrorists. Over the years since 1968, ETA had assassinated more than 800 people, including members of the armed forces and the police, as well as politicians and other civilians. The peak years of the violence occurred in the late 1970s, during the transition to democracy. After ETA killed a total of ninety-two people in 1980, the level of assassinations fluctuated between about thirty and fifty per year, with the threat of terrorist attacks continually hanging over Spanish society. Some leaders in the Basque region, already enjoying greatly increased local powers under the new constitution, came to see armed struggle as outmoded and counterproductive, especially since many recent victims of ETA were local politicians opposed to armed struggle or members of the locally controlled police force – the Ertzaintza. A hard core of militants refused to abandon armed struggle, however, financing their efforts with "revolutionary taxes" extorted from Basque businesses. Some local politicians even relied on the threat of continued violence as a tool in their political wrangles with the central government, whichever party happened to be in power at the national level.

The political party representing ETA began life as Herri Batasuna in 1978. Over the years, as terrorism continued, many Spaniards came to view HB as no more than a cynical front organization for the terrorists. In the heightened world awareness of terrorism in the late 1990s, the Spanish judiciary, in particular the examining magistrate Baltasar Garzón, found proof linking HB leaders to ETA and had many of them arrested and tried. In June 2001, a new party called Batasuna replaced HB, but with the same outlook and leadership. Since then, the judiciary and militant ETA supporters have sparred repeatedly, with the judiciary outlawing one party, only to have the leadership regroup and form a new party. The Aznar government refused to negotiate for peace until ETA leaders formally renounced armed struggle, since periodic truces seemed to have no lasting effect. The first Zapatero government was more willing to pursue a political approach to finding a solution, even as it worked with other members of the European Union to arrest fugitive terrorists.

In the first decade of the new millennium, Spain's population grew from about 40 to 46 million, in a society that increasingly represents a diverse mixture of people from all over the world. From 1995 to 2010, the number of foreign-born residents of Spain rose from 5 percent to more than 12 percent, a major shift in such a short period. Other major changes include the prominence of women in all aspects of Spanish life, including business and politics. In addition to female mayors and regional leaders all over Spain, José María Aznar of the conservative Popular Party appointed several women to his cabinet, including Foreign Minister Ana Palacio, and women from the Popular Party presided over both houses of the Cortes. The first cabinet of José Luis Rodríguez Zapatero in 2004 included seven women, plus a female Vice-President of the Government, all of whom had risen through the ranks of the Socialist Party. When Zapatero won a second term with the general elections of March 2008, he appointed a woman as Minister of Defense – Carme Chacón Piqueras, who had already served as the vice-president of the lower house of the Cortes and Minister of Housing in his first administration.

Various other economic and social measures also situate Spain solidly within the norms of the European Union, and in some cases in the forefront. In 2005, the average life expectancy for women in Spain was 83.7 years, the highest in the EU. In that same year, the Spanish Cortes amended its laws to allow marriages between two people of the same sex, linking Spain with the Netherlands as the two European countries with the most liberal laws affecting homosexuals and lesbians. The Catholic Church strongly objected to the new law, because it considers marriage a sacrament and not merely a civil union, but a large majority of Spaniards favored the change, because it signified the end of legal discrimination based on gender.

Spaniards' faith in the future came under stress in the economic crisis that began in 2008, when a combination of financial blows hit Spain along with other European countries. Disruption and near collapse in the previously booming construction and banking sectors brought growth to a halt and caused increasing distress and political discontent. Rising unemployment, especially among young people seeking their first jobs, offered the most visible indication of the profound economic difficulties affecting Spanish society. Zapatero and his government underestimated the extent of the growing crisis and were slow to respond, as he himself later admitted. The Popular Party, led by Mariano Rajoy, focused on the socialists' failure to address the faltering economy and easily won the election of 2011. Rajoy's new government immediately made efforts to stem the crisis at home and to secure financial support from the European Union. In the short term, Rajoy's cost-cutting measures caused widespread discontent and played out against a background of financial and personal scandals among Spain's elite, including members of the royal family.

King Juan Carlos I and the constitutional monarchy enshrined in Spanish democracy provided key elements of stability amid the challenges of modern life. Until recently, the king enjoyed widespread popularity, boosted by his public activities and by memories of his widely admired actions opposing the failed coup of 1981. Every Christmas Eve, television stations in Spain broadcast the king's annual message in which he typically touched on matters of recent concern to the country as a whole and his shared hopes for its future. Yet during the period of severe economic crisis, the popularity of Juan Carlos began to wane. He lost further support in the aftermath of a previously unreported hunting trip to Botswana in 2012, where he suffered a broken hip. In addition to the unpopularity of wild game hunting, the trip itself seemed an affront to Spaniards still suffering from the economic crisis. His health remained a concern even as the royal family worked to regain its former standing in the public eye. Queen Sofía's popularity remained high, thanks to her unflappable demeanor and tireless energy, and Prince Felipe and his family continued to enjoy widespread support as they fulfilled their official duties. The sisters of the prince, however, no longer enjoyed the popularity of their earlier years. Elena is divorced and not as active in public life. Cristina's husband has been accused in a financial scandal that is still under investigation.

Early in June 2014, King Juan Carlos I announced his intention to abdicate. He had never publicly noted that retirement was on his mind, but his decision followed a series of high-profile resignations and retirements, including the almost unprecedented retirement of Pope Benedict XVI in February 2013 and the abdications of Queen Beatrix of the Netherlands and King Albert of Belgium later in the same year. In Spain, rapid preparations and favorable votes in both houses of the legislature prepared the way for the abdication of Juan Carlos I and the ceremony installing the new king, Felipe VI, on June 19. Public opinion polls suggested strong support for the changeover and a widespread belief that the new king would restore the standing of the monarchy.

Felipe VI and Queen Letizia already had considerable experience in handling the official and ceremonial aspects of royal life. Moreover, Felipe had extensive preparation for kingship through his military and academic training in Spain and graduate education in diplomacy at Georgetown University in the United States. His ability to speak Catalan, as well as Spanish and several other languages, will be of benefit. Felipe and Letizia have two daughters, making it likely that Spain will some day have another ruling queen, a prospect that seems to appeal to many Spaniards. The Bourbon dynasty has had an interesting and somewhat conflicted career in Spain, disappearing and reappearing at intervals over the past three hundred years. For the moment at least, the future of the dynasty appears secure, because Spaniards of all political stripes seem to recognize that a modern monarchy within a modern democracy provides a symbol of stability for society and a visible link between the present and the past.

The New Spaniards seem comfortable dealing with that past, not just the civil war and the Franco regime, but also with the full range of issues related to two thousand years of history. Popular history magazines share space at every kiosk with newspapers and magazines featuring political analysis, celebrity gossip, sports, and pornography. These magazines feature articles by today's most respected scholars, some of whom are as well known to the Spanish public as they are to their students. A typical issue juxtaposes articles about Spanish history with articles about various other places in the world, subtly reminding Spaniards that their long history is embedded in a broader context. Convinced of their own uniqueness, they are also keenly aware of the value of being just like everyone else in the developed world, after several generations of isolation during the Franco years.

By late 2013, economic reforms to deal with the crisis of 2008 were having a measurable effect, and forecasters predicted gradual improvements in the Spanish economy. Spain continues to be a country of surprising contradictions, with a strong moralistic core and, at the same time, a thriving pornography and sex industry. In fact, many Spaniards see no particular contradiction in upholding strong morals in every aspect of their lives except their sexuality. In politics, the restrained dialogue during the transition to democracy has given way in recent years to an increasingly strident style of political discourse, which often gets in the way of the compromises necessary to run the country effectively. The new confrontational style of politics provides evidence that the New Spaniards are not afraid that their strong disagreements will endanger the continued development of democracy. Nonetheless, like their counterparts in the rest of the developed world, Spaniards will have to adjust to a future in which few things are certain. They seem equal to the challenge.

FIGURE 8.1 The juxtaposition of old and new in modern Spain shows clearly in this view of Mérida. The Roman bridge over the Guadiana River was used for automobile traffic until 1991, when the Puente Lusitania by Santiago Calatrava replaced it.

FIGURE 8.2 Huge investments in the infrastructure of Spain in recent decades have transformed the skylines of many cities. The stunning Alamillo bridge over the Guadalquivir River in Seville was designed by Santiago Calatrava as part of the building projects for the World Exposition of 1992.

FIGURE 8.3 The terrorist bombings in and around Madrid on March 11, 2004, caused outrage all over the country. The next day, an estimated 11 million people publicly demonstrated their solidarity with the victims and their revulsion at the attacks. In Madrid alone, some 2 million people marched through the center of town in the rain, filling the streets with a sea of umbrellas.

FIGURE 8.4 The increased presence of women in government and the professions is one of the most notable changes in recent Spanish history. María Teresa Fernández de la Vega, shown holding a document in the center of the photo, was Vice-President under President José Luis Rodríguez Zapatero in the socialist government elected in 2004. She appears here with female reporters and government workers at the Moncloa Palace, the seat of government, in 2004.

CHRONOLOGY AND RULERS

The land and early inhabitants

1.2–1.1 million years old	Earliest human remains in Iberia (Atapuerca)
200,000–24,000 years ago	Neanderthals in Iberia
45,000–10,000 years ago	Upper Paleolithic period
c. 800 BCE	Phoenicians in Iberia
Sixth century BCE	Emporion founded, first Greek city in Iberia
Third century BCE	Carthaginians in Iberia
206 BCE	Romans drove Carthaginians from Iberia

Ancient legacies

Third century BCE through fourth century CE	Romans in Spain
409–15	Suevi, Vandals, Alans entered Spain
Fifth century to 711	Visigothic rule in Spain

Diversity in medieval spain

711–1492	Muslim rule in parts of Spain
Eighth century	Growth of the Christian kingdoms began

756–88	'Abd al-Raḥmān I, declared al-Andalus an independent emirate
929	'Abd al-Raḥmān III, 912–61, declared himself caliph
1031	Caliphate abolished, period of *taifa* kingdoms began
1085	Alfonso VI of León (1065–1109) and Castile (1072–1109) conquered Toledo
1094	Rodrigo Díaz de Vivar, El Cid, conquered Valencia
1104–34	Alfonso I of Aragon; conquered Zaragoza
1137	Aragon and Barcelona joined
1232–1492	Nasrid dynasty in Granada
1236	Fernando III of Castile, 1217–52 (king of León 1230–52), conquered Córdoba and (1248) Seville

The rise of Spain to international prominence

Castile

1252–84	Alfonso X
1284–95	Sancho IV
1295–1312	Fernando IV
1312–50	Alfonso XI
1350–69	Pedro I (the Cruel)
1369–79	Enrique II of Trastámara
1379–90	Juan I
1390–1406	Enrique III

1406–54	Juan II
1454–74	Enrique IV
1474–1504	Isabel I
1504–6	Juana I and Felipe I
1506–16	Fernando II (of Aragon, as regent for Juana)

Aragon

1213–76	Jaume I
1276–85	Pere III
1285–91	Alfonso III
1291–1327	Jaume II
1327–36	Alfonso IV
1336–87	Pere IV
1387–95	Joan I
1395–1410	Martín I
1412–16	Fernando de Antequera (reigned as Fernando I of Trastámara)
1416–58	Alfonso V
1458–79	Joan II
1479–1516	Fernando II

Spain as the first global empire

The Habsburg dynasty – 1516–1700

| 1516–56 | Carlos I (Emperor Carlos V) |
| 1556–98 | Felipe II |

1598–1621	Felipe III
1621–65	Felipe IV
1665–1700	Carlos II

The Bourbon dynasty – 1700 to present, with several interruptions

1700–24	Felipe V
1724	Luis I
1724–46	Felipe V (second time)
1746–59	Fernando VI
1759–88	Carlos III
1788–1808	Carlos IV
1808	Fernando VII

Toward modernity: from the Napoleonic invasion to Alfonso XIII

French occupation and War of Independence

| 1808–13 | Joseph Bonaparte (José I) |

Bourbon dynasty restored

| 1813–33 | Fernando VII |
| 1833–68 | Isabel II |

Provisional government, after forcing Isabel II into exile

| 1869–70 | Francisco Serrano (regent) |
| 1870–73 | Amadeo I (elected by the Cortes) |

First Republic

February 1873–January 1874

Bourbon dynasty restored

1875–85   Alfonso XII

1885–1931   Alfonso XIII

1923–30   Dictatorship of Miguel Primo de Rivera

The struggle for the Spanish soul: Republic, civil war, and dictatorship

1930–1   "Dictablanda" of Dámaso Berenguer and Juan Bautista Aznar

1931   Exile of Alfonso XIII began

Second Republic

1931–9

Presidents:

1931–6   Niceto Alcalá Zamora

1936–9   Manuel Azaña

Dictatorship of Francisco Franco

1939–75

New Spain, new Spaniards: European, democratic, and multicultural

Bourbon dynasty restored

1975–2014   Juan Carlos I

2014–present   Felipe VI

Presidents of the Government:

15 July 1976–29 January 1981	Adolfo Suárez
29 January 1981–2 December 1982	Leopoldo Calvo Sotelo y Bustelo
2 December 1982–5 May 1996	Felipe González
5 May 1996–17 April 2004	José María Aznar
17 April 2004–21 December 2011	José Luis Rodríguez Zapatero
21 December 2011–present	Mariano Rajoy

GUIDE TO FURTHER INFORMATION

There is a wealth of scholarship in many languages regarding Spain and, from the fifteenth to the nineteenth century, its overseas ventures. The internet is also an excellent source of further information and illustrations for all of the people and places mentioned here and in the text. In what follows, we list a few general books related to each substantive chapter, plus additional works on specific topics, presented in rough chronological order. The lists are not exhaustive. Instead, they provide an introduction to the work available in English. For Chapters 3–8, we mention representative cultural figures as well, both Spaniards and others whose work had important connections to Spain. We also mention places with examples of the material and cultural developments discussed in each chapter.

The land and its early inhabitants

Ecology is a relatively new interest for historians, although specialists in geography, archeology, and various earth sciences have long concerned themselves with aspects of that broad field. The best way to learn about the varied landscapes of Spain is to explore them in person, from the rain-drenched valleys of Galicia in the northwest to the deserts of Almería in the southeast, and from the impressive mountains of the Picos de Europa near the northern coast to the prehistoric caves at Nerja (Andalusia) near the southern coast. Entry points into the published work about the geography of Spain and its Mediterranean neighbors include the following:

Karl W. Butzer, *Archaeology as Human Ecology* (Cambridge University Press, 1982).

John Robert McNeill, *The Mountains of the Mediterranean World: An Environmental History* (Cambridge University Press, 1992).

Fernand Braudel, *The Mediterranean and the Mediterranean World in the Age of Philip II* (New York: Harper and Row, 1972–73), vol. I.

Carla Rahn Phillips and William D. Phillips Jr., *Spain's Golden Fleece: Wool Production and the Wool Trade from the Middle Ages to the Nineteenth Century* (Baltimore, MD: Johns Hopkins University Press, 1997), ch. I.

The archeological site at Atapuerca in Castile-León has yielded the oldest human remains thus far discovered in Europe. The caves at Altamira near Santander (Cantabria) contain spectacular wall paintings that date from about 18,500 to 14,000 years ago. Celtic megaliths at Ulaca (Castile-León) mark a settlement dating from about the fifth to the second century BCE. Some archaeological sites are open to visitors, but many are closed to all but qualified researchers while excavations continue. The open-cast mines at Río Tinto near Huelva in Andalusia have been in operation at least since Phoenician times, though they were abandoned during the medieval period and were fully developed only after the Industrial Revolution. They continue in operation today, mostly for the extraction of iron and copper, though silver and other minerals also exist there. Often billed as the oldest mines in the world, and certainly some of the richest, the Río Tinto operations may have been the site of King Solomon's mines in the Bible. Over the millennia, the mines have contributed to economic development but they have also transformed a huge swath of southwestern Andalusia into a moonscape devoid of vegetation, where the rivers run wine-red, as the name implies. Certain areas are open to visitors.

The magnificent Iberian stone sculptures of the "Dama de Elche" and similar figures from Valencia are presumed to date from the fourth century BCE and are housed in the National Archeological Museum in Madrid. The much cruder large stone sculptures known as the "Toros de Guisando" (Bulls of Guisando) near Ávila date from about the second century BCE, and some scholars think the Romans moved them to their current site. Additional reading on Spain's prehistoric peoples includes:

Juan Luis de Arsuaga, Eudald Carbonell, and José María Bermúdez de Castro, *The First Europeans: Treasures from the Hills of Atapuerca* (Valladolid: Junta de Castilla y León, 2003).

María Cruz Fernández Castro, *Iberia in Prehistory* (Oxford: Blackwell, 1995).

Ann Neville, *Mountains of Silver and Rivers of Gold: The Phoenicians in Iberia* (Oxford: Oxbow Books, 2007).

Richard J. Harrison, *Spain at the Dawn of History: Iberians, Phoenicians, and Greeks* (New York: Thames and Hudson, 1988).

Roger Collins, *Spain: An Oxford Archaeological Guide* (Oxford University Press, 1998).

Ancient legacies

Scholarly work on Roman Spain is already substantial and expands with every new archeological find. Much of the work is published in scholarly articles, which is typical of the field of archeology. A few of the published books include:

Leonard A. Curchin, *Roman Spain: Conquest and Assimilation* (New York: Routledge, 1991).

Michael Kulikowski, *Late Roman Spain and its Cities* (Baltimore, MD: Johns Hopkins University Press, 2004).

J. S. Richardson, *The Romans in Spain* (Cambridge, MA: Blackwell, 1996).

Roman civilization left traces in nearly every corner of Spain, and virtually every provincial museum includes a collection of artifacts from the period. In Castile-León, the Roman aqueduct in the city of Segovia is perhaps the best-known structure, but

Roman bridges are still in use in numerous cities, towns, and villages in many parts of Spain. The city of Soria in Castile-León houses an excellent small museum with finds from the nearby archeological site of Numancia, which is also open to visitors. In Catalonia, the cities of Tarragona and Barcelona contain important Roman remains. Of particular note are the in situ ruins of Barcino in the Museum of the City of Barcelona. The best single location for Roman materials is the city of Mérida in Extremadura, which houses the National Museum of Roman Art (Museo Nacional de Arte Romano) as well as an impressive theatre and coliseum complex and other remains. In Andalusia, ruins of the Roman city of Itálica near Seville contain impressive mosaics, and the fish-processing station at Baelo Claudia near Tarifa provides an interesting window into industrial production and Mediterranean trade during the Roman period. Also instructive are the remains of Roman hydraulic gold-mining at Las Médulas near Ponferrada in Castile-León, which show the ecological consequences of that operation.

Very few scholars working on Visigothic Spain publish in English. Among the available books are the following:

Roger Collins, *Visigothic Spain, 409–711* (Oxford and Malden, MA: Blackwell, 2004).

Peter J. Heather, *The Visigoths from the Migration Period to the Seventh Century: An Ethnographic Perspective* (Woodbridge and Rochester: Boydell Press; San Marino: Center for Interdisciplinary Research on Social Stress, 1999).

Karen Eva Carr, *Vandals to Visigoths: Rural Settlement Patterns in Early Medieval Spain* (Ann Arbor: University of Michigan Press, 2002).

Kenneth Baxter Wolf, *Conquerors and Chroniclers of Early Medieval Spain* (Liverpool University Press, 1999).

As Chapter 2 indicated, the primary legacies of the Visigoths in Spain were their law codes and additions to Latin and vernacular language. Although the Visigoths founded cities in

Iberia and selected Toledo as their capital, only a very few extant structures provide a visible reminder of their presence, most of them churches in Castile-León. One example is the church of San Juan near Palencia, which dates from the seventh century.

Diversity in medieval Spain

The Muslim invasion and the subsequent implantation of Islamic culture in Spain have attracted generations of modern scholars working in English, and that interest remains strong. Scholars who have worked on Christian or Jewish Spain in the medieval period are even more numerous. Older generations tended to specialize in one religious community or another. By contrast, many modern scholars include the full cultural diversity of medieval Spain. A sampling of the published work in English includes:

Roger Collins, *Early Medieval Spain: Unity in Diversity, 400–1000* (London: Macmillan Education, 1995).

Norman Roth, *Jews, Visigoths, and Muslims in Medieval Spain: Cooperation and Conflict* (Leiden and New York: E. J. Brill, 1994).

Jerrilynn Denise Dodds, *Al-Andalus: The Art of Islamic Spain* (New York: Metropolitan Museum of Art, 1992).

Joseph F. O'Callaghan, *A History of Medieval Spain* (Ithaca, NY: Cornell University Press, 1975).

Reconquest and Crusade in Medieval Spain (Philadelphia: University of Pennsylvania Press, 2004).

B. F. Reilly, *The Medieval Spains* (Cambridge University Press, 1993).

R. A. Fletcher, *The Quest for El Cid* (New York: Oxford University Press, 1991).

Hugh Kennedy, *Muslim Spain and Portugal: A Political History of al-Andalus* (London: Longman, 1996).

Olivia Remie Constable, *Trade and Traders in Muslim Spain: The Commercial Realignment of the Iberian Peninsula, 900–1500* (Cambridge University Press, 1994).

Thomas F. Glick, *From Muslim Fortress to Christian Castle: Social and Cultural Change in Medieval Spain* (Manchester University Press, 1995).

Robert Ignatius Burns, SJ, *Muslims, Christians, and Jews in the Crusader Kingdom of Valencia: Societies in Symbiosis* (Cambridge University Press, 1984).

Heath Dillard, *Daughters of the Reconquest: Women in Castilian Town Society, 1100–1300* (Cambridge University Press, 1984).

James F. Powers, *A Society Organized for War: The Iberian Municipal Militias in the Central Middle Ages, 1000–1284* (Berkeley: University of California Press, 1987).

Teofilo F. Ruiz, *From Heaven to Earth: The Reordering of Castilian Society, 1150–1350* (Princeton University Press, 2004).

Jonathan Ray, *The Sephardic Frontier: The Reconquista and the Jewish Community in Medieval Iberia* (Ithaca, NY: Cornell University Press, 2006).

Material remains from the long medieval period are impressive and widespread. Undoubtedly the most famous Islamic remnants are the palace complex in the city of Granada, the great mosque in the city of Córdoba, and the watchtower known as La Giralda in Seville, all of them in Andalusia. In addition, there are various structures in many other parts of Spain that contain Islamic elements, whether they were built for communities of Muslims, Christians, or Jews.

The cultural fusion between Christian and Islamic architectural styles resulted in structures built by Mudéjars (Muslims living under Christian rule) and Mozarabs (Christians living under Muslim rule). The city of Toledo (Castile-La Mancha) contains fine examples of Mudéjar architectural elements and decorative motifs, as well as several large Jewish synagogues and Christian churches from the medieval period. The city of Calatayud and other towns in Zaragoza province (Aragon) contain some fine examples of Mozarab structures. Calatayud itself also has a neighborhood that was the medieval Jewish quarter, as do many other municipalities. The most famous is probably the Barrio de Santa Cruz in Seville, but many smaller towns and cities also retain remnants of Jewish quarters from the medieval period, among them Hervás in Extremadura.

Christian churches and monasteries from the medieval period, as well as secular structures, still exist throughout Spain, even though many of them have been changed considerably over the centuries. Some of the best examples of true Romanesque architecture are the numerous churches in the countryside along the pilgrimage routes toward Santiago de Compostela (Galicia).

Towns founded or expanded during the medieval period retain other visible remnants of their distant past as well. The winding streets characteristic of Islamic towns and Jewish neighborhoods were designed to provide shade in the brutal heat of summers in the south. The central plazas and more regular street patterns of Christian towns founded during the reconquest echo traditions established during the Roman period. Elements of both traditions still exist in many modern urban settings. The city of Barcelona has its famous "Gothic Quarter," and the village of La Alberca in Salamanca province preserves much of its medieval character. Both Islamic and Christian towns were commonly surrounded by walls during the medieval period, both for defense and to control the flow of people and goods. Many modern cities retain remnants of their medieval walls, and the city of Ávila has refurbished the full circlet of walls that surrounded its medieval center.

Memories of the medieval centuries also persist in the tradition of mock battles between "Moros y Cristianos" (Moors and Christians) that recall the intermittent warfare of the reconquest. Festivals of Moors and Christians are still held in many parts of Spain and Portugal, and as far away from Iberia as Peru, Papua-New Guinea, and the Philippines. In Spain, one the most elaborate festivals takes place every April in the city of Alcoy (in Valencian, Alcoi) in Alicante province (Valencia).

The rise of Spain to international prominence

Scholarship on the crucial period from the fourteenth to the late fifteenth century has produced a wide range of general and specific studies. The work available in English includes the following:

Angus MacKay, *Spain in the Middle Ages: From Frontier to Empire, 1000–1500* (New York: St. Martin's, 1977).

L. P. Harvey, *Islamic Spain, 1250 to 1500* (University of Chicago Press, 1990).

John Edwards, *The Spain of the Catholic Monarchs, 1474–1520* (Malden, MA, and Oxford: Blackwell, 2000).

Jocelyn N. Hillgarth, *The Spanish Kingdoms, 1250–1516*, 2 vols. (Oxford: Clarendon Press, 1976–8).

Teofilo F. Ruiz, *Spanish Society, 1400–1600* (Harlow and New York: Longman, 2001).

Helen Nader, *The Mendoza Family in the Spanish Renaissance, 1350 to 1550* (New Brunswick, NJ: Rutgers University Press, 1979).

Henry Kamen, *The Spanish Inquistion: A Historical Revision* (New Haven, CT: Yale University Press, 1998).

Norman Roth, *Conversos, Inquisition, and the Expulsion of the Jews from Spain* (Madison: University of Wisconsin Press, 1995).

Felipe Fernández Armesto, *Before Columbus: Exploration and Colonization from the Mediterranean to the Atlantic, 1229–1492* (Philadelphia: University of Pennsylvania Press, 1987).

Peggy K. Liss, *Isabel the Queen: Life and Times*, rev. edn. (Philadelphia: University of Pennsylvania Press, 2004).

William D. Phillips Jr., and Carla Rahn Phillips, *The Worlds of Christopher Columbus* (Cambridge University Press, 1992).

Barbara F. Weissberger, *Isabel Rules: Constructing Queenship, Wielding Power* (Minneapolis: University of Minnesota Press, 2004).

The Spanish Renaissance employed hundreds of writers, artists, and musicians. These included both Spaniards and foreigners who came to Spain for the opportunities provided by economic growth and the cultural investment in the royal court and noble households. Among the most notable figures were the composer and musician Juan del Encina (1468–1530); the sculptor Gil de Siloe (late 1440s to 1501); and the painters Pedro Berruguete (1450–1504) and Juan de Flandes (*c.* 1460–1519). The Prado Museum (Madrid) and the National Museum of Art of Catalonia (Museu Nacional d'Art de Catalunya, Barcelona) have excellent holdings from the late medieval and Renaissance periods.

The late fifteenth century saw the development of the plateresque, Spain's version of Renaissance architecture. Named because its ornate decorative schemes were much like the work of silversmiths (*plateros*), the plateresque style featured motifs from Northern European, Islamic, and Italian Renaissance traditions and reached its height in the early sixteenth century. The cities of Salamanca, Valladolid, and Granada contain fine examples of plateresque façades, as do many other towns and cities that shared in the period's economic expansion.

Spain as the first global empire

Scholarly work on the three-century period covered in this chapter is vast. Two excellent starting points for the Habsburg period are J. H. Elliott, *Imperial Spain* (New York: St. Martin's, 1963), and John C. Lynch, *Spain under the Habsburgs*, 2 vols. (New York University Press, 1981 [1964]). The latter's *Bourbon Spain, 1700–1808* (Oxford: Blackwell, 1989) brings the story to 1808. Both authors have a distinguished list of publications on specific topics as well. For Spain's empire in the Americas, an excellent overview is Mark A. Burkholder and Lyman L. Johnson, *Latin America to 1830*, 6th edn. (New York: Oxford University Press, 2007). The bibliography included therein provides an introduction to many other scholars of Latin America working in English. For Spain, additional authors who have published on the period in English include the following:

Carla Rahn Phillips and William D. Phillips Jr., *Spain's Golden Fleece: Wool Production and the Wool Trade from the Middle Ages to the Nineteenth Century* (Baltimore, MD: Johns Hopkins University Press, 1997).

Helen Nader, ed., *Power and Gender in Renaissance Spain: Eight Women of the Mendoza Family, 1450–1650* (Urbana: University of Illinois Press, 2004).

Richard Kagan and Fernando Marías, *Urban Images of the Hispanic World, 1493–1793* (New Haven, CT: Yale University Press, 2000).

Jonathan Brown, *Painting in Spain: 1500–1700* (New Haven, CT: Yale University Press, 1998).

Antonio Domínguez Ortíz, *The Golden Age of Spain, 1516–1659* (New York: Basic Books, 1971).

William S. Maltby, *The Reign of Charles V* (Basingstoke: Palgrave, 2002).

M. J. Rodríguez-Salgado, *The Changing Face of Empire: Charles V, Philip II, and Habsburg Authority, 1551–1559* (Cambridge University Press, 1988).

Sara T. Nalle, *God in La Mancha: Religious Reform and the People of Cuenca, 1500–1650* (Baltimore, MD: Johns Hopkins University Press, 1992).

Geoffrey Parker, *Philip II* (Chicago: Open Court, 2002).

Peter Pierson, *Philip II of Spain* (London: Thames and Hudson, 1975).

Pablo Emilio Pérez-Mallaína Bueno, *Spain's Men of the Sea: Daily Life on the Indies Fleets in the Sixteenth Century* (Baltimore, MD: Johns Hopkins University Press, 1998).

Garrett Mattingly, *The Armada* (Boston: Houghton Mifflin, 1959).

Margaret Greer and Walter Mignolo, *Rereading the Black Legend: The Discourses of Religious and Racial Difference in the Renaissance Empires* (University of Chicago Press, 2007).

Antonio Feros, *Kingship and Favoritism in the Spain of Philip III, 1598–1621* (Cambridge University Press, 2000).

Jonathan Brown and John Huxtable Elliott, *A Palace for a King: The Buen Retiro and the Court of Philip IV*, rev. edn. (New Haven, CT: Yale University Press, 2003).

JoEllen Campbell, *Monarchy, Political Culture and Drama in Seventeenth-Century Madrid: Theater of Negotiation* (Farnham, Surrey: Ashgate, 2006).

Allyson M. Poska, *Regulating the People: The Catholic Reformation in Seventeenth-Century Spain* (Leiden and Boston: Brill, 1998).

Ruth MacKay, *"Lazy, Improvident People": Myth and Reality in the Writing of Spanish History* (Ithaca, NY: Cornell University Press, 2006).

Carla Rahn Phillips, *The Treasure of the San José: Death at Sea in the War of the Spanish Succession* (Baltimore, MD: Johns Hopkins University Press, 2007).

Richard Herr, *The Eighteenth-Century Revolution in Spain* (Princeton University Press, 1958).

John Huxtable Elliott, *Empires of the Atlantic World: Britain and Spain in America, 1492–1830* (New Haven, CT: Yale University Press, 2006).

Suzanne L. Stratton and Ronda Kasl, *Painting in Spain in the Age of Enlightenment: Goya and his Contemporaries* (Indianapolis Museum of Art; New York: The Spanish Institute, 1997).

David R. Ringrose, *Spain, Europe, and the "Spanish Miracle," 1700–1900* (Cambridge University Press, 1997).

Many of the literary figures from Spain's "Golden Age" have works available in English: Miguel de Cervantes Saavedra (1547–1616); Mateo Alemán (1547–1614?); Luis de Góngora (1561–1627); Lope Félix de Vega Carpio (1562–1635); Francisco de Quevedo (1580–1645); and Diego de Saavedra Fajardo (1584–1648), among others. During the period, theatres all over Spain, and especially in Madrid, performed plays (*comedias*) for a diverse audience of fans in venues called *corrales de comedia*, much like the theatres in Shakespeare's England. One of the best venues to see plays from this period is the restored theatre in Almagro (Castile-La Mancha). The eighteenth century arguably produced no Spanish writers equal to those of the Golden Age. However, the playwright Leandro Fernández de Moratín (1760–1828) wrote acute portraits of the pretensions of the rising Spanish middle class.

Representative artists associated with Spain from the early sixteenth through the eighteenth century include some of the most famous painters in all of European history: Alejo Fernández (1475–1545); Titian (Tiziano Vecelli, *c.* 1485–1576); Sofonisba Anguissola (1532–1625); El Greco (Domenikos Theotokopoulos, 1541–1614); Peter Paul Rubens (1577–1640); Anton van Dyck (1599–1641); Juan Bautista Maíno (*c.* 1578–1649); Diego Velázquez (1599–1660); Francisco de Zurbarán (1598–1664); Bartolomé Esteban Murillo (1617–82); Claudio Coello (1642–93); and Francisco Goya (1746–1828). Their works appear in major museums all over the world, but the Prado Museum in Madrid is the best venue to view most of them in one location.

The political and economic connections between Spain and Northern Europe meant that the work of artists such as Hieronymous Bosch (*c.* 1450–1516) and various members of the Breughel painting dynasty became popular among royal and noble collectors in Spain. Their works are also well represented at the Prado Museum. Notable composers and musicians from the three centuries include Juan del Encina (1468–1530); Diego Pisador (1509–57); Luis Milán (*c.* 1500–1561); Antonio de Cabezón (1510–66); Gaspar Sanz (1640–1710); and Domenico Scarlatti (1685–1757).

Buildings, bridges, monuments, and urban quarters from the Habsburg period still exist all over Spain. The cities of Salamanca, Valladolid, Madrid, Seville, and Valencia are particularly rich in representative churches, monasteries, and other buildings from the sixteenth and seventeenth centuries. The elaborate plateresque decorations of the early sixteenth century gave way to more austere styles during the late sixteenth century; the best-known example is the royal palace of El Escorial near Madrid. The seventeenth century saw a return to elaborate stonework and surface decoration in the Spanish Baroque style, which can be seen in urban centers throughout Spain. Churches and other structures built or remodeled in the seventeenth century, such as the cathedral in Santiago de Compostela, provide examples of the Spanish Baroque and its more flamboyant successor, known as Churrigueresco (after the Churriguero family of architects). The major cities of Latin America also have a stunning array of Spanish Baroque buildings, with decoration by highly skilled local artisans.

For the eighteenth century, the royal palaces in Madrid, La Granja, Riofrío, and Aranjuez exemplify the French and Italianate styles favored by the Spanish Bourbons. The church of the Salesas Reales in Madrid is a fine example of eighteenth-century religious architecture in Spain.

Toward modernity: from the Napoleonic invasion to Alfonso XIII

The nineteenth and early twentieth centuries have attracted a wide variety of scholars in various fields. Richard Herr's *An Historical Essay on Modern Spain* (Berkeley: University of California Press, 1974 [1964]) gives an excellent overview of nineteenth-century politics, although it was first published nearly half a century ago. John D. Bergamini's *The Spanish Bourbons: The History of a Tenacious Dynasty* (New York: Putnam, 1974), also a classic, focuses on the personal histories and foibles of the royal family. The essay collection *Spanish History since 1808*, edited by José Álvarez Junco and Adrian Shubert (London: Arnold; New York: Oxford University Press, 2000), contains essays by more than two dozen current historians working on modern Spain. Additional books in English include:

Raymond Carr, *Spain, 1808–1975* (Oxford: Clarendon Press, 1982).

Christopher J. Ross, *Spain, 1812–1996* (London: Arnold; New York: Oxford University Press, 2000).

Charles J. Esdaile, *Spain in the Liberal Age: From Constitution to Civil War, 1812–1939* (Oxford: Blackwell, 2000).

Nicolás Sánchez-Albornoz, *The Economic Modernization of Spain, 1830–1930* (New York University Press, 1987).

Adrian Shubert, *A Social History of Modern Spain* (London and Boston, MA: UnwinHyman, 1990).

Mary Vincent, *Spain 1833–2002: People and State* (Oxford University Press, 2007).

Adrian Shubert, *Death and Money in the Afternoon: A History of the Spanish Bullfight* (New York: Oxford University Press, 1999).

David Mackay, *Modern Architecture in Barcelona, 1854–1939* (New York: Rizzoli, 1989).

Carolyn P. Boyd, *Historia Patria: Politics, History, and National Identity in Spain, 1875–1975* (Princeton University Press, 1997).

Praetorian Politics in Liberal Spain (Chapel Hill: University of North Carolina Press, 1979).

William J. Callahan, *The Catholic Church in Spain, 1875–1998* (Washington, DC: Catholic University of America Press, 2000).

Joseph Harrison and Alan Hoyle, *Spain's 1898 Crisis: Regenerationism, Modernism, Post-colonialism* (Manchester University Press; New York: St. Martin's, 2000).

Enrique A. Sanabria, *Republicanism and Anticlerical Nationalism in Spain* (New York: Palgrave Macmillan, 2009).

Deborah L. Parsons, *A Cultural History of Madrid: Modernism and the Urban Spectacle* (New York: Berg, 2003).

Teresa-M. Salas, *Barcelona 1900* (Ithaca, NY: Cornell University Press; Amsterdam: Van Gogh Museum, 2008).

Joan Connelly Ullman, *The Tragic Week: A Study of Anticlericalism in Spain, 1875–1912* (Cambridge, MA: Harvard University Press, 1968).

Edmund Peel, ed., *The Painter Joaquín Sorolla y Bastida* (London: Sotheby's Publications, 1989).

William H. Robinson and Jordi Falgàs, *Barcelona and Modernity: Picasso, Gaudí, Miró, Dalí* (New Haven, CT: Yale University Press; Cleveland Museum of Art, 2006).

Francisco J. Romero Salvadó, *The Foundations of Civil War: Revolution, Social Conflict and Reaction in Liberal Spain, 1916–1923* (New York: Routledge, 2008).

Alejandro Quiroga, *Making Spaniards: Primo de Rivera and the Nationalization of the Masses, 1923–30* (Basingstoke and New York: Palgrave Macmillan, 2007).

For Spanish literary production during the nineteenth century, writers available in English include Gustavo Adolfo Béquer (1836–70); Benito Pérez Galdós (1843–1920); and Leopoldo Alas (a.k.a. "Clarín," 1852–1901). Many Spanish writers were involved in exploring the distinctive character of Spain as well as its regional identities and languages, an approach characteristic of European Romanticism. For example, Rosalía de Castro (1837–85) wrote often in Gallego, and Joaquim Rubió y Ors (1818–99) was a guiding force in the Catalan Renaissance (Renaixença). Unfortunately, few of the works written in languages other than Castilian Spanish are available in English. Writers representing the conflictive period from the end of the nineteenth century to about 1930 include Vicente Blasco Ibáñez (1867–1928); Miguel de Unamuno (1864–1936); Ramón María del Valle-Inclán (1866–1936); and Pío Baroja (1872–1956).

In painting, Francisco Goya continued to work well into the nineteenth century, and his powerful and disturbing later paintings are well represented in the Prado Museum in Madrid. No Spanish artists in the generations that followed Goya came near his stature, although they kept up with artistic trends elsewhere in Europe and documented the political turmoil and social changes of their times. In Barcelona, the National Museum of Art of Catalonia has a sizeable section devoted to the nineteenth and early twentieth centuries, as does the Prado. In the early twentieth century, Joaquín Sorolla (1863–1923) painted a series of regional scenes for the Hispanic Society in New York that captures the timelessness of Spanish rural life. Sorolla's house–museum in Madrid provides a glimpse of comfortable upper-middle-class family life in the capital, and the Lázaro-Galdiano Museum displays the wealth and artistic tastes of Sorolla's contemporary, the writer, financier, and art collector José Lázaro-Galdiano (1862–1947).

In music, Fernando Sor (1778–1839), Pablo Sarasate (1844–1908), Isaac Albéñiz (1860–1909), and Enrique Granados (1867–1916) helped to define a distinctive Spanish idiom within the framework of European Romanticism. The period also saw the peak production and popularity of the *zarzuela* genre, Spain's national musical theatre. Part opera, part musical comedy, and of varying lengths and themes, the *zarzuela* dates from the late seventeenth century, but it was largely eclipsed by French and Italianate forms under the early Bourbons. The great revival began in the mid nineteenth century and lasted well into the twentieth, with dozens of prominent composers and librettists from all over Spain, and thousands of examples of their works are still extant. Although little known outside Spain and Latin America, *zarzuelas* continue to be performed to enthusiastic audiences, and their plots provide an excellent entry point into the popular culture of Spain. The Zarzuela Theatre in Madrid, one of the best places to see performances, has a regular annual season.

The struggle for the Spanish soul: Republic, civil war, and dictatorship *and* New Spain, new Spaniards: European, democratic, and multicultural

The period from the Second Republic to the end of the Franco dictatorship is difficult to separate from the transition to democracy after Franco's death, although we have done so in this book for the sake of clarity. For political events, there is a certain justification for the separation. Historical scholarship concerned with the civil war and the Franco period includes the following:

Chris Ealham, *Class, Culture and Conflict in Barcelona, 1898–1937* (London: Routledge, 2005).

Paul Preston, *The Coming of the Spanish Civil War: Reform, Reaction, and Revolution in the Second Republic* (London and New York: Routledge, 1994).

Jordana Mendelson, *Documenting Spain: Artists, Exhibition Culture, and the Modern Nation, 1929–1939* (University Park: Pennsylvania State University Press, 2005).

Martin Blinkhorn, *Democracy and Civil War in Spain, 1931–1939* (London: Routledge, 1996).

Stanley G. Payne, *The Collapse of the Spanish Republic, 1933–1936: Origins of the Civil War* (New Haven, CT: Yale University Press, 2006).

George R. Esenwein and Adrian Shubert, *Spain at War: The Spanish Civil War in Context, 1931–1939* (London and New York: Longman, 1995).

Michael Seidman, *Republic of Egos: A Social History of the Spanish Civil War* (Madison: University of Wisconsin Press, 2002).

Gerald Howson, *Arms for Spain: The Untold Story of the Spanish Civil War* (New York: St. Martin's, 1999).

Gijs Van Hensbergen, *Guernica: The Biography of a Twentieth-Century Icon* (New York: Bloomsbury, 2004).

Ronald Radosh and Mary R. Habeck, *Spain Betrayed: The Soviet Union in the Spanish Civil War* (New Haven, CT: Yale University Press, 2001).

Paul Preston, *Franco: A Biography* (New York: Basic Books, 1994).

Sheelagh M. Ellwood, *Spanish Fascism in the Franco Era: Falange Española de las Jons, 1936–76* (New York: St. Martin's, 1987).

Michael Richards, *A Time of Silence: Civil War and the Culture of Repression in Franco's Spain, 1936–1945* (Cambridge University Press, 2006).

Stanley G. Payne, *Franco and Hitler: Spain, Germany, and World War II* (New Haven, CT: Yale University Press, 2008).

The Spanish Civil War, the Soviet Union, and Communism (New Haven, CT: Yale University Press, 2004).

Lesley Ellis Miller, *Balenciaga* (London: V&A, 2007).

Inbal Ofer, *Señoritas in Blue: The Making of a Female Political Elite in Franco's Spain: The National Leadership of the Sección Femenina de la Falange (1936–1977)* (Brighton: Sussex Academic Press, 2009).

Sasha D. Pack, *Tourism and Dictatorship: Europe's Peaceful Invasion of Franco's Spain* (New York: Palgrave Macmillan, 2006).

Cristina Palomares, *The Quest for Survival after Franco: Moderate Francoism and the Slow Journey to the Polls, 1964–1977* (Brighton: Sussex Academic Press, 2006).

Historical scholarship that deals mostly with the period from the transition to democracy into the present includes:

José Luis de Villalonga, *The King: A Life of King Juan Carlos of Spain* (London: Weidenfeld and Nicolson, 1994).

Charles T. Powell, *Juan Carlos of Spain: Self-Made Monarch* (New York: St. Martin's, 1996).

Paul Preston, *The Triumph of Democracy in Spain* (London: Routledge, 1987).

Juan Carlos: Steering Spain from Dictatorship to Democracy (London: Harper Perennial, 2005).

Laura Desfor Edles, *Symbol and Ritual in the New Spain: The Transition to Democracy after Franco* (Cambridge University Press, 1998).

John Hooper, *The New Spaniards* (London and New York: Penguin Books, 1995).

Oriol Bohigas and Peter Buchanan, *Barcelona, City and Architecture, 1980–1992* (New York: Rizzoli, 1991).

Olympia Bover and Pilar Velilla, *Migrations in Spain: Historical Background and Current Trends* (Madrid: Bancode España, Servicio de Estudios, 1999).

Kathryn Crameri, *Catalonia: National Identity and Cultural Policy, 1980–2003* (Cardiff: University of Wales Press, 2008).

Victoria L. Enders and Pamela B. Radcliff, eds., *Constructing Spanish Womanhood: Female Identity in Modern Spain* (Albany: State University of New York Press, 1999).

José María Garrut Romá, *Casa-Museu Gaudí* (Barcelona: Andres Moron, 2002).

Selma Holo, *Beyond the Prado: Museums and Identity in Democratic Spain* (Liverpool University Press, 2000).

Kenneth MacRoberts, *Catalonia: Nation Building without a State* (New York: Oxford University Press, 2001).

Edward F Stanton, *Culture and Customs of Spain* (Westport, CT: Greenwood Press, 2002).

Giles Tremlett, *Ghosts of Spain: Travels through Spain and its Silent Past* (New York: Walker, 2006).

Alexander Tzonis, *Santiago Calatrava: The Poetics of Movement* (New York: Universe, 1999).

Cultural trends are best understood by considering the twentieth century as a whole. Many important cultural figures in modern Spain were born fairly early in the twentieth century, lived through the civil war, and worked into the new millennium, grappling with the enormous changes in Spanish society during their lifetimes. Other important figures, born during the Franco dictatorship, nonetheless began their professional lives in the shadow of the civil war. To understand the evolution of their work, it is necessary to consider the whole period covered by Chapters 7 and 8.

In literature, Spaniards produced work in the twentieth century that continues to enjoy critical acclaim and a wide readership. Federico García Lorca (1899–1936), active in the cultural life of the Second Republic, was arrested by the nationalists and killed at the start of the civil war, yet he remains one of the iconic figures in twentieth-century Spanish literature. Other writers went into exile during the civil war or chose to live largely outside Spain while Franco held power: Juan Ramón Jiménez (1881–1958); Ramón Sender (1902–82); Jorge Guillen (1893–1984); Juan Goytisolo (1931–). Others decided to live and work in Spain for most of their careers for a variety of reasons, regardless of their relationship with the Franco regime. Writers whose works are available in English include: José Ortega y Gasset (1883–1955); Gonzalo Torrente Ballester (1910–99); Carmen Martín Gaite (1925–2000); Camilo José Cela (1916–2002); Ana María Matute (1926–); and Vicente Aleixandre (1898–1984), among others.

Painters and other artists also had to choose where and how to pursue their careers during the civil war and its aftermath; their politics, like their artistic styles, covered a broad spectrum. For example, the Basque Ignacio Zuloaga (1870–1945), best known for his portraits and genre scenes from the worlds of bullfighting, flamenco dancing, and other romanticized aspects of Spanish life, was also known for his support of the nationalists during the civil war. In part for that reason, he was out of favor in the international art community during the Franco regime, though many museums in Europe and elsewhere display his work. There are also small museums associated with Zuloaga in Zumaya in the Basque country and in Pedraza near Segovia (Castile-León).

Pablo Picasso (1881–1973), whom many call the greatest Spanish artist since Goya, produced brilliant works in a variety of mediums and styles, though he is probably best known for his Cubist works. Born in Málaga and trained in a variety of venues, he lived in France for most of his adult life, yet he was already comfortable in an international environment long before the civil war. Although a longtime member of the Communist Party, he did not demonstrate a particular commitment to that cause. Museums devoted to his work exist in France (Antibes and Paris), Germany (Berlin and Münster), and Spain (Barcelona and Málaga), and many other important museums hold examples of his work.

Salvador Dalí (1904–89), known for surrealism in both his life and his art, allied with fashionable leftist political movements at the start of his career but later turned conservative, much to the outrage of his fellow surrealists. After spending the civil war years abroad, he returned to his native Catalonia in 1942, where he spent the rest of his life, comfortable with the Franco regime and therefore at odds with most of the international art community. Many important museums hold examples of his work, as do the Dalí Theatre-Museum that he built in Figueras (Catalonia) and the Dalí Museum in St. Petersburg, Florida. Another prominent Catalan artist, Joan Miró (1893–1983), also spent most of his working life in Catalonia, but he kept his distance from the Franco regime. Influenced by the major artistic movements of the early twentieth century, he found his major inspiration in Catalan themes and primitive art. Many major museums hold examples of his work in various mediums, as does the Joan Miró Foundation in Barcelona.

Among composers, Joaquín Rodrigo (1901–99) is probably the most important Spanish figure from the generations after Granados and Albéniz. His work, like theirs, forms part of the standard repertoire of musicians throughout the Western world, evoking the musical idiom of Spain and its quintessential instrument, the guitar. Spanish guitarists such as Andrés Segovia (1893–1987) established Rodrigo's music in the classical repertoire, and international guitarists continue that tradition. Other Spanish musicians of international acclaim in the twentieth century include Pablo Casals (cellist and conductor 1876–1973); Alicia de Larrocha (pianist, 1923–2009); Alfredo Kraus (tenor, 1927–99); Monserrat Caballé (soprano, 1933–); Rafael Frühbeck de Burgos (conductor, 1933–); Teresa Berganza (mezzo-soprano, 1935–); Plácido Domingo (tenor and conductor, 1941–); and José Carreras (tenor, 1946–). Their performances are readily available on recordings.

Spaniards such as Luis Buñuel (1900–83) helped to pioneer the new artistic medium of film, although many, including Buñuel, chose to live outside Spain during the Franco period. Those who made their careers in Spain, such as Carlos Saura (1932–) and Pilar Miró (1940–97), had to deal with the difficult and often capricious censorship system, though films remained a popular form of entertainment. In the New Spain, film

433

directors such as Fernando Colomo (1946–) and Pedro Almodóvar (1949–) reflect the openness of cinema and society, and the latter in particular has a devoted international following in the English-speaking world.

Some of the most lasting examples of Spain's cultural production in the twentieth century are the buildings and monuments from previous centuries restored for modern uses. Government-owned hotels known as "Paradores" (lit., stopping places), a venture begun in 1928, are often situated in castles, monasteries, hostels, palaces, and other historic structures. Many privately owned hotels and hotel chains have also refurbished historic structures for modern use, benefiting from the boom in tourism. The net result is a stunning network of lodging places throughout Spain that preserve examples of architecture over the millennia. Similarly, historic structures in many cities and towns have been restored and remodeled as museums, concert venues, and commercial establishments, with support from the government and teams of well-trained experts in architectural restoration. In Madrid, the National Library and Atocha railway station provide examples of intelligent restoration efforts. The remodeling of the venerable Prado Museum complex includes a brilliant set of additions by Rafael Moneo (1937–), visually connected to the nearby Jeronymite church that dates from the Habsburg period.

Several other modern Spanish architects have achieved international prominence, in addition to designing stunning structures in Spain. Among them are Antoni Gaudí (1852–1926), creator of the still unfinished basilica of the Sagrada Família in Barcelona as well as other iconic structures; Josep Lluís Sert (1902–83), a pioneer in modern urban design; Ricardo Bofill (1939–); and Santiago Calatrava (1951–), known for bridges that redefine the form, and for the City of Arts and Sciences complex in his native Valencia. The 1992 Olympics in Barcelona, and the World Exposition in Seville that same year, provided numerous opportunities for Spanish architects and city planners to display their visions for the

434

new Spain. In Barcelona, the historic but neglected waterfront district was rebuilt to house Olympic athletes and transformed into an attractive promenade for city residents. In Seville, the Guadalquivir River, which had been diverted from its course for flood control, was restored to its original channel and spanned by a collection of new bridges, among them the breathtaking Alamillo bridge by Calatrava. Towns and cities throughout Spain also embarked on ambitious plans to restore buildings and reroute traffic patterns to preserve historic structures and enhance the urban core for pedestrians. As a result, the venerable Spanish custom of the evening stroll, or *paseo*, has gained added appeal.

At the same time that the New Spain settles comfortably into modernity, centuries-old art forms such as the bullfight and flamenco music and dance are enjoying a popular renaissance and experimenting with new forms. The fabric of Spanish life thus continues to be a seamless texture of old and new.

INDEX

CAMBRIDGE CONCISE HISTORIES

Titles in the series:

A Concise History of Switzerland
Clive H. Church and *Randolph C. Head*

A Concise History of the United States of America
Susan-Mary Grant

A Concise History of Wales
Geraint H. Jenkins

A Concise History of the World
Merry Wiesner-Hanks